DTLR
TRANSPORT
LOCAL GOVERNMENT
REGIONS

The Implementation of National Planning Policy Guidance (PPG7) in Relation to the Diversification of Farm Businesses

Final Report

Prepared by Land Use Consultants
in association with
The University of the West of England and
Royal Agricultural College Enterprise

October 2001

Department for Transport, Local Government, and the Regions: London

Following the General Election in June 2001 the responsibilities of the former Department of the Environment, Transport and the Regions (DETR) in this area were transferred to the new Department for Transport, Local Government and the Regions (DLTR).

Department for Transport, Local Government and the Regions
Eland House
Bressenden Place
London SW1E 5DU
Telephone 020 7944 3000
Web site www.dtlr.gov.uk

Further copies of this publication are available from:

Department for Transport, Local Government and the Regions
Publications Sales Centre
Cambertown House
Goldthorpe Industrial Estate
Goldthorpe
Rotherham S63 9BL
Tel: 01709 891318
Fax: 01709 881673

or online via the Department's web site.

The free executive summary is available from:
Department for Transport, Local Government and the Regions,
PO Box 126
Wetherby
West Yorkshire
LS23 7NB
Tel: 0870 1226 236
Fax: 0870 1226 237
Textphone: 0870 1207 405
E-mail: dtlr@twoten.press.net

ISBN 1 85112 511 6

Printed in Great Britain on material containing 75% post-consumer waste and 25% ECF pulp (cover), and 100% post-consumer waste (text).

October 2001

Product Code 01PD0716

ACKNOWLEDGEMENTS

This study was commissioned by the Department of the Environment, Transport and the Regions (DETR), now the Department for Transport, Local Government and the Regions (DTLR). We are particularly grateful for the support and guidance provided by Martyn Mance, the nominated officer for the study and by Richard Longman (DETR, Planning Policies Division) as Chair of the Steering Group. We are also very grateful for the help and guidance provided by the other members of the Steering Group: Joanna Russell (Countryside Agency); Mark Jones (Country Land and Business Association); Peter Greenfield (DETR); Crispin Moore (Local Government Association); Mark Edwards (MAFF); Lindsay Roberts (National Assembly for Wales); Brian McLaughlin (National Farmers' Union) and David Green (Planning Officers' Society).

We are also indebted to the 21 Local Planning Authorities who agreed to form our sample for this research. We are particularly grateful to the local authority officers who assisted us with the collection of information and who were prepared to meet us at short notice to discuss the issues relevant to the study.

Our particular thanks goes to those who attended the various workshops through this research study and to those applicants who agreed to be interviewed as a case study example.

This research has been undertaken by Land Use Consultants (LUC) with Lyndis Cole acting as Research Director, the work of the University of the West of England, Bristol (UWE) led by James Shorten and that of Royal Agricultural College Enterprise (RACE) led by Graham Smith.

CONTENTS

CHAPTER 3

Development plan policies 39

CHAPTER 4

Development control process adopted for farm diversification applications 73

CHAPTER 5

CHAPTER 6

CHAPTER 7

Conclusions and best practice

BIBLIOGRAPHY

APPENDIX 1

Methodology for choosing the sample of Local Planning Authorities (LPAs)

APPENDIX 2

Postal questionnaire to applicants

APPENDIX 3:

Methodology for the farmer/landowner telephone interviews

APPENDIX 4:

Results of the farmer/landowner telephone interviews

APPENDIX 5:

Plans reviewed

APPENDIX 6:

Applications database structure

APPENDIX 7:

Application details by local authority

APPENDIX 8:

Case studies

APPENDIX 9:

Appeals

TABLES

FIGURES

BOXES

EXECUTIVE SUMMARY

PURPOSE

This fact-finding research has been undertaken by Land Use Consultants in association with the University of the West of England, Bristol and the Royal Agricultural College Enterprise on behalf of the Department of Environment, Transport and the Regions (DETR) – now the Department for Transport, Local Government and the Regions (DTLR) – with the majority of the data collected between October and December 2000.

The aims of the research have been to:

- Assess the extent to which national planning policy guidance set out in PPG7 (1997, prior to its amendment in March 2001) for the diversification of farm businesses, is reflected in development plans and in development control decisions;

- Identify where, in the operation of the planning system, and in what circumstances, problems may lie; and

- Establish the extent to which planning authorities are proactively assisting farm diversification.

DEFINITION

The research has specifically looked at those aspects of farm diversification subject to planning control (ie activities involving a change of use of land, or buildings, or new development not falling within the definition of agriculture). It has been concerned with diversification developments (including tourism accommodation) occurring on working farms (ie farms involved with the husbandry of land and/or animals) or in buildings or on land previously associated with farming but now separated from a working farm.

RESEARCH METHOD

The research has focused on 21 sample Local Planning Authorities (LPAs) spread across urban fringe, accessible rural and remote rural areas in England. The relevant policies of 14 Regional Planning Guidance (RPG) documents, 16 structure plans and 24 local plans (relating to the sample LPAs) were examined. Local plan officers, development control officers, economic development officers and members were interviewed within each LPA. Details on all (1397) farm diversification applications made within the sample LPAs between February 1997 and February 2000 were collected. More detailed information was collected on a stratified random sample of 20 applications within each sample LPA, including a postal questionnaire sent to each applicant, with a return of 181. Twelve case studies were examined in detail. In addition 554 farmers were contacted by telephone of which 67 provided information for this research. Finally, workshops were held with planners, with farm advisors and representatives and with farmers who have considered diversification in some form.

CONTEXT

There is now very strong national policy support for farm diversification (as contained in the *England Rural Development Programme* (ERDP) 2000-2006; the Government's *Strategy for Agriculture: An Action Plan for Farming,* and the Rural White Paper – *Our Countryside: The Future – A fair deal for rural England*). This is underpinned by funding streams and advice to farmers, combined with a supportive planning policy framework, set out in PPG7 (1997) and a policy statement issued by DETR on 21st March 2001, clarifying PPG7 (1997).

KEY FINDINGS

Farm diversification activity

This research confirms that tourism is by far the most common farm diversification activity subject to planning controls (31% of all planning applications). Equestrian (17%), storage/haulage and offices (both 10%) and manufacturing (8%) are the next most common. The nature of applications indicates that, with the exception of tourism, the majority are responding to the vibrancy of urban-based economies, rather than adding value to land-based products or responding to their rural location. Innovation is generally lacking.

Diversification activity in different areas: Remote rural areas have over six times the number of applications for farm diversification per head of population, compared to the urban fringe, highlighting the importance of farm diversification to the economy of remote areas. Conversely urban fringe areas receive nearly three times as many farm diversification applications per unit area (many of which are retrospective), highlighting the greater development pressure in these areas.

On average farm diversification makes up only 1.5% of all planning applications determined by LPAs – but ranging from only 0.9% in urban fringe areas to 5.1% in National Parks.

In remote rural areas tourism developments make up 53% of all farm diversification applications. Indeed, a key concern expressed at the planning workshops is the saturation of the tourism market and the lack of other diversification opportunities in these remote areas. In more accessible rural areas equestrian applications are the most common (average 30%), followed by tourism, storage and offices.

Development plan policies for rural and farm diversification

Farm diversification policies: Rural issues are poorly addressed in older RPG, but the strong support for diversification of the rural economy in PPG7 (1997) is addressed in all the more recent RPG documents, and is well reflected in the majority of structure and local plans reviewed. **Farm diversification** while explicitly mentioned in 60% of the more recent RPG documents, is only addressed in policy by 50% of structure plans and 54% of local plans reviewed. Significantly, 40% of post-1997 local plans still do not contain specific policies on farm diversification.

Variation by category of LPA: The over-riding characteristic of farm diversification policies in development plans is that of variability. Generally plans do not reflect the full policy content of PPG7. The local plans of accessible rural and urban fringe areas tend to contain more detailed and more restrictive policies on rural and farm diversification compared to remote rural areas. In remote rural areas, farm diversification may not be covered in local plan policy at all and, where it is, policies tend to be brief and not particularly restrictive (the exceptions are the full farm diversification policies of the National Parks).

More restrictive policies for farm diversification most frequently relate to Areas of Outstanding Natural Beauty (AONBs) and Green Belts, and situations where development plans place greater emphasis on environmental conservation over local social and economic needs. The key area of potential policy conflict though, is that between farm diversification and the need to reduce reliance on the private car, as expressed in PPG13 (1994).

Responding to local circumstances: Currently RPG and development plans treat rural areas as homogeneous, failing to recognise the considerable differences in rural areas across regions and within authority areas. None of the structure or local plans reviewed demonstrate an understanding of local social and economic needs in the development of farm and rural development policies. This is significant in that it lessens the ability of plans to make a pro-active and integrated response to local needs, identifying and promoting those types of development suitable to different localities.

The planning process

Planning applications: 90 – 95% of applicants receive some form of advice (other than from the LPA) before submitting a planning application for farm diversification. 60% of these applications are made on behalf of clients by professional advisors. Most farm diversification applications are adequate in terms of the information provided and there is little evidence that this affects approval rates.

Advice from the LPA: 85% of would-be applicants seek advice from the LPA before submitting an application. In the majority of cases this contact is with a planning officer and over 70% of this advice is substantial involving a site visit or meeting. Both planning officers and applicants feel that this advice is helpful but there is concern that it may be curtailed by the Government's Best Value regime. Once an application has been made this dialogue usually continues but is felt less helpful by applicants as subsequent advice may contradict that given earlier.

Delegated Powers: 60% of farm diversification applications are determined by committee, although there is a clear indication that committees normally follow officer recommendations.

Development control decisions

From this study, the average approval rate for farm diversification applications is 83%. This compares with a national average approval rate for all planning applications in England in 1999-2000 of 88%, or just over 90% for minor developments, excluding dwellings. The highest approval rates for farm diversification relate to tourism (85%) and equestrian activities (84%), and the lowest approval rates to storage and haulage (71%).

In remote rural areas, where policies for farm diversification are generally less detailed, 87% of farm diversification applications are approved, while in accessible rural and urban fringe areas, where policies are generally fuller (but more restrictive) reflecting the higher development pressure, approval rates are 84% and 68% respectively.

Approval rates for farm diversification in Green Belts (71%) are similar to those in urban fringe areas more generally. The approval rate in AONBs (76%) is 7% below the average for all farm diversification activities. No other designation appears to affect approval rates for farm diversification, including National Parks and local landscape designations.

Where applications are refused, the most common reasons for refusal relate to: landscape and visual impact (62% of applications refused), development inappropriate in the countryside (52% of refusals), traffic and highways (51% of refusals), and inappropriate development in AONBs/Green Belts (33% of refusals).

Similar issues are reflected in the most frequent conditions applied to approvals, namely: design and materials (57% of approvals), landscape and screening (46%), restrictions on activities (43%), and restrictions on car parking (35%).

Problem areas

Issues of policy identified through this research are:

- *Large scale developments:* Development control officers are concerned about the increasing size of buildings coming forward for re-use and the lack of policy guidance on this, both at the national level and within local plans. 28% of diversification activities involving modern (and often large) farm buildings are refused, compared to 13.5% for traditional farm buildings. This is accentuated in accessible rural areas where the refusal rates for modern farm buildings is 33% (reflecting a greater concern about intensification of use) compared to only 15% in remote rural areas.

- *Attachment to a working farm:* In local plan policy and determination, LPAs are often keen to see a clear relationship between a diversification activity and support for a working farm, especially where large or significant new building is involved. This is not directly addressed in PPG7. 83% of applications which relate to a working farm are approved, compared to 68% where there is no clear relationship. Of those approvals that have been implemented, only 39% are bringing additional income to a farm business.

- *Traffic generation and farm diversification:* In the past development control officers have dealt with the potential conflict in guidance between PPG7 (1997) and PPG13 (1994) by the simple expedient of supporting farm diversification. The main exception has been development likely to generate significant amounts of traffic. The recent revision of PPG13 (March 2001) has helped resolve this issue.

- *Lack of vision:* Lying at the heart of the above issues is a desire on the part of planners to be clear about what farm diversification should be delivering to whom and why. It is for this reason that the planning workshops pointed to the need for LPAs to have a vision for their rural areas, based on a clear understanding of economic and social, as well as environmental, needs.

Issues of process identified through this research are:

- *Perception of the role of planning:* It is evident from this research that there is often a poor understanding of the planning system amongst farmers.

- *Understanding of farming amongst planners:* Planning officers are rarely trained in agricultural and diversification issues, records of pre-application advice are frequently not retained, and the lack of clarity in policy in key areas can result in unclear and inconsistent advice being given to farmers. This is often compounded by the lack of co-ordination between planning advice and other sources of support given to farmers.

- *Availability of guidance:* There is little written guidance which LPAs or the farming community feel able to draw on.

- *Determination times:* By whatever measure, the determination of farm diversification applications is slow.

It has to be concluded from this research that the majority of LPAs are not proactively assisting farm diversification. Neither in development plan policies, other publications, or in the delivery and coordination of advice to farmers, is the full potential to identify and promote farm diversification suitable to its locality being taken up. LPAs are not unwilling to act proactively, rather they lack the resources to do so.

BEST PRACTICE

Examples of best practice that demonstrate how things might be improved include:

- The survey of local social and economic needs in a range of integrated rural development initiatives, such as the Forest of Bowland and the Countryside Agency's Land Management Initiatives

- The development of clear, criteria-based policies for farm diversification, as in the National Parks

- The development of first stop shops for farmer advice, covering planning and economic development

- The preparation of written advice alerting the farming community to relevant planning issues.

- The use of agricultural liaison officers, as in the National Parks, to act as facilitators and help break down the barriers between local authorities and the farming community.

RECOMMENDATIONS

The over-riding message that emerges from this research is the need for greater clarity of purpose for farm diversification and its role in wider rural diversification. This clarity of purpose is required at all levels, in defining the parameters under which farm diversification should operate; what it should deliver at the local level and for whose benefit; and clarity and consistency in the communication between LPAs and the farming community.

In the light of the study findings it is recommended that:

1: *The Government should consider the feasibility of providing a clearer, but flexible, definition of sustainable farm diversification which, amongst other things, addresses issues of scale of development and the differences between farm diversification which is and is not attached to a working farm.*

2: *National policy guidance should clearly acknowledge that different approaches to farm diversification may be required to achieve sustainability objectives in different areas – responding to the different needs and pressures of different areas.*

3: *DEFRA/DTLR and the Countryside Agency at the national level, and local authorities at the more local level, should consider how the range of farm plans now being produced in support of farm business development and environmental protection, might be used in support of planning applications for farm diversification.*

4: *LPAs should develop a clear vision for the integrated rural development of their rural areas, based on a rigorous understanding of local social and economic, as well as environmental, needs. This may require further emphasis in PPG7.*

5: *LPAs should have clear criteria-based policies for farm diversification which reflect local needs and which differentiate, where appropriate, between the types of diversification activity appropriate in different types of rural area. This information might be better provided as Supplementary Planning Guidance.*

6: *Subject to any clearer national definition of sustainable farm diversification, development plans should address the scale of development appropriate to their rural area and how (if at all) farm diversification activities should relate to a working farm.*

7: *The value of pre-application advice should be fully taken into account in any Best Value review of LPA services.*

8: *Within LPAs there should be consistent linking of pre- and post-application advice.*

9: *LPAs should consider training for development control officers in farm diversification, or the identification of a specialist officer to deal with inquiries and applications.*

10: *LPAs should establish clear coordination with other bodies offering assistance and advice on farm diversification, such as DEFRA, local Economic Development Departments, the Farm Business Advisory Service and the Rural Enterprise Scheme.*

11: *Local authorities, the Regional Development Agencies, DEFRA and other relevant bodies should consider establishing first stop shops where applicants can gain planning and economic development advice under one roof.*

12: *LPAs should develop closer partnerships with the farming community through agricultural or farming fora, or regular liaison meetings between planners and the farming community.*

13: *LPAs should consider producing written advice (a leaflet or similar) that explains how farm diversification applications will be dealt with and the issues that will be taken into account in their determination reflecting local circumstances.*

14: *LPAs should take planning advice out to the farming community, perhaps through planning clinics, or the work of agricultural liaison officers, or by working with those who are already in close liaison with the farming community, for example, planning advisors operating under the Rural Enterprise Scheme.*

In making these recommendations it is realised that it would not be appropriate or practical for all LPAs to follow all the recommendations directed at them to the same degree. It will be for individual local authorities to decide the actions which are most appropriate for them depending on local circumstances. Under the ERDP, the Action Plan for Farming, the Rural White Paper and the response to Foot and Mouth Disease there are a broad range of activities being undertaken by a wide range of organisations. In many cases the actions identified above could and should be shared as part of these initiatives, rather than falling to local authorities alone.

CHAPTER 1

Brief and purpose of study

1.1 This fact-finding research study has been undertaken for the (then) Department of the Environment, Transport and the Regions (DETR), now the Department for Transport, Local Government and the Regions (DTLR), with the majority of the data collected between October and December 2000.

THE BRIEF

1.2 The Government's national Planning Policy Guidance (PPG 7 revised) *The Countryside – Environmental Quality and Economic and Social Development* published in February 1997, seeks to promote sustainable development in the countryside. It encourages rural economic diversification and emphasises its increasing importance to farmers, and the potential benefits for the local economy, of diversification of farm businesses into non-agricultural enterprises. However, there has been some anecdotal evidence that these positive messages are not always adequately translated into policies and decisions at the local level, and that the planning system could be more supportive of farmers wishing to diversify, particularly in the light of the *Government's Action Plan for Farming* (Chapter 2).

Aims

1.3 Against this background, the aims of this research as set out in the brief dated 10 August 2000, have been to:

● *"Assess the extent to which national planning policy guidance set out in PPG7 in relation to the diversification of farm businesses is reflected in development plans and in development control decisions;*

● *Identify where, in the operation of the planning system, and in what circumstances, problems may lie; and*

● *Establish the extent to which planning authorities are proactively assisting farm diversification."*

Issues

1.4 As far as possible, the research has also sought to address the following issues identified in the brief:

● *"The extent to which current national planning policies and guidance in respect of farm diversification are reflected in local planning policies through development plans, and whether local planning authorities are interpreting and applying these national policies in ways which are more or less restrictive than in PPG7.*

- *Where PPG7 is not adequately reflected in local plans, is this because of conflicting regional planning guidance or structure plan policies?*

- *Does the presence of other policies, in particular, on transport and the environment, in local plans or the way in which these policies are applied to development control decisions, undermine positive farm diversification policies?*

- *Whether any particular aspect of guidance in PPG7 is being applied inconsistently, or is causing interpretative difficulties for users and, if so, why?*

- *The number and proportion of planning applications for farm diversification schemes which are approved/refused, on initial application and appeal, or withdrawn/not proceeded with; the nature and the frequency of the conditions attached to a permission; the reasons given for decisions to refuse permission, and whether reasons for refusal are adequately explained.*

- *The comparison of this success/failure rate with applications for other types of development in the countryside (outside the main settlements).*

- *Whether there is evidence of planning committees disagreeing with officers' recommendations in respect of farm diversification proposals, and whether there are any significant variations between the terms of delegated powers for determining farm diversification proposals as compared with other rural business applications?*

- *The correlation between development control decisions and current national planning guidance (PPG7) and local planning policies.*

- *Whether there are significantly different issues, policies and decisions arising in the countryside adjacent or near to urban areas, compared with remoter rural areas; in National Parks or designated Areas of Outstanding Natural Beauty; or in different parts of the country (regional or sub-regional variations). And to what extent is the presence of Best and Most Versatile agricultural land an issue in the success or otherwise of diversification proposals?*

- *Whether there appear to be problems associated with particular types, or scales, of farm-based development, including business expansion; with proposals for new building development; or with certain types of existing buildings (such as those erected under permitted development rights).*

- *To what extent is accessibility (with reference to PPG 13) a key issue in farm diversification proposals?*

- *Are there any particular planning-related issues arising in relation to diversification on tenanted farms?*

- *Is the quality of applications submitted by farmers a significant factor?*

- *Do local planning authorities and farmers feel that they give and receive helpful advice and information, or could more be done in this area? Is there evidence of awareness and use of any particular guidance issued by central or local government, or by any other bodies?*

- *To what extent have local initiatives been taken to improve understanding and dialogue between local planning authorities and farmers (eg discussion forums, rural/farm liaison officers) and how successful are they?*

- *What other measures or changes of practice would farmers/applicants find most helpful as a means of further facilitating appropriate farm diversification schemes?*

CHANGING CONTEXT

1.5 Since preparation of the brief for this study, there has been a number of further policy developments, in particular:

- the launch of the England Rural Development Programme in October 2000 by the (then) Ministry of Agriculture, Fisheries and Food (MAFF) – now the Department for Environment, Food and Rural Affairs (DEFRA); and

- the launch of the Rural White Paper *Our Countryside: The Future – A fair deal for rural England* by the DETR and MAFF in November 2000.

1.6 Both of these place increasing emphasis on farm diversification as outlined in Chapter 2. Fundamentally, since the preparation of the draft final report for this study at the beginning of February 2001, livestock farming and the tourism industry in the UK have been dramatically affected by the Foot and Mouth Disease epidemic. The full implications of this are yet to be assessed but the Prime Minister publicly highlighted at the beginning of April 2001, that once the crisis is over, there will be a need for a fundamental reappraisal of agriculture and agricultural policy and its role within the wider rural economy. In turn, a number of commentators in the press and media, Government agencies, including the Countryside Agency, and Non Governmental Organisations (NGOs) such as the World Wide Fund for Nature, have emphasised the need for further and more fundamental review of the Common Agricultural Policy (CAP), combined with greater diversification of the agricultural and rural economy. This serves to underline the increasing importance that is likely to be placed on farm diversification in the future.

DEFINITION OF FARM DIVERSIFICATION

1.7 A range of different definitions have been developed for farm diversification (eg Ilbery 1992, CPRE 2000). Essentially there is **on-farm diversification** which may involve the introduction of different methods of agricultural production or the use of new and novel crops, or the adding of value to farm products (on-farm agricultural diversification); or it may involve non-agricultural activities that utilise agricultural land or buildings, such as tourism or the leasing of land or buildings to other non-agricultural businesses (on-farm non-agricultural diversification). In addition, there are **off-farm sources of income** which may nonetheless help support the farm business. These off-farm sources include alternative employment, self-employment and investments.

1.8 This study is specifically concerned with those aspects of **farm diversification subject to planning control. It is concerned with economic diversification activities occurring on working farms (on-farm diversification), or in buildings or on land previously associated**

with farming but which are now separated from a working farm unit (not strictly on-farm diversification but contributing to rural diversification more generally). In this context, a working farm unit is defined as one which is still involved with the husbandry of land and/or animals as a means of gaining an income.

1.9   The study is not concerned with economic development within or on the edge of rural settlements, other than those directly associated with a farm unit; nor has it been concerned with the sale of farmland for residential or industrial development in these locations. Although such developments are vital to an overall understanding of rural diversification, they require separate investigation.

1.10   Thus the specific **types of development** that have been investigated through this study are:

- new buildings (associated with a farm diversification activity)

- extension of an existing agricultural building

- economic re-use of agricultural buildings

- change of use of agricultural land

- signage in support of a farm diversification activity

- residential accommodation in support of economic farm diversification.

1.11   In turn, the study has looked at the following types of **diversification activity** which may be associated with one or more of the above types of development:

- tourism
- recreation
- retail (farm shops and pick your own)
- workshops
- manufacturing/industry
- food processing

- storage/haulage
- machinery/vehicle repair
- office/studio
- equestrian
- energy
- (plus other miscellaneous activities, such as dog kennels and catteries)

1.12   Written as a list, economic farm diversification subject to planning permission may appear easily classifiable. Yet it embraces a wide range and differing combinations of development types and diversification activities, from minimal change to an existing agricultural building to provide industrial storage to the change of use of land to provide for sporting activities.

SAMPLE LOCAL PLANNING AUTHORITIES (LPAs)

1.13   The majority of this research has focused on the relevant policies and performance within 21 sample Local Planning Authorities (LPAs). These sample LPAs are listed in **Table 1.1**.

1.14   The methodology by which this LPA sample was selected is set out in **Appendix 1**. In summary, the LPAs were chosen to reflect:

- *different locations relative to main centres of population* covering the urban fringe, accessible rural and remote rural areas[1];

- *different geographical areas* with at least one LPA selected from each English administrative region;

- *different designations and categories of countryside* within the LPA areas, covering National Parks, Areas of Outstanding Natural Beauty (AONBs), Green Belts, and Best and Most Versatile (BMV) agricultural land;

- *different types of farming* including areas dominated by large estates and owner occupation, upland and lowland farming, and different farm types covering both livestock and arable areas;

- *less favoured or disadvantaged areas* ie Rural Development Areas (RDAs) – now known as Rural Priority Areas – and EU Objective 1, 2, and 5b funded areas;

- *farm diversification initiatives* with the sample reflecting areas where there has been a significant focus on farm diversification and integrated rural development, such as the Forest of Bowland Upland Experiment, work in the Peak District National Park and the Countryside Agency's Land Management Initiatives, as in the High Weald AONB focused on parishes within Wealden District Council, East Sussex.

---

[1] The classification of 'urban fringe', 'accessible rural' and 'remote rural' LPAs has been derived from Tarling et al (1993, RDC) and also checked against the classification developed by Bramley et al (1995, RDC) and subsequently used by Elson et al (1998, RDC).

Table 1.1: Sample Local Planning Authorities (LPAs)

Region/County	Urban fringe	Accessible rural	Remote rural
South West: Cornwall			Caradon
Somerset	Bath & N E Somerset (BaNES)	Sedgemoor	Exmoor National Park
East of England: Norfolk			North Norfolk
South East: East Sussex		Wealden	
Kent	Maidstone		
Hampshire	Eastleigh	Basingstoke & Deane	
East Midlands: Lincolnshire			East Lindsey
Leicestershire	Blaby		
Derbyshire			Peak District National Park
West Midlands: Warwickshire	Warwick	Stratford on Avon Wychavon	
North East: Northumberland			Berwick on Tweed
North West: Lancashire		West Lancashire	Ribble Valley
Cheshire	Ellesmere Port & Neston		
Yorkshire & Humberside: North Yorkshire		Harrogate	North York Moors National Park
Totals: 14 (Counties)	6	7	8

RESEARCH METHODOLOGY

1.15 The research has involved the following activities.

Literature review

1.16 A thorough desk study was undertaken of publications relating to farm diversification and the planning system. This included previously commissioned research by the Department of the Environment/DETR, the former Rural Development Commission and the Planning Officers' Society, and surveys undertaken by the National Farmers' Union (NFU) and Country Landowners' and Business Association (CLA). It also included all related work by other Government departments, agencies and NGOs including MAFF, Countryside Agency, Council for the Protection of Rural England (CPRE), the National Trust, the Soil Association and research bodies such as the Joseph Rowntree Foundation. Consultancy studies undertaken on behalf of these organisations were also reviewed. Electronic searches of agricultural, planning and environmental databases and journals of academic work in the field were supplemented by a review of work by universities undertaking planning and agricultural research (for example, Cambridge University, University of Newcastle Upon Tyne, University of Exeter, University of Plymouth and Oxford Brookes University).

National consultations

1.17   Consultations were held (either by telephone or in person) with:

- British Horse Society (BHS)

- Countryside Agency

- Country Land and Business Association (CLA)

- Council for the Protection of Rural England (CPRE)

- Farm and Rural Conservation Agency (FRCA)

- Local Government Association (LGA)

- Ministry of Agriculture, Fisheries and Food (MAFF) – now the Department for Environment, Food and Rural Affairs (DEFRA)

- National Farmers' Union (NFU)

- National Trust (NT)

- Planning Inspectorate

- Planning Officers' Society (POS)

- Royal Institution of Chartered Surveyors (RICS)

- Royal Town Planning Institute (RTPI)

- Rural Design and Building Association (RDBA)

- Tenant Farmers' Association (TFA)

- Thoroughbred Breeders Association

Review of planning appeals

1.18   With the assistance of the Planning Inspectorate all appeals in England relating to farm diversification for the three-year period February 1997 – February 2000 were identified. This involved a three-stage process: first, the Planning Inspectorate undertook a search of their database for any planning appeals with 'change of use' in the title; second, this list was manually reviewed by the research team for those appeals relating to farm diversification; third, from this list the Inspectorate selected approximately 40 cases across England which represented the range of activities and developments covered by the research. Nineteen of these were selected for more detailed review and 12 have been written up (**Appendix 9**).

Review of statutory development plans

1.19 The Local Plans (total 24), Structure Plans (total 16) and Regional Planning Guidance (RPG) (total eight plus six further draft documents) relating to the 21 sample LPAs were reviewed to assess their policy content on rural and farm diversification and their conformity with current national planning guidance, as set out in PPG7 (1997). The approach followed in the plan review is considered further in **Chapter 3.**

Review of development control decisions and practice for farm diversification

1.20 Within each of the 21 sample LPAs the following activities were undertaken:

- Structured interviews were held with the local plans officer, development control officer(s) and the economic development officer, to explore the local plan policies for farm diversification and how these are implemented through the development control process.

- The planning register was reviewed in each LPA for the last three years, February 1997 – February 2000, with all farm diversification enterprises identified entered onto a summary database.

- Within each LPA a stratified random sample of 20 applications for farm diversification (total 420) was selected for more detailed investigation, with a fuller database being completed on each, based on reference to the case files.

- A short postal questionnaire (**Appendix 2**) was sent by the University of the West of England (UWE) to each applicant relating to the sub-sample of 420 applications. This questionnaire explored the planning process followed, the applicant's views on this process and, where the application had been implemented, the nature of the development and the farm that it was attached to. In total 181 returns were received representing a response rate of 43% – this is a high return for a postal questionnaire of this type, where a response of 30% is considered good. In this report this is referred to as the postal questionnaire.

Case studies

1.21 From the sub-sample of 420 applications for farm diversification, 12 were identified with the help of the project Steering Group for more detailed investigation as case studies (**Appendix 8**). These involved interviews with the applicant and the relevant development control officer. These case studies are **not** representative of the total sample but have been chosen to exemplify diversification involving:

- equestrian activities

- developments typical of what may be anticipated in the future (eg 'B1' uses, manufacture and farm shops)

- large scale developments or those with significant expansion

- applications that were refused

- applications that were refused and then approved

- applications resulting in personal permissions.

Farmer surveys and workshops

1.22 The data collected from the above activities provided information on how farm diversification interacts with the planning system and, through the postal questionnaire to applicants and the case studies, picked up on the applicants' experience of the planning system. But other than anecdotal evidence from previous studies, the data did not reveal the more general concerns of the farming community and the reasons why farmers may be put off from diversifying. To try and address these concerns further work was undertaken in three of the sample LPAs:

- Maidstone, Kent (urban fringe)

- Stratford, Warwickshire (accessible rural)

- North Yorkshire Moors National Park (remote rural)

This work, which was undertaken by the Royal Agricultural College Enterprise (RACE), involved a farmer telephone survey and farmer workshops:

1.23 **Farmer telephone survey:** A telephone interview was conducted with a randomly selected sample of farmers, drawn from a marketing database. The purpose of these interviews was first, to collect data from farmers on their experience of diversification and the planning system and second, to identify those farmers willing to attend a workshop. The methodology and questionnaire used are set out in **Appendix 3,** while **Appendix 4**, sets out the full results of this telephone survey. In this report this survey is referred to as the farmer telephone survey.

1.24 **Farmer workshops:** Following on from the above, two workshops were held in each of the three local authority areas. The first afternoon workshop was for farming advisors and representatives including land agents and NFU and CLA representatives, while the second evening meeting was for farmers identified through the telephone survey. The aim was to have 8 to 12 attendees per workshop to discuss their experience of farm diversification and the planning system.

Planning workshops

1.25 Finally, three planning workshops for planning officers were held in Bristol, London and Manchester in January 2001, with the purpose of discussing the findings of the research, allowing sharing of experience and the testing of conclusions. Each had 8-10 participants.

Data collected

1.26 In summary, the data on which this study is based, in addition to that collected through consultations and a literature review, are as follows:

- Review of all extant RPG and all revision documents (total 14 documents); 16 Structure Plans, and 24 Local Plans relating to 21 Local Planning Authorities (including two National Park Authorities (NPAs)).

- A database of **1397 planning applications** for farm diversification across 21 sample LPAs in England, made over the three years February 1997 – February 2000. Of these **420** were looked at in detail.

- **12 case studies** of planning applications for farm diversification, drawn from the sample of 420.

- Statistics on **all appeals** relating to farm diversification in England over the three years February 1997 – February 2000 (approximately 300) of which 19 were looked at in detail and 12 written up.

- A postal questionnaire response from **181** out of 420 applicants contacted (43% response rate).

- A telephone questionnaire response from **67** farmers out of 554 contacted (12.1% response rate).

This is supported by data collected through national consultations, interviews with 21 LPAs, and planning and farmer workshops.

1.27 This suggests that the findings of this study are robust when compared to previous studies which have addressed the same topic. For example, the authoritative RDC-commissioned study on *Rural Development and Land Use Planning Policies* (Elson et al. 1998) was based on a review of 5 RPG, 10 Structure Plans and 32 Local Plans including two NPAs; interviews with 17 LPAs; development control data collected from eight LPAs covering 316 applications; combined with telephone interviews with a range of planning consultants and agents, and national consultations.

STRUCTURE OF THIS REPORT

1.28 The following Chapters set out the findings of the research:

Chapter 2: Background and trends: Provides context to the study, setting out background trends and issues identified primarily through the literature review and national consultations.

Chapter 3: Development plan policies: Focuses on the review of the statutory development plans and the degree to which their policies for rural and farm diversification reflect the guidance in PPG7 (1997). It also reviews Regional Planning Guidance.

Chapter 4: Development control process adopted for farm diversification applications: Looks at the process adopted by applicants in making a planning application (drawing on the results of the postal questionnaire, case studies and the telephone interviews with farmers) and follows the process adopted by LPAs in determining such applications.

Chapter 5: Results of the planning register review: Examines the results of the planning system, the approval rates for farm diversification planning applications, the use of conditions and reasons for refusal. This Chapter largely draws on the database built up from the planning registers of the sample LPAs, cross referred to the case studies and appeals.

Chapter 6: Perceptions and opportunities: Looks at the perceptions of the farming community with regard to farm diversification in general and the planning process in particular. It identifies some potential positive measures put forward by the farming community and planners. This Chapter draws on the results of the postal questionnaire, telephone survey, farmer workshops, and the planning workshops.

Chapter 7: Conclusion: Summarises the conclusions of this fact-finding research, including recommendations and best practice.

CHAPTER 2
Background and trends

2.1   This Chapter briefly sets out the policy context to farm diversification, the extent of farm diversification to date, and the influence of planning on this activity.

THE AGRICULTURAL ECONOMY

2.2   The economy of rural England is changing. British farming is in crisis having experienced a rapid and deepening decline in farm incomes since the mid 1990s. Over the last five years farm incomes have fallen by over 60% (DETR/MAFF, 2000) and are now at their lowest level for 20 years. For example, in 1995 the typical farm income in the South East was £270/hectare: by 1997 this had fallen to £32/hectare[2]. For hill farmers in England, Net Farm Income dropped by nearly 50% between 1997/98 and 1998/99 and a further 20% over the following year (MAFF, 2000). According to the *Annual Farm Business Survey* for the period March 2000 – February 2001 (MAFF) overall farm incomes fell by a further 10% over the year, bringing the average farm income down to £5,200. At the same time, in October 2000 Deloitte's[3] predicted a national average Net Farm Income of minus £22/hectare for the financial year 2000/2001(without taking account of the effects of the Foot and Mouth epidemic).

2.3   This decline in farm incomes is the result of both short and long-term causes. Exchange rates, the legacy of BSE, reduced price support under the CAP and a fall in international commodity prices have combined to drive down prices and support, and drive up costs.

2.4   Agriculture's relative importance in the UK economy has been declining. At publication of the *Rural White Paper* (November 2000) it accounted for only 4% of GDP in rural areas, although it has greater significance in terms of employment in some parts of the country, especially in upland and more remote rural areas dependant on livestock farming. On the other hand, the range of rural employment opportunities outside agriculture is increasing, with rural areas having a generally lower unemployment rate than normally seen in urban areas (Countryside Agency, 2000). But important disparities in economic activity and unemployment still exist between different rural areas. Rural wages are lower on average, jobs are more likely to be seasonal or casual than in urban areas, unemployment in lower skill sectors is relatively high and remote rural areas are generally more disadvantaged. These problems have been compounded by the different sectoral and geographical impacts of the current agricultural crisis, as poorer more marginal areas of the country have been hit hardest – a problem that has been significantly compounded by the Foot and Mouth epidemic.

[2] MAFF *England Rural Development Plan – South East Region* (2000)

[3] Deloitte and Touche News. October 12th 2000. *Rural Landscape Under Threat*

Figure 2.1: Farm incomes in the UK, Economic Trends

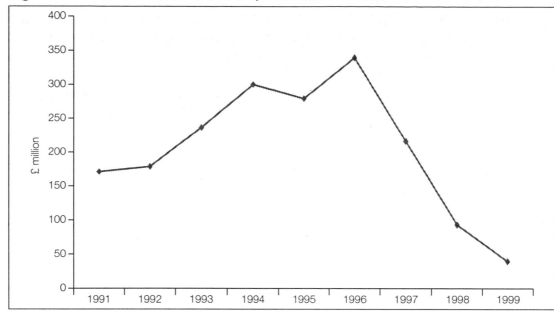

Source: *Farm Incomes in the UK, Economic Trends*, various years

POLICY CONTEXT

2.5   Farm diversification is not a new phenomenon. Farming has long played a key role in tourism and many other aspects of the rural economy. But it is only within the last two decades that it has been promoted in national policy as a means of contributing to farm incomes.

2.6   Three important aspects of national policy set the framework for farm diversification and this study:

● *The England Rural Development Programme* (ERDP) 2001-2006. MAFF. October 2000

● *The Government's Strategy for Agriculture: An Action Plan for Farming.* MAFF. March 2000

● The Rural White Paper – *Our Countryside: The Future – A fair deal for rural England.* DETR/MAFF. November 2000.

The England Rural Development Programme

2.7   Under Agenda 2000, the Rural Development Regulation (RDR) has been introduced as the second pillar of the CAP across the EU, providing the start in the redirection of agricultural support from commodity support to schemes which boost the broader rural economy; advance environmentally beneficial farming practices; and help to modernise and restructure the farming industry. In England this is being taken forward by the England Rural Development Programme (ERDP) which was launched on 3rd October 2000, following publication of the England Rural Development Plan earlier in the year. This programme provides £1.6bn for agriculture over the next seven years and is the main plank in the delivery of the Government's *Action Plan for Farming* (outlined below). It provides four new support schemes to assist in the development of the rural economy, plus enhanced budgets for existing schemes, as follows:

New schemes

- *The Rural Enterprise Scheme:* delivers £152 million over the programme period, providing targeted support for the development of more sustainable, diversified, enterprising rural economies and communities

- A *Processing and Marketing Grant:* gives a total of £44 million to encourage innovation and investment to achieve added value for English primary products

- A *new Vocational Training Scheme* with a total of £22 million available for training activities that broaden the skills base of agricultural and forestry workers

- A *new Energy Crops Scheme* for establishing energy crops and producer groups.

Additional support

- For the *Woodland Grant Scheme* and *Farm Woodland Premium Scheme*

- For *Agri-environment Schemes,* including *Organic Farming Schemes*

- For the new *Hill Farm Allowance Scheme* to help preserve the farmed upland environment

In addition, as announced in the *Action Plan for Farming*, MAFF launched the Farm Business Advice Service to deliver business advice and assistance to farmers.

The Government's strategy for agriculture – An Action Plan for Farming

2.8 In response to the deepening decline in farm incomes at the beginning of 2000, the Government launched its *Action Plan for Farming* in March 2000. This set out a five-point plan of action, building on the activities being undertaken as part of the England Rural Development Programme (ERDP). These actions are:

i) *Partnership – building a broad partnership of interest.*

ii) *Measures to provide relief for the hardest-hit sectors throughout the UK and help ease the process of change*

iii) *Measures to ensure that the England Rural Development Programme steers the industry towards its new priorities and new directions*

iv) *Government support for a range of measures to give farmers better advice and support to promote diversification (see above)*

v) *Measures to ensure that the Government, farmers and the food industry work together to find ways to improve profitability in the industry*

vi) *Work in Brussels for further market-orientated CAP reform, removal of production controls and simplification of bureaucracy.*

A central tenet of the *Action Plan* is the promotion of farm diversification ((iii) &(iv) above.):

"The entrepreneurial family farm will continue to thrive – but it will often be supported by adding value to farm products or income from non-farming activity. In many more areas farmers will look to turn a positive approach to the environment to their own economic advantage."

2.9 To help in the delivery of farm diversification, the *Action Plan* announced a range of improvements and assistance to help farmers diversify, including the potential revision of national planning guidance on farm diversification as set out in PPG7 (1997). These are now being taken forward under the ERDP, with further assistance and advice confirmed in the Rural White Paper.

2.10 At a seminar hosted by Nick Raynsford, Minister for Planning, in May 2000 to discuss farm diversification and the planning system, it was generally agreed that national planning guidance on the countryside as set out in PPG7 (1997) is broadly satisfactory and not a priority for immediate, major revision (the notes of this seminar are available on the DTLR website at www.dtlr.gov.uk/planning/seminar/01.htm). There was greater concern, however, that the guidance in PPG13 (1994) on transport tended to be interpreted in such a way as potentially to undermine policies in favour of farm diversification. It was also recognised that there was a shortage of information on how national policies for farm diversification were reflected in local plans and implemented through the development control process. This is the purpose of this study.

The Rural White Paper. Our Countryside: The Future

2.11 This White Paper launched in November 2000 has the aim of sustaining and enhancing the distinctive environment, economy and social fabric of the English countryside for the benefit of all, with the vision of a *"living, working, protected and vibrant countryside"*. The support and encouragement of farm diversification in the *Action Plan for Farming* and the *ERDP* is restated. In reviewing the planning environment for farm diversification, the White Paper [Chapter 8] states that the Government will be:

● providing free consultancy advice on planning for farmers pursuing diversification projects under the Rural Enterprise Scheme;

● revising PPG 13 to clarify the interrelationship between transport policy and rural development proposals (published 27 March 2001);

● providing a planning policy statement clarifying the positive approach which local authorities are expected to take towards farm diversification (issued 21 March 2001 – para 2.18 below); and

● publishing a revised edition of *A Farmer's Guide to the Planning System*.

Other initiatives

Following the *Action Plan for Farming* and the *ERDP*, a range of other actions have and are being undertaken in support of farm diversification including:

Nationally

● MAFF published (December 2000) a free leaflet *New Directions – Farm Diversification* as a forerunner to a forthcoming guide on the same subject.

- The Countryside Agency and Regional Development Agencies issued a joint statement in September 2000 explaining how they would work together to assist the rural economy.

- DETR, through the Government's Regional Offices, promoted a series of on-going workshops during 2000/01 in co-operation with MAFF, the Countryside Agency, NFU, CLA and other regional partners, to encourage dialogue and better understanding between farmers, planners and local authorities at the regional level.

- The Local Government Association (LGA) has produced a *Charter for Agriculture* which provides a checklist of the many ways that local authorities, both rural and urban, interact with agriculture.

- CPRE published *Farm Diversification: Planning for success* in May 2000.

- RICS has been holding seminars to raise the awareness of its members to the needs of farm diversification.

- The Rural Design and Building Association continues to hold conferences and farm visits to promote farm diversification.

Locally
- The Planning Officers Society (POS) has been encouraging planning officers to contact their local NFU and CLA branches to develop agricultural fora and potentially appoint farm liaison officers.

- The National Trust has recently appointed new farming and countryside officers in each of its regions to offer advice and assistance to the National Trust's tenant farmers.

2.12 In addition, there are a large and growing number of local initiatives promoting farm diversification and integrated rural development, including the MAFF Upland Experiments (Forest of Bowland and Bodmin) and the Land Management Initiatives (LMIs) being supported by the Countryside Agency, as well as a number of well documented projects initiated under Objective 5b, such as that in the Marches area of Shropshire. Individual local authorities have also been developing their contacts with the farming community through the promotion of farmers' markets and other positive initiatives (often under the banner of Local Agenda 21) and through farming fora and other methods of liaison, explored further in Chapter 4.

2.13 It is too early to identify the full Government response to the re-building of agriculture in the worst affected areas following the Foot and Mouth epidemic but local authorities in association with the Regional Development Agencies are developing early recovery programmes. For example, Cumbria County Council has established a Foot and Mouth Task Force which is looking at ways of combining and enhancing measures under the ERDP, the Objective 2 programme and other rural regeneration programmes administered by the Countryside Agency and the North West Regional Development Agency, with the aim of developing new ways of 're-engineering' agriculture, tourism and the rural economy[4].

---

[4] WWF. Press information: Foot and Mouth Addendum. April 2001

Sustainable development

2.14 A theme running through much of the above policy development and action and through national planning policy, is that of sustainable development. The Government's strategy for sustainable development in the UK is set out in *A Better Quality of Life* (May, 1999). This seeks a better quality of life for everyone, now and for generations to come. It is driven by four objectives as set out in the Government's strategy:

- *Social progress that recognises the needs of everyone;*

- *Effective protection of the environment;*

- *Prudent use of natural resources; and*

- *Maintenance of high and stable levels of economic growth and employment.*

2.15 Within rural areas, sustainable development is sometimes described by practitioners as integrated rural development which seeks the integration of economic, social and environmental objectives. This integration is evident in the aims of the Rural White Paper.

2.16 The importance of sustainable and integrated development is highlighted in PPG12: *Development Plans* (December, 1999):

Paragraph 4.1 notes "... *The planning system, and development plans in particular, can make a major contribution to the achievement of the Government's objectives for sustainable development*" and in paragraph 4.2 goes on to note that "*The Development Plan Regulations require local authorities to have regard to environmental, social and economic considerations when preparing development plans.*" Paragraph 4.3 stresses that " *In all cases, it is necessary to consider the interaction of policies within the plan, so that, for example, the environmental and social implications of policies designed to encourage economic growth are fully considered*".

National planning guidance

2.17 The national planning guidance for rural areas is provided by PPG7 (1997) which gives clear support for farm diversification. Despite this support, over the last few years, there have been some suggestions that there should be a fundamental review of planning as it relates to farm diversification. In particular suggestions:

- in the report *Rural Economies* (1999) by the Performance and Innovation Unit (PIU) of the Cabinet Office, that farm developments should be placed in the B1 Use Class (offices and light industrial) so that their re-use for such purposes would not require planning permission, provided that all new agricultural buildings were subject to full planning control (ie., no longer covered by Permitted Development Rights under Part 6 of the T&CP General Permitted Development Order 1995);

- by the RTPI that a Rural Business or Enterprise Use Class should be introduced. This would incorporate a wide range of permitted uses appropriate to a rural area but with conditions to ensure that intensification of activity would trigger a threshold requiring planning permission.

Another suggestion from the Rural Design and Building Association is that equestrian development should not require planning permission because of its intrinsic similarities with farming.

2.18   Nevertheless, the supportive context to farm diversification provided by PPG7 (1997) was recognised at the May 2000 seminar noted above (para 2.10), and has been fully endorsed by those consulted through this study. More recently, the Government's encouragement of farm diversification has been strengthened in national planning policy by revision to PPG 11: *Regional Planning* (October, 2000), revision to PPG 13: *Transport* (March, 2001) (para 3.65), and a policy statement issued by DETR on 21ˢᵗ March 2001 clarifying PPG7 (1997). In the latter policy statement[5] stress is placed on the importance of LPAs supporting *"farm diversification schemes for business purposes that are consistent in their scale with their rural location"* and reflects the *"importance that the Government attaches to effective planning for sustainable farm diversification projects and the re-use of redundant farm buildings"*. This is specifically set out in revisions to paragraphs 2.8 and 3.4 of PPG7 (1997):

Paragraph 2.8 *"..encourage rural enterprise, including the diversification of farm businesses"*

Paragraph 3.4A, having introduced the context for farm diversification provided by the ERDP and the Government's *Action Plan for Farming* advises that *"Local planning authorities should be supportive of well-conceived farm diversification schemes for business purposes that are consistent in their scale with their rural location."*

Paragraph 3.4B *"...........it is usually preferable for farm diversification schemes to re-use good quality existing buildings and put them to a new business use, rather than build new buildings in the countryside. New buildings, either to replace existing buildings or to accommodate expansion of enterprises, may also be acceptable provided that they satisfy sustainable development objectives and are of a design and scale appropriate to their rural surroundings."*

2.19   The full policy guidance provided by PPG7 for farm diversification is returned to in Chapter 3.

2.20   Nevertheless, as acknowledged in the Rural White Paper [paragraph. 8.4.5], there is anecdotal evidence that farmers are sometimes discouraged from making planning applications for farm diversification by the attitude of LPAs. This has been reflected in a number of recent reports. An NFU survey in England (1999) indicated that 17% of farmers cited planning restrictions as a reason not to diversify. The CLA in a survey of its members (2000) across England and Wales, found that 52% of respondents who had approached their LPA concerning farm diversification had been discouraged from pursuing their proposal by the advice received and of these 52%, only 45% had gone on to make a planning application. These concerns are picked up in Chapter 6.

Tenant farmers

2.21   The one area where considerable concern has been expressed about the whole concept of farm diversification is amongst tenant farmers. As noted by the Tenant Farmers Association, there are three main concerns. Firstly, the majority of farm tenants are bound by agreements that restrict their use of land to agricultural activity. The majority of

---

[5] DETR Press Notices *Farmers Get Greater Flexibility in New Planning Guidance* www.press.dtlr.gov.uk/0103/0155.htm and www.planning.dtlr.gov.uk/ppg/ppg7/index.htm

tenancies are still under the 1986 Agricultural Holdings Act. This legislation and the contracts of tenancy together specify that tenants can only be involved in agricultural activity. While the 1995 Agricultural Tenancies Act was meant to provide a better platform for landlords and tenants to agree farm diversification, user clauses imposed by some landlords in these agreements has made them even more restrictive than the 1986 tenancies[6].

2.22   Secondly, diversification could affect succession. Under the old legislation many tenants have the ability to pass on the tenancy to the next generation. There are statutory tests that have to be passed by the successor, including that the principal source of livelihood of the successor in five out of the last seven years has been from the farm. It is argued that in many cases, diversified activities will be run by the very individuals who may succeed to the tenancy. If their principal livelihood has been non agricultural this may jeopardise their succession.

2.23   Thirdly, there is concern that if there was relaxation of planning in favour of farm diversification, this would give landlords a greater opportunity of obtaining planning permission and thereby serving a notice to quit on the tenant.

2.24   A survey of CLA members conducted by the CLA between December 1999 and January 2000 indicated the potential caution of tenant farmers to farm diversification, with only 14.6% of tenants identified in the survey having approached their landlords to discuss diversification. But the survey also shows that an overwhelming majority (94%) of landlords are willing to consider proposals by tenants for farm diversification in a positive light, with only a very small number of landlords having refused consent for diversification (para 4.4). The survey also suggests that user clauses inserted in contracts of tenancy under the 1995 Agricultural Tenancies Act do not provide a barrier to diversification by tenants.

FARM DIVERSIFICATION ACTIVITY

Views on farm diversification

2.25   Against the policy background described above, all the national consultees, with the exception of the Tenant Farmers Association, gave strong support to farm diversification (eg Countryside Agency, NFU, CLA, NT, RTPI, POS, LGA, RICS, CPRE). But there was a recognition that it is not appropriate for everyone, nor a panacea for agriculture (NFU, CLA, RICS). It is the view of the NFU and CLA that farm diversification needs to be seen as part of broader agricultural reform. In the recently published (March 2001) report of the Hills Task Force – set up in November 2000 by the then Minister for Agriculture – there is a clear view that diversification must be wide ranging and integrated:

"..diversification must have its widest possible meaning to be relevant: wives working off the farm, odd days of contracting and part-time work, niche markets, tourism and trying to secure more of the premium from breeding, processing and marketing quality stock – they can all play a part. There is no panacea, but scope for a thousand different flowers to bloom" [X1.2]. The report goes on to recommend that a farm's appropriateness for diversification should be very carefully

---

[6] According to the TFA this is particularly because landlords do not want to loose control of their land and because taxation relief (particularly for Capital Gains and Inheritance Tax) could be put at risk if any tenancy granted offered the tenant the ability to be involved in activities that are not strictly agricultural.

considered including, amongst other things, its assets; the attributes of the farm household; location; planning policy; access to local markets; market capacity; and impact on the core business and that *"particular care must be taken not to apply diversification blueprints in the hills where every situation is different"* [recommendation 20].

2.26   This focus on integration was re-iterated in discussion with the Countryside Agency, CPRE and LGA who recognised that farm diversification should be of a type that is innovative, based on sound business planning, and which maximises benefits for the farm business, the wider rural economy, the local community, and re-enforces local character and identity. It was also recognised that the character and quality of the countryside are vital economic assets which, aside from environmental arguments, should be conserved for economic reasons alone.

2.27   As noted in the NFU survey of farm diversification (1999), an important feature of farm income diversification is to provide an element of financial stability in a business subject to high volatility in the primary income source. Generally, while farm income is subject to sudden changes, income from non-agricultural sources tends to be more consistent and therefore increases stability.

Extent of farm diversification

2.28   The most comprehensive study to-date on the extent of farm diversification is that produced by ADAS *English Agriculture: Opportunities for Change and Diversification* (2000) which draws on a range of existing surveys[7]. This concluded that over 50% of farms in England have some form of diversified enterprise (covering on-farm agricultural enterprises such as organic cropping, on-farm non-agricultural enterprises, and off-farm income). This is supported by a separate NFU survey (1999) which identified that in 1998, 62% of farmers received income from sources outside agriculture, compared to 50% in 1993 (again this survey includes off-farm income including investments).

2.29   Leaving aside pensions, investments and social payments, the MAFF Farm Business Survey for 1997/98 suggests that nationally:

● 5% of full-time farms have **on-farm diversification activities** (including both agricultural and non-agricultural income), contributing on average £6,000 per farm, or 45% of farm income;

● 20% of full-time farms gain **income earned off the farm** by the farmer or spouse, contributing on average £11,500 per farm, or 78% of farm income.

(These figures would be significantly higher if part-time farms were included).

2.30   For on-farm non-agricultural diversification, by far the most common activity is tourism. This is confirmed by the ADAS study and the findings of this study (Chapter 5), as well as previous studies of rural diversification (Elson, 1995) and rural building re-use (LUC, 1995). Farm tourism is particularly prevalent in more remote rural areas of high landscape

[7] The main surveys identified in this report are:
● Exeter University 1989. 5,800 postal questionnaires. England
● Exeter University 1991. 488 interviews. GB
● Nat West UK 1992. 25,799 postal questionnaires. GB
● Produce Studies. 1994. 801 interviews. GB
● ADAS Farmers' Voice. 1999. 2352 postal questionnaires. England

quality, such as the National Parks. Co-incidentally these are also the areas which are dominated by small livestock farms that have been at the forefront of the Foot and Mouth epidemic.

2.31 For off-farm income the ADAS study identified that farm services and agricultural contracting are by far the most popular form of farm diversification overall, involving a third of all farmers under the age of 25. This growth in farm contracting is being encouraged by four interlinked trends – farm amalgamations; loss of full-time farm labour as farm businesses rationalise; the purchase of farmland by non-farmers who then require assistance in the management of the land; and the retirement of farmers who use farm diversification as their pension plan, with the land managed under contract and the agricultural buildings leased out for business use.

2.32 From the Farm Business Survey it appears that all sizes of farm benefit from non-farm income, although lower income farms have tended to diversify their income sources more, compared to higher income farms. Other commentators have suggested that the amount of farm income derived from farm diversification has been increasing over the last few years as a percentage of overall farm income. But this is likely to be more a reflection of declining agricultural incomes than a significant increase in diversified incomes.

2.33 In conclusion, there is now very strong national policy support for farm diversification underpinned by funding streams and advice to farmers, combined with a supportive planning policy framework. Much of this support is new and has yet to be felt and so, to-date, farm diversification activity has been relatively limited. Where it has occurred, the primary emphasis has been on tourism development (concentrated in the more remote rural areas). The main sources of diversified income though, comes from off the farm, primarily agricultural contracting. The limited market opportunities for farm diversification in some areas has caused the NFU and CLA to comment that farm diversification is not the panacea for the future of farming – a view shared by the Government's Task Force for the Hills. Nevertheless, as the recently introduced support for farm diversification beds down, there is likely to be a considerable increase in diversification activity, especially in the light of the Foot and Mouth epidemic, which is likely to accelerate further government support in this area.

CHAPTER 3

Development plan policies

3.1 This Chapter reviews the Regional Planning Guidance (RPG) and statutory development plan policies relating to rural and farm diversification across the 21 sample LPAs, and reports on the interviews with development plan officers. It specifically focuses on how Regional Planning Guidance compares with the national guidance contained in PPG 11 (2000) and how local plan policies compare with the national guidance contained in PPG7 (1997). A full list of the plans reviewed is set out in **Appendix 5.**

REGIONAL PLANNING GUIDANCE

3.2 All RPG in England, both extant and draft versions, have been examined as part of this study and compared with the comments of planning officers on RPG.

3.3 PPG11: *Regional Planning* (2000), sets the context for rural policy within Regional Planning Guidance (RPG) noting in paragraph 9.3 that:

"In preparing regional or sub-regional rural policies in RPG it will be important to identify and take account of environmental, economic and social needs, opportunities and capacities. RPG should take account of the diverse nature of rural areas with policy being focussed on finding ways to address the needs of rural communities while respecting environmental quality and enhancing the quality of life."

3.4 It continues in paragraph 9.4 to say:

"Farming makes a major contribution to the economy of rural areas but increasingly farm businesses need to diversify and new businesses need to be established in order to maintain the economic vitality of rural communities. This is something which the Government wishes to encourage."

3.5 At paragraph 9.5 it summarises that amongst other things, RPG should:

"define regionally significant rural economic diversification and regeneration priorities consistent with those set by the RDA's economic strategy, where possible building on the economic and social potential of conservation and environmental activities."

3.6 Thus PPG11 sets a clear requirement that RPG should provide a firm regional context for farm diversification, in both its broader economic circumstances and geographical variation. However, PPG11 is very recent and will only have had a small impact on even the most recent RPGs. As indicated in **Table 3.1**, the majority of the RPGs date from the early or mid-1990s. RPG11 (1998) for the West Midlands and RPG6 for the East of England are more recent and, at the time of the study, were the only RPGs not currently under review.

Table 3.1: Status of RPGs

Region	Extant RPGs	Draft RPGs available
North East	RPG7 1993	Draft 1999
North West	RPG13 1996	Draft 2000
Yorkshire & Humberside	RPG12 1996	Draft 1999
West Midlands	RPG11 1998	None
East Midlands	RPG8 1994	Draft 1999
East of England	RPG6 2000	None
South West	RPG10 1994	Draft 2000
South East	RPG9 1994	Draft 2000

Rural and farm diversification

3.7 The older extant RPGs rarely pay detailed attention to farm diversification. All of the six RPGs which are now being replaced encourage diversification of the rural economy and mention the role of farm diversification in doing so, but rarely go beyond such general support. RPG8 (1994) for the East Midlands is typical:

".... Changes to the European Community Common Agricultural Policy and the need to put less emphasis on food production will increase the already existing possibilities for which farmland and rural buildings can be used to provide alternative income and employment as well as environmental benefits. Development plan policies should therefore be framed to enable farming and other rural industries to develop and diversify. Not only will this allow farmers to continue managing the countryside for the benefit of the whole community but it will help retain young people in the community, maintain rural services and reduce the necessity for long-distance commuting..." [paragraph 4.20]

3.8 The more recent RPG documents examined, comprising two extant RPGs (6 and 11) and six draft documents, all stress the need to diversify the rural economy. RPG9 (South East) frames this in the context of a *"multi-purpose countryside"* but stresses the need for controlled rural development so as not to dilute the 'Urban Renaissance'. Draft RPG7 (North East) states that *"employment in complementary industries such as tourism, leisure and sport provision, cultural industries (particularly craft based), food processing, catering and distribution should also be encouraged through the provision of workspaces through new buildings and conversions"* and encourages LPAs to promote diversification of the rural economy by allowing more varied employment opportunities, while avoiding the need for excessive commuting. The advice in draft RPG13 (North West) is very similar, while RPG11 (West Midlands) adds that such policies should be tailored to the local geography:

"Authorities should, with partners, assess the specific needs and opportunities for rural diversification in different parts of their areas, having regard to the economic differences between accessible and remote rural areas. Development plan policies should then reflect the type of development needed and likely to arise in each area, and the particular characteristics of the local environment." [paragraph 6.3].

3.9 Five of the recent RPG documents specifically address farm or agricultural diversification. RPG11 (West Midlands) is relatively general in its advice: *"Local authorities can help agricultural businesses adapt to such changes by adopting a positive approach to agricultural development and farm diversification proposals"*. Draft RPG10 (South West) advises that local authorities should *"set out policies for supporting sustainable farm diversification schemes which help to maintain the viability of the agriculture sector and rural economic vitality"*. RPG6 (East

Anglia) urges authorities to: *"promote farm diversification appropriate to the environmental and ecological setting, in particular uses which support the local economy through increased employment"* and acknowledges that dispersed patterns of development lead to many rural communities having few alternatives to car-based transport. Draft RPG13 (North West) suggests that local authorities should develop policies for agricultural diversification, recognising the need for a flexible and efficient agricultural industry. Potential diversification activities suggested include farm tourism, farm accommodation, farm shops, on-farm processing and farm woodland management and products. Draft RPG9 (South East) by comparison is more cautious – whilst encouraging small-scale activities and initiatives that will *'add value'* to farm produce, it highlights the need to consider the scale of activity relative to its setting.

3.10　　Many of the development plan officers interviewed, suggested that RPG's coverage of rural issues in general, and of farm diversification in particular, was weak. This view may have been based on the earlier RPGs. On the other hand, there was a concern that if the RPG policies became too detailed they would usurp the role of structure plans.

3.11　　Overall, PPG11 suggests that RPG should base its policies for rural diversification on a clear understanding of the differing needs and characteristics of rural areas within the region. This is beginning to happen in the emerging RPGs, where the coverage of rural diversification is fuller than in the earlier RPGs. But still only five of the eight most recent RPG documents make specific reference to farm diversification. It is important that the new RPGs do address these issues more fully, providing important regional context for development plan policies. Although concern was raised about the interplay between RPG and structure plans, more detailed policies at the regional level, clearly help focus attention on rural areas and help articulate a strategy for rural and farm diversification, which can frame more detailed policies at the structure and local plan level.

DEVELOPMENT PLANS

3.12　　This section looks at the structure and local plan policies relating to the 21 sample LPAs. Sixteen structure plans were reviewed: five pre-1997 plans and 11 post-1997 plans, reflecting the revision of PPG7 in February 1997 (plans adopted in 1997 have been included as pre-1997 plans). Twenty four local plans were examined (two authorities still did not have area-wide plans): seven were pre-1997 plans and 17 post-1997 plans (see **Appendix 5** and **Figure 3.1).**

3.13　　This analysis was based on a systematic review of each plan against a series of questions reflecting the guidance in PPG7. The overall stance of each plan was also assessed. Structure plans cannot be expected to reflect the policy detail in PPG7 and the analysis reflects this. Where development plan officers made specific comments on their policies these are included.

Figure 3.1: Distribution of local plans by age and category of rural area

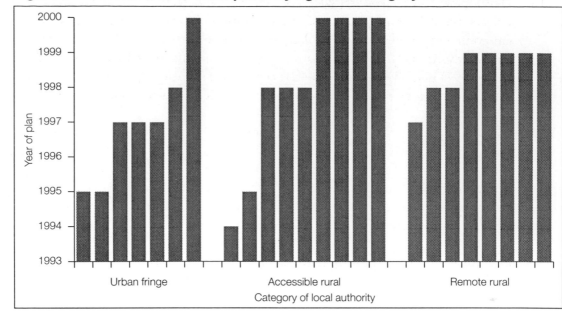

NB. Each bar represents one local plan

Sustainable development and the general approach to development in the countryside

3.14 The Government's objectives for sustainable development are contained in *A Better Quality of Life* (para 2.14) while PPG7's general approach to sustainable rural development is set out in paragraphs 1.3 and 1.4 of that document. Broadly, PPG7 encourages economic growth and diversification which meets the economic and social needs of people who live and work in rural areas, while protecting the rural environment, and states that *"Building in the open countryside, away from existing settlements or from areas allocated for development in development plans, should be strictly controlled."* [paragraph 2.3]

Structure Plans

3.15 The pre-1997 structure plans tend to focus on environmental conservation while post-1997 plans address economic, social and environmental issues. Nevertheless, there are a few post-1997 structure plans that do not make explicit reference to sustainable development. But all structure plans promote rural enterprise.

Local Plans

3.16 **Sustainable development:** The majority of local plans incorporate policies or text explicitly addressing sustainable development although most do not make specific reference to *A Better Quality of Life*. Interpretation of the principles of sustainability varies however, with seven LPAs putting a greater emphasis on environmental protection than on achieving integration between environmental protection and meeting the social and economic needs of the community.

3.17 A few plans do not explicitly address sustainable development. Examples include Cheddar and Bridgwater Local Plans (Sedgemoor District Council) and Bath and North East Somerset (BaNES) (pre-1997), and Ribble Valley and Ellesmere Port and Neston (post-1997). The strategic aims of both Ribble Valley and Ellesmere Port and Neston though, are clearly related to sustainable development.

3.18   **Development in the countryside:** The general approach to development in the countryside reflects the LPA's interpretation of sustainability, with several putting a strong emphasis on environmental protection, particularly in Green Belt areas. The plans of the three National Park Authorities (NPAs) all contain strict environmental restraints, although the Exmoor Plan (1997) notably strives, within the constraints of the designation, for a reconciliation between environmental protection and meeting social and economic needs.

3.19   Encouraging economic development whilst protecting the rural environment is a policy stance that has been at the heart of rural planning policy for some time and thus is fairly reflected in the majority of structure and local plans, although some plans have greater emphasis on environmental conservation than economic concerns. In contrast, promoting living rural communities and recognising the interdependence of urban and rural policies are more recent concerns and are not found in the majority of plans.

Economic development in rural areas

3.20   PPG7 (1997) strongly supports economic development in rural areas and rural diversification. Addressing rural diversification, paragraph 3.8 states *"The range of businesses that can be successfully located in rural areas is expanding"* and gives general support for new firms in the countryside as they contribute to the local and national economy and *"bring new life and activity to rural communities"*. Paragraph 2.10 notes that *"The main focus of new development should be on existing towns and villages (including networks of small villages) and other areas allocated in development plans, where employment, housing (including affordable housing) and other facilities can be provided close together"*. This advice is little changed from that of PPG7 (1992).

3.21   In paragraph 2.9 of the PPG, LPAs are advised to take account of the then DOE, 1995 Good Practice Guide, *Planning for Rural Diversification*, which notes the importance of local authorities *"assessing the economic and social needs of their areas; devising policies for economic activity which respects the countryside; and taking a constructive approach to planning applications"*. Paragraph 3.9 (PPG7) notes that assessments of local social and economic needs can be carried out under Sections 11 or 30 of the Town and Country Planning Act 1990, and may set out priorities for the types of economic development appropriate to particular areas.

3.22   Paragraph 3.10 (PPG7) advises on small-scale commercial development in the countryside, and 3.11 on the expansion of existing businesses.

Structure Plans

3.23   Most structure plans identify the importance of diversifying the rural economy, but most lack detailed policy. In general structure plans reflect the overall strategy of wishing to concentrate commercial development in settlements and to restrict development in the open countryside.

3.24   The Cornwall, East Sussex and Brighton and Hove, Kent, Lancashire, Leicestershire, Lincolnshire and Norfolk plans contain general criteria for assessing the suitability of commercial development in rural areas. Criteria typically include environmental and landscape impacts, provision of infrastructure, requirements for the development to be small-scale and in keeping with the character of its surroundings, avoidance of Best and Most Versatile agricultural land and encouragement of the re-use of buildings, or justification for requiring new buildings. The Lancashire Structure Plan contains one of the most comprehensive rural development policies, addressing many of the issues variously covered by other structure plans:

> "(c) *Development in the open countryside outside Green Belts will be limited to:*
> *(i) that needed for the purposes of agriculture, forestry or other uses appropriate to a rural area, including ones which will help diversify the rural economy while being in keeping with the rural environment; (ii) the rehabilitation and reuse of buildings subject to this not having adverse effects on the rural economy; (iii) the reuse or redevelopment of major developed sites."*
> *(extract, Lancashire Structure Plan, Policy 1).*

Like the majority of other plans, the Leicestershire Structure Plan requires that employment development should "...*not lead to the dispersal of employment activities which would undermine the vitality of the rural centre."* [Employment Policy 9]

Local Plans

3.25 **Rural economic development:** All local plans, both pre and post-1997, with the exception of one pre-1997 and two post-1997 plans, explicitly outline an approach to rural diversification and most plans contain policies for new small-scale commercial and industrial development in rural areas. Plans favour locations for such development which are in or adjacent to settlements, though some occasionally stipulate the specific circumstances in which small-scale development might be allowed in other locations (including on farms).

3.26 Criteria-based policies for employment development in rural areas are found in both pre- and post-1997 plans, though some contain criteria which are more restrictive than those in PPG7. Examples of additional criteria include; design, appearance and materials, noise pollution and general amenity issues. Maidstone and Eastleigh (pre-1997 and both urban fringe authorities) contain policies specifically prohibiting new buildings in the countryside.

3.27 45% of local plans contain policies for the future expansion of businesses in rural areas. The Peak District local plan includes a criterion that development outside settlements "*.....should not expand the physical limits of the established use".* Maidstone also prohibits expansion of existing businesses, and Eastleigh contains very strict criteria for the same. Sedgemoor's (post-1997) criteria for expansion of businesses in the countryside are, in contrast, less restrictive than PPG7, being only that the use:

- *"is in scale with the existing use*

- *does not generate excessive traffic and/or a significant number of additional trips; and*

- *does not increase the environmental impact of the site"* (policy E7).

3.28 Of the few authorities with development area designations, either European or English, such as Objective 1 status or Rural Development (Priority) Area status, only West Lancashire contains any clearly related policy, though paragraph 4.18 of PPG7 suggests that plans should take account of such designations.

3.29   Overall, therefore, PPG7's strong support for diversification of the rural economy is well covered in most local plans, both pre and post-1997, reflecting that this is a well-established component of rural planning policy. By comparison, this support is less forthright in structure plans.

3.30   **Addressing local circumstances and the tailoring of policy:** Although suggested in the *Good Practice Guide, Planning for Rural Diversification*, and PPG7 paragraph 2.9, that LPAs should assess local economic and social needs to inform rural development policies, this approach is not generally reflected in the sample of plans examined. The Wansdyke and Exmoor (pre-1997) and Harrogate and North York Moors (post-1997) plans contain evidence of assessments of economic trends and recreation and amenity needs in supporting text. Wealden has also conducted a survey on the re-use of rural buildings within the District[8], which has influenced the local plan policies, and will undertake an updated survey to inform the plan review. No plans, though, clearly demonstrated the use of a more comprehensive assessment which has systematically informed policies for rural development.

3.31   Some plans do differentiate between different landscape character areas but this does not extend to considering local economic and social needs.

3.32   When development plan officers were asked about social and economic assessments used to inform plan policies, ten LPAs pointed to relevant studies, although these were often not referred to in the local plan. These included housing needs surveys (four), a survey of business floorspace needs, an agricultural survey, a rural business survey, work for a Single Regeneration Budget bid, and use of village appraisals. LPAs also cited local plan review background papers and piecemeal research as identifying local needs. Whilst useful, it is clear that none had undertaken a more comprehensive needs assessment of the type encouraged by the Good Practice Guide. However, two LPAs suggested that consideration of local needs and circumstances could be addressed at the development control stage within the flexibility provided by local plan policies.

3.33   As part of forthcoming plan reviews, Stratford, Warwick and Wychavon are planning to address variations across their rural areas, with clear differentiation in policy. BaNES is hoping to place more emphasis on local economic development, and East Lindsey is hoping that parish councils will undertake a SWOT analysis of the new plan proposals. Similarly the Peak District NPA intends to use stakeholder groups to give the next plan a more specific local identity. No authority, though, indicated that they intended to undertake a full assessment of rural economic and social needs to inform the plan review. While useful, the piecemeal work described by planning officers cannot wholly fulfil the role of more detailed assessments which combine topic-specific information with, potentially, a more integrated vision of local needs.

3.34   This general lack of information on social and economic needs in rural areas is significant, in that it greatly lessens the ability of plans to make a pro-active and integrated response to local needs in rural areas (as suggested in PPG7 and PPG11). In turn, plans are not in a position to develop an overview for their area and promote particular types of development suitable to the locality or, to tailor policies to reflect local circumstances.

---

[8] This demonstrated that those parts of the District in the Rural Development Area had had fewer economic conversions than other parts of the District, despite the availability of grant aid.

Farm diversification

3.35 National policy guidance on farm diversification was developed considerably in the 1997 revision of PPG7. Paragraph 3.4 stated: *"Farmers increasingly look to diversify beyond agriculture to diversify their incomes. Much farm-based work is now concerned with activities such as woodland management, farm shops, equestrian businesses, sporting facilities, nature trails, craft workshops and holiday accommodation. This provides potential benefits for the local economy and environment."*. The guidance suggested that development plans should state **criteria** for farm-based diversification. It also noted that appropriate new buildings may be considered, as well as the re-use of existing buildings, so long as the operational needs of farming were taken into account. As noted in Chapter 2 this advice was updated and further amplified in March 2001.

3.36 Annex C of PPG7 gives further guidance on development specifically related to farm diversification, such as farm shops and food processing.

Structure Plans

3.37 A significant proportion of Structure Plans contain general policies for diversifying or strengthening the rural economy, as discussed above, but do not specifically address farm diversification. In these cases farm diversification development is left to be considered under the more general heading of rural diversification and, sometimes, rural building re-use. However, others such as Cornwall, Lancashire, Somerset and Exmoor, and Cheshire make specific mention of farm diversification, although the references are often brief and general. For example:

"In rural areas provision should be made for development which creates or enhances local employment, shopping or community facilities, including development necessary for the purposes of agriculture and development associated with the diversification of agricultural units." [Somerset and Exmoor National Park Joint Structure Plan Review, Policy 19]

"In the countryside, proposals for farm diversification schemes well related to existing buildings, and proposals for the change of use of buildings for employment and tourism uses, will be encouraged where the scale and character of the proposal is in keeping with the existing buildings and their surrounding area." [County Durham Structure Plan, Policy 24]

3.38 The Kent Structure Plan goes further and requires that farm diversification development should be connected to and primarily serve a working farm:

"Development which will assist in supporting Kent's agricultural and horticultural industry will normally be permitted, subject to transport, landscape and other planning considerations. Any such development should:

(a) be part of, and primarily serve, an individual viable or potentially viable farm or horticultural unit, or

(b) be well-related to the primary or secondary route networks, and normally be in or adjoining a settlement or located on land identified in local plans for employment uses."
[The Agricultural and Horticultural Industry, Policy ED5]

3.39 The East Sussex and Brighton and Hove Plan requires the provision of a farm or enterprise plan, while Cornwall has an additional policy requiring that '…*development should not prejudice the efficiency of farming*' (Replacement Cornwall Structure Plan, Policy E7).

3.40 Overall, as might be expected, the policies in structure plans for farm diversification are often brief and quite general. Again, it may be that opportunities to indicate how farm diversification can contribute to the meeting of local economic, social and environmental circumstances are being missed.

Local Plans

3.41 Of the 24 local plans examined only 54% specifically addressed farm diversification (three pre- and 10 post-1997 plans). It is particularly surprising that seven post-1997 plans do not cover farm diversification, given the relative prominence of this issue in PPG7 1997.

3.42 Where farm diversification is mentioned, plans generally give positive encouragement, subject to conditions or criteria. Policies usually include restrictions based on landscape/wildlife/character impacts, particularly in Green Belt, AONBs and National Parks. There is also a frequent requirement that traffic generation should not be of an unacceptable level. Where specific criteria are listed, they typically reflect the general tenor of PPG7 (1997) applicable to farm diversification, addressing issues such as building re-use, traffic and access, agricultural operational needs, amenity, and landscape/visual impacts. A broad range of additional criteria are also found in plans, including details on the goods which may be sold by farm shops and requirements for equestrian development. Examples of some of the more comprehensive criteria-based policies are given in **Box 3.1**.

3.43 Within the policies for farm diversification there are also other noticeable variations (examples of which are also given in **Box 3.1**):

- Some policies are clearly more restrictive than the generally supportive tone of PPG7 (1997). This is a characteristic of pre and post-1997 plans.

- Some policies offer only limited guidance and may require conformity with other specified or all other policies in the plan, making it difficult for applicants to understand the expectations of the development. This particularly relates to pre-1997 plans. In post-1997 plans policies are usually fuller and based on detailed criteria for farm diversification. But several post-1997 plans still rely on general policies.

- A recurrent feature of the fuller policies for farm diversification is that development should either be attached to or complimentary to a working farm; or that existing employment on the farm should be retained; or that the development should have a long-term benefit to the agricultural enterprise; or the development should not fragment a farm holding. Thus policies are seeking, in different ways, to establish that farm diversification development is related to an agricultural business which it assists or at least does not disrupt. In discussions with planning officers the need to maintain the viability of farms was widely recognised and Exmoor, for example, commented that a more lenient approach will be taken when a diversification activity is obviously supporting a working farm.

- The Peak District NPA also adds that development shall be restricted to a specific use or range of uses rather than to a more general use class.

3.44   The majority of development plan officers interviewed felt that their policies do not take a significantly different approach to farm diversification from the generally supportive approach taken to broader rural diversification, of which it forms a part. This may be why some even recent plans do not specifically mention farm diversification or only address it in general terms. Furthermore, in some urban fringe authorities, it was noted that farm diversification was difficult to distinguish from other forms of development, as farm buildings and land are often separated from working farms. This contrasts with more remote rural areas where the distinction between farm diversification and other development is more clear cut, allowing authorities such as Exmoor NPA to comment that isolated farms are treated more favourably than other similarly isolated developments.

3.45   **Farm plans:** Paragraph C24 of PPG7 (1997) suggests that farm plans may usefully support farm diversification applications. But within the sample LPAs, only three (Wealden, West Lancashire and Ribble Valley, all post-1997) encourage the use of farm plans. In the case of Wealden, this reflects a similar policy in the East Sussex Structure Plan (para 3.39). In addition, Ellesmere Port and Neston Local Plan makes reference to an agricultural appraisal and notes that this would be expected to accompany particular types of planning application.

3.46   **Policies for specific activities:** Pre-1997 plans contain few policies for specific farm diversification activities. Where activities are referred to, policies most commonly deal with holiday conversions. Of the post-1997 plans, most refer only to a few specific activities, most commonly farm shops, holiday conversions and equestrian activities. Only Harrogate, Caradon, Exmoor and Wealden have a policy for energy crops. In addition, Wealden has detailed additional policies relating to motor and gun sports. An example of a policy for farm shops is included in **Box 3.1**. Discussions with planning officers suggested that these more specific policies were included where a particular type of development was prevalent. However, the point was repeatedly made that the range of activities covered by farm diversification is potentially enormous, both in terms of type and scale of activity. In consequence, it was best to rely on more general policies with in-built flexibility to deal with different types of application.

3.47   Overall, farm diversification is only specifically mentioned in 54% of local plans reviewed. Even in some post-1997 plans, it may not be mentioned or policies may be of a very general nature. Where criteria-based policies have been used, they usually reflect the issues identified in PPG7 and often reflect the desirability of such development being linked to a working farm. These criteria bring clarity to the process and allow local circumstances to be addressed. Nevertheless, the overall tenor of farm diversification policies (where they exist) is to be more restrictive than suggested in PPG7, either through specific policies, or criteria within policies, or because there is a requirement for the proposals to comply with all other policies in the plan.

Box 3.1: Sample local plan policies for farm diversification

More comprehensive policies for farm diversification:

North York Moors National Park

"Proposals for farm diversification enterprises will be approved where:

(1) the scale, location, and design of a proposal and the nature of the use proposed is not detrimental, individually or cumulatively, to the character and appearance of the locality and is compatible with the two National Park purposes; and

(2) the proposed activity is compatible with agricultural operations on the farm and would not prejudice the efficient functioning of surrounding land uses; and

(3) the proposal does not unacceptably impact upon the amenities of residents or cause an unacceptable level of noise, light, air or water pollution or an unacceptable impact on water quantity; and

(4) the proposed access and level of traffic generated by the proposal is within the capacity of existing approach roads and would not be detrimental to the amenity of the locality or prejudice highway and pedestrian safety; and

(5) the proposal does not involve a significant, irreversible loss of the best and most versatile agricultural land; and

(6) the proposal does not result in demonstrable harm to the landscape, nature conservation interests, cultural heritage features or the use and enjoyment of public rights of way; and

(7) building requirements are met through the conversion of a suitable existing building which meets criteria under Policies BE13 and BE16 or F8. New buildings will only be approved where the activity proposed cannot be met through the conversion and alteration of an existing building and where the proposal is ancillary to agricultural enterprises on the farm.

Proposals for recreational and tourist based diversification enterprises also provide appropriate links to and reinforcements of the surrounding public rights of way and public access network."
[North York Moors Local Plan, 2000, Farm Diversification, Policy F5]

Wychavon District Council

"In conjunction with other agencies, the Council will aim to support farm diversification where it does not conflict with environmental protection or countryside or recreation policies contained within the District Local Plan." [Policy AG15]

"Applications for farm diversification projects will need to be evaluated in the light of the following criteria:

(1) Development will not normally be permitted on the best and most versatile agricultural land (Policy AG1);

(2) The Council will need to be satisfied that the quality of the landscape is preserved particularly with regard to conservation areas, Areas of Great Landscape Value and the Area of Outstanding Natural Beauty where the proposal should not cause any environmental damage;

(3) The Council will need to be satisfied that the proposal is environmentally acceptable and does not affect the local environment by virtue of its own activities or by cumulative effects with neighbouring proposals. For this reason, mixed uses on site will not be encouraged;

(4) Existing suitable accommodation should be used where possible, thereby reducing the need for new buildings;

(5) Traffic generation should not be excessive, creating pressure on or adding to pressure on the existing highway network. Adequate access, servicing and parking should be provided within the curtilage of the application site;

(6) Landscaping and screening should be provided where necessary to minimise the visual impact of a proposal, for example, car parking associated with the development;

(7) There will be no detrimental impact on the landscape and features of nature conservation, wildlife habitats and historic features." [Policy AG16]

[Wychavon District Local Plan, 1998, Farm Diversification, Policies AG15 & AG16]

Extracts from policies which are more restrictive than PPG7 (1997) suggests.

Exmoor National Park

"no conversions of isolated buildings permitted except for camping barns"

[Exmoor National Park Local Plan, 1997, Conversion of Rural Building, Policy CBS4]

Basingstoke and Dean Borough Council

"permission will not normally be granted for non-agricultural industrial, storage or distribution development in the countryside unless it can be demonstrated to the satisfaction of the borough council that it cannot be reasonably located in an existing employment area, or within or adjoining the policy boundaries"

[Basingstoke and Deane Borough Local Plan, 1998, Employment in the Countryside, Policy C42]

Policies which give more limited guidance and/or make reference to conformity with other policies in the plan.

Harrogate District Council

"Proposals for farm diversification will be permitted provided they meet all the following criteria:

B)   The proposal should wherever possible re-use existing farm buildings. (In the event of existing buildings being incapable of conversion any new building should conform with Policy C13 on agricultural and forestry development).

C)   The proposals will not have an adverse effect on residential amenity or the character and amenity of the area.

D)   That the likely level of traffic generation is acceptable, taking account of the existing access and approach roads."

[Harrogate District Local Plan, 2000, Farm Diversification, Policy C14]

North Norfolk District Council

"Development proposals for farm diversification will be permitted where:

(a)   they are in accordance with the other policies of the Local Plan; and

(b)   they would not prejudice the future agricultural operation of the farm."

[North Norfolk Local Plan, 1998, Farm Diversification, Policy 76]

Policies which require that development should either be attached or complimentary to an active farm, or would not fragment a farm holding.

Blaby District Council

"Within the area identified as countryside on the proposals map, planning permission will not be granted for built development, or other development which would have a significantly adverse effect on the appearance or character of the landscape. Planning permission will, however, be granted for limited small scale employment and leisure development (including dwellings essential for these needs), providing that all of the following criteria are met:

(i)   it is sited, designed and landscaped in a manner which limits the effect on the appearance and character of the landscape;

(ii)   it is in keeping with the appearance and character of nearby built development;

(iii)   it would have a satisfactory relationship with nearby uses, including considerations of vibration, emissions, hours of working, vehicular activity, privacy, lights, illumination, noise, disturbance and an overbearing effect;

(iv)   it would not unacceptably sever or fragment an agricultural holding."

[Blaby District Local Plan, 1999, Other Development in the Countryside, Policy C2]

Peak District National Park

(a) "Diversification of economic activity on a farm will be restricted to the specific use or range of uses for which permission is given rather than to a use class.

(b) New buildings will not be permitted if the diversified use can be appropriately located in existing vernacular buildings or in a non-vernacular building which would remain appropriate to the area despite its removal from agriculture.

(c) The location and size of an existing non-vernacular building and its relationship to other buildings and features will be important when judging whether it is appropriate for a new use. Where a new use is acceptable, the development should include any improvements to the building and its setting that are needed to ensure that its impact on the landscape and on the character and appearance of the farm is not more harmful than if a new building had been permitted.

(d) Development will not be permitted unless there is sufficient certainty of long-term benefit to the farm business as an agricultural operation."

[Peak District National Park Local Plan, 1999, Farm Diversification, Policy LC14]

Sedgemoor District Council

"Proposals to diversify the range of economic activities on a farm will be permitted if all the following criteria are met:

a) the proposal is complementary to the agricultural operations on the farm and is operated as part of the farm holding;

b) the proposal should re-use or adapt any existing farm buildings, which are available;

c) if a new building is justified it should be sited in or adjacent to an existing group of buildings, be of compatible design and blend satisfactorily into the landscape in design, siting and materials;

d) there would be no harm to the residential amenity of neighbouring property, landscape, wildlife or highway safety; and

e) uses that would attract a significant number of people will be accessible by public transport."

[Sedgemoor Local Plan, 2000, Farm Diversification, Policy E8]

> **Policy for a specific farm diversification activity.**
>
> *Ribble Valley District Council*
>
> *"The Borough Council will approve the development of farm shops which are linked to genuine farm diversification proposals, subject to the following criteria:*
>
> i) *any new building should be minimal, well related to existing farm buildings and reflect the landscape character of the area in terms of materials and design.*
>
> ii) *the proposal should be well related to the primary transport route system. It should not generate additional traffic movements of a scale and type likely to cause undue problems or disturbance.*
>
> iii) *the site should be large enough to accommodate the necessary car parking service areas and appropriate landscaped areas.*
>
> iv) *the range of goods sold must be linked to the farming nature of the enterprise.*
>
> v) *where possible the proposal should incorporate the use of existing farm buildings. These should:*
>   a) *have a genuine history of use for agriculture or other rural enterprise;*
>   b) *be structurally sound and capable of conversion for the proposed use without the need for major alterations which would adversely affect the character of the building;*
>
> vi) *the proposed use will not cause unacceptable disturbance to neighbours in any way."*
>
> [Ribble Valley Local Plan, 1998, Farm Shops, Policy S7]

Re-use of rural buildings

3.48   Rural building re-use has been of long standing concern to planning policy and is very important in the context of this study, as it forms a part of most farm diversification developments. Paragraphs 3.14 to 3.17 of PPG7 give specific guidance on the re-use of buildings in the countryside. Support for business re-use is strong (with business re-use favoured over residential re-use) provided that: the buildings are of permanent and substantial construction; conversion does not lead to dispersal of activity away from existing towns and villages; they are in keeping with their surroundings; objections can be adequately addressed through conditions; and buildings in the open countryside do not involve major reconstruction. Local planning authorities are encouraged to compile and promote registers of buildings available for business re-use.

3.49   Annex G of PPG7 gives additional specific guidance on the re-use and adaptation of rural buildings, clarifying that there should be no requirement for a building to be redundant before it can be considered for re-use except where there is a suspicion of attempted abuse of agricultural Permitted Development Rights (PDRs); that re-used buildings should not have a significant adverse landscape impact; that local authorities should consider formulating policies for complexes of buildings with a large aggregate floor area (taking local economic and social needs, environmental and traffic considerations into account); and that the cumulative impacts of the re-use of a series of buildings should be considered. It is also suggested that in certain circumstances Permitted Development Rights for new agricultural buildings might be removed or re-used buildings might be tied to their holding, to prevent the proliferation of new agricultural buildings and the fragmentation of farm holdings.

Structure Plans

3.50 Like farm diversification policies, structure plan policies support rural building re-use but tend to be general in nature. Exceptions are the East Sussex and Brighton and Hove, and Derby and Derbyshire Structure Plans, both of which contain specific criteria for assessing proposals for re-use of existing buildings, for example:

> "(b) *in the countryside, conversions and/or changes of use of existing buildings for employment, recreation, tourist accommodation and facilities, and institutional uses will be supported, without the need to demonstrate that a countryside location is necessary, provided:*
>
> (i) *their form, bulk and general design are in keeping with their surroundings; and (ii) the use is appropriate to the area in terms of scale, type and impact on its surroundings (including traffic impact and impact on the vitality of towns and villages)."*

[East Sussex and Brighton and Hove Structure Plan, Policy S10]

3.51 Several plans contain a clear preference for the re-use of existing farm buildings over the erection of new buildings, and others reflect PPG7's preference for change of use to employment rather than residential use.

Local Plans

3.52 **General policies for building re-use:** Pre-1997 plans contain a mix of more positive (three) and less encouraging (six) policies for re-use of rural buildings than suggested by PPG7. Generally plans only refer to the PPG7 criteria relating to: the permanence of the building; its form, bulk and design; and the proviso that buildings in the open countryside be capable of conversion without major or complete reconstruction. Other PPG7 (1997) criteria occur only infrequently, although additional criteria are listed in some cases, including: traffic concerns, accessibility, restricting open storage areas, and impact on amenity.

3.53 In post-1997 plans, the tone is generally closer to that of PPG7 (1997) with eight more positive and six less encouraging policies. Again, the most commonly mentioned criteria relate to: permanence; form, bulk and design; and the proviso relating to buildings in the open countryside. Only Sedgemoor and Harrogate mention criteria preventing dispersal of activity that might prejudice town or village vitality – Wealden tackles the same problem in a criterion stating that where a development would generate many jobs, it must be located close to a town or village. In addition, only five plans explicitly suggest the use of conditions to overcome legitimate planning objections which would otherwise outweigh the advantages of re-use, although the Harrogate local plan suggests that personal planning permissions could serve the same purpose. Several plans list additional conditions for re-use, typically relating to: traffic/access issues, amenity, intensity of use and compatibility of use with location. Where these additional criteria are introduced they can bring greater restrictions as well as greater refinements to the policy.

3.54 As might be expected, plans covering designated landscapes, ie. National Parks and AONBs, put extra emphasis on preserving the character, design and appearance of existing buildings, while in Green Belts emphasis is placed on the importance of maintaining the openness of the countryside.

3.55   Examples of criteria-based policies, some including greater restriction than PPG7 (1997) guidance, are included in **Box 3.2**. Exmoor's policies are particularly noteworthy as they demonstrate the potential for more sophisticated policies to address the full detail of local circumstances and provide clear guidance for applicants, despite the National Park designation setting more stringent tests for such development.

3.56   **Size and cumulative impact:** There is a growing trend for larger, modern farm buildings and complexes of farm buildings to come forward for re-use (para 4.45-4.46), yet the issue of size and cumulative impact is not generally dealt with in either pre or post-1997 plans. Exceptions include Maidstone (pre-1997) which contains criteria precluding the expansion or extension of existing buildings, and four post-1997 plans which note the need to be aware of potential cumulative impacts. In the case of Ribble Valley specific reference is made to incremental urbanisation, while the North York Moors Plan has a specific policy that modern farm buildings may only be re-used for B1 uses, providing the buildings do not have an already unacceptable impact on the landscape.

3.57   **Register of buildings for re-use:** In the sample, only the Wealden local plan specifically mentions a register of buildings with extant permissions for re-use. Whilst this is only one of several suggestions in PPG7 (1997) for the promotion of farm diversification, it is significant that it has not been taken up more widely (para 4.60).

3.58   **Residential re-use:** Approximately 50% of pre-1997 plans make no distinction between residential and economic re-use, with only three plans having specific policies resisting residential in favour of economic re-use of rural buildings.

3.59   By comparison, most post-1997 plans indicate a general preference for economic over residential re-use, although this is not always explicitly expressed in policy. Exceptions are Wealden, North York Moors, Ribble and East Lindsey which have clear policies in favour of economic re-use. On the other hand, Sedgemoor has no clear priority for economic re-use and Stratford on Avon only resists conversion to residential use in the open countryside. Harrogate goes so far as to specifically state that paragraph 3.15 of PPG7 has been ignored because of the long-winded process required to prove that every effort has gone into securing a business use before planning permission for residential use is granted.

3.60   Overall, both structure and local plans reflect that building re-use has been a long established concern of planning policy. In the local plans reviewed, the policies in the pre-1997, as well as post-1997, plans are usually criteria-based and relatively full. The criteria used in post-1997 plans closely reflect the concerns set out in PPG7 (1997), but where additional criteria are introduced they can bring greater restrictions. Thus across all local plans reviewed, 45% are strongly supportive of rural building re-use, while the remainder are more restrictive than the guidance set out in PPG7. Significantly, there are a considerable number of plans which still fail to actively promote economic over residential re-use. As noted in PPG7, residential re-use is likely to have a minimal impact on the local economy and may bring little benefit in terms of local employment.

Box 3.2: Sample local plan policies for building re-use

Policies which may set more restrictive tests than PPG7 (1997), or which are undermined by other elements of the plan:

Warwick District Council

"Proposals for the re-use or adaptation of existing rural buildings will be considered favourably provided that the District Council is satisfied that:

a) *The condition of the building, its nature and situation make it suitable for re-use or adaptation; and*

b) *The proposed use or adaptation can he accommodated without extensive rebuilding, alteration or extensions to the building; and*

c) *The appearance and the setting of the building following conversion, protects and where possible, enhances the character and appearance of the countryside; and*

d) *Safe vehicular access from the public highway is readily available or achievable without major modification or detriment to the landscape; and*

e) *The proposed use or adaptation would not give rise to environmental or traffic problems which would outweigh the benefits of re-use or adaptation."*

[Warwick District Council Local Plan, 1995, District-Wide Policy C3]

Eastleigh Borough Council

"Proposals for the use for employment purposes of buildings in the countryside will be permitted provided:

i) the building is of a sound construction with a reasonable expectation of life and lends itself to conversion without significant building work being required;

ii) the design of any conversion or alterations retains the intrinsic qualities of the building and avoids inappropriate external alterations;

iii) the proposal takes the form of a self-contained conversion, with no new buildings and any extensions comply with policy 13.CO;

iv) the development does not result in an unacceptable level of traffic generation, including heavy goods vehicles, or endanger existing road users, or necessitate changes to the highway network that are considered unacceptable; and

v) the proposal does not include extensive hard surfaced areas or open storage."

[Eastleigh Borough Local Plan, 1997, Re-use of Buildings in the Countryside, Policy 11CO]

This policy, however, may be undermined by the following supporting text later in the plan:

"Rural Buildings

8.28 The Council recognises that the re-use and adaptation of rural buildings for commercial or business uses can encourage new enterprises and can provide jobs needed in rural areas. Central Government advice in PPG7 (1992) supports this.

8.29 Nevertheless it is also important to reduce the demand for use of the private motor car....

8.30 In order to reconcile these two statements the Council proposes to discourage the re-use for employment purposes of rural buildings which are not well served by public transport or readily accessible from an existing settlement by means other than the private motor car."

Examples of additional restrictive criteria in policies:

East Lindsey District Council

"The re-use of farm and other buildings in the countryside for commercial or community uses will be permitted provided:.......

g) it would not result in the dominance of non-agricultural uses in the countryside."

[East Lindsey Local Plan, 1999, Re-use of Buildings in the Countryside, Policy DC6]

Wealden District Council

"Proposals for non-residential development (including workshops, offices, tourist accommodation and recreational use) through the conversion of agricultural or other rural buildings in the countryside (outside the development boundaries as defined on the Proposals Map) will be permitted where the building's form, bulk and general design are in keeping with its surroundings. In addition, all proposals should meet the following criteria:......
proposals which would be likely to create a significant number of jobs should be well located in relation to towns and villages."

[Wealden Local Plan, 1998, Conversion for Non-Residential Uses, Policy DC7]

A detailed set of policies providing clear guidance:

Exmoor National Park Local Plan

"The re-use or physical adaptation of soundly constructed permanent rural buildings for appropriate non-residential purposes, including holiday accommodation will be permitted provided that:

1)   the form, bulk and general design of the building do not detract from its setting

2)   proposals for such buildings do not adversely affect the character of the locality or residential amenities;

3)   sites have satisfactory accessibility and adequate space for parking and associated activities, which must not impair important qualities of the surrounding countryside;

4)   alterations respect the scale and form and any special feature of the existing building."

[Exmoor National Park Local Plan, 1997, Conversion of Rural Buildings, General Principles, Policy CBS1]

"Changes of use of buildings, including residential re-use within the settlements listed under Policies HI, H2 and H3 will be acceptable in principle provided they comply with Policies E3 and CSF2. Any associated building conversions and activities should not adversely affect the character of the locality or residential amenities. Sites should have satisfactory accessibility and parking. Alterations should respect the scale and form and any special features of the existing building."

[Exmoor National Park Local Plan, 1997, Conversion of Rural Buildings Within Settlements, Policy CBS2]

"Changes of use of buildings located in hamlets or farm groups where there is an existing dwelling, for purposes which benefit the rural economy of the National Park will be permitted. Building conversions should observe the criteria of Policy CBS 1. Changes of use for residential purposes will not be permitted unless:

1)   reasonably ancillary to an existing dwelling; or

2)   necessary for the needs of agriculture or forestry or an appropriate farm diversification scheme."

[Exmoor National Park Local Plan, 1997, Conversion of Rural Buildings in Farm Groups or Hamlets, Policy CBS3]

"Proposals for the conversion of buildings standing alone in the countryside which are not part of a farm group or hamlet will not he permitted unless the proposal is for a camping barn which complies with the terms of Policy RT4."

[Exmoor National Park Local Plan, 1997, Conversion of Rural Buildings Standing Alone in the Countryside, Policy CBS4]

"Proposals for the conversion of rural buildings to camping barns will be permitted provided that:

1) *the building is well related to the footpath/ bridleway network;*

2) *the proposal does not involve significant alterations to the external fabric and surroundings of the building which would materially affect its character or appearance;*

3) *overground utility services or new vehicular access are not proposed;*

4) *the proposal conforms with Policy CBS1."*

[Exmoor National Park Local Plan, 1997, Camping Barns and Backpackers' Camp Sites, Policy RT4]

"The use of land for small back-packers' camp sites will be permitted provided the site is well screened, related to a village or farm, does not require the provision of new vehicular access or buildings and is well related to the existing network of footpaths and bridle-ways."

[Exmoor National Park Local Plan, 1997, Camping Barns and Backpackers' Camp Sites, Policy RT5]

Policy which does not favour commercial re-use over residential (PPG7 paragraph 3.15).

Harrogate District Council

"Outside development limits (as defined on the proposals map) and the built-up confines of settlements referred to in Policy H6, all proposals for the re-use and adaptation of rural buildings should have regard to the following criteria:

A) *The proposal, by virtue of any physical changes, access and servicing arrangements, and the level of activity associated with the proposed use, should not harm the character or appearance of the countryside or of the building itself.*

Any proposal for residential use will not be permitted where:

B) *The building is not of a permanent and substantial construction, and is not of a type capable of conversion to the new use without requiring extensive alteration, extension, demolition and/or rebuilding works: or*

C) *An associated residential curtilage would harm the character or appearance of the countryside: or*

D) *The premises are suitable for business use and there is an identified local need for business premises: or*

E) *There is a local need for affordable housing, the building is suitable for such purposes and the proposal is not an affordable housing scheme.*

Proposals for business use, in addition to having regard to criterion A, will be permitted where:

F) *The building is of a permanent and substantial construction: and*

G) *Any alterations, extensions or rebuilding are minimised and are essential to the operational requirements of an identified user: and*

H) *It would not lead to dispersal of activity on such a scale as to prejudice nearby town and village vitality: and*

I) *There is no adverse effect on residential amenity."*

[Harrogate District Local Plan, 2000, The Re-use and Adaptation of Rural Buildings, Policy C16]

Transport and highways

3.61 PPG7 (1997) echoes the advice in PPG13 *Transport* (1994) that development generating significant traffic movements should not be located in inaccessible locations [PPG7 paragraph 3.9] where it will increase reliance on the private car.

3.62 Several, but not all, **structure plans** make specific note of the potential traffic implications of rural development. Examples include Lancashire, Norfolk, Lincolnshire, Somerset and Exmoor, and Derby and Derbyshire.

3.63 60% of **local plans** have policies referring to PPG13, over half of which are post-1997 plans. Nevertheless, a total of six plans (three pre-1997, three post-1997) make no explicit reference to PPG13, and a further five have only vague references.

3.64 While the main thrust of PPG13 (1994) was to reduce dependency on the car and concentrate new development in accessible locations, it provided little specific advice for rural planning beyond addressing the balance between housing and employment opportunities. Plans with policies that incorporate PPG13's objectives therefore tend to only address these broad issues. In particular, the policies of urban fringe and accessible rural authorities are primarily aimed at urban settlement issues, and do not fully address the different transport issues of rural areas. Where rural transport is addressed it is usually in relation to large developments for B1, B2 and B8 uses where significant traffic generation is expected. Transport issues in relation to more general and smaller developments are seldom explicitly addressed. This often means that policies could be interpreted as placing restrictions on commercial development, including farm diversification. This is a particular problem in more remote areas.

3.65 Since the research phase of this study was completed, and too late to influence any of the plans reviewed, PPG13 was revised (March 2001). The new PPG13 (2001) contains considerably expanded guidance for rural areas, noting that:

"In rural areas, the potential for using public transport and for non-recreational walking and cycling is more limited than in urban areas". [paragraph 40]

and specifically addressing farm diversification:

"In order to reduce the need for long-distance out-commuting to jobs in urban areas, it is important to promote adequate employment opportunities in rural areas. Diversification of agricultural businesses is increasingly likely to lead to proposals for conversion or re-use of existing farm buildings for other business purposes, possibly in remote locations. PPG7 indicates that for development related to agriculture and for farm diversification, appropriate new buildings may also be acceptable. In plan policies and development control decisions, local authorities should encourage farm diversification proposals particularly, but not exclusively, where this enables access by public transport, walking and cycling. They should be realistic about the availability, or likely availability, of alternatives to access by car. Similarly, they should not reject proposals where small-scale business development or its expansion would give rise to only modest additional daily vehicle movements, in comparison to other uses that are permitted on the site, and the impact on minor roads would not be significant." [Paragraph 43]

3.66   Prior to this advice being given, both development plan officers and development control officers interviewed, raised the concern that under the policies of PPG7 (1997) and the old PPG13 (1994), as incorporated into their development plans, it was not clear how to reconcile the traffic generation of farm diversification development with its often inaccessible location. No plan policies specifically addressed this issue, which has meant that it is left to development control officers to seek ways of determining applications against a background of apparently contradictory policies. This is discussed further in Chapter 4. The new PPG13 (2001), and development plan policies which should flow from it, should alleviate this tension considerably.

3.67   In addition to traffic generation concerns, 13 plans also include highway safety policies (five pre-1997, eight post-1997 plans), although most are phrased in general terms about pedestrian and cyclist safety. Wychavon is unusual in having a highway safety policy that specifically relates to the re-use of rural buildings, placing some restrictions on those that are likely to generate higher levels of traffic such as farm shops. More detailed policies of this nature could well be useful in addressing these issues elsewhere.

Design/appearance of buildings

3.68   PPG7 (1997) requires that new development in the countryside should not have a negative impact on its surroundings and should respect local building styles and materials [paragraph 2.11]. It also suggests that other existing buildings with an adverse impact on the landscape might be removed as part of a planning application or improved in appearance through the use of conditions [paragraphs 2.13 and Annex G (G4)].

3.69   Reflecting PPG7 (1997), and the central importance of such policies to all rural development, all plans have guidance and design criteria for the alteration of existing buildings and the erection of new buildings, though for Ellesmere Port and Neston this is not rural-specific. Plans with AONB or National Park designations have stricter design criteria, especially in AONBs – with the exception of Ribble Valley where there are no specific policies for the Forest of Bowland AONB.

3.70   The only plans with a policy for the improvement or removal of poor quality redundant buildings are Basingstoke and Deane, BaNES (pre-1997), and Wychavon and Caradon (post-1997). In an interesting departure from PPG7, text in the pre-1997 Exmoor plan notes that derelict traditional agricultural buildings in the countryside are not necessarily unwelcome as they can become interesting landscape features.

3.71   Thus although the importance of the design and appearance of new rural buildings is recognised in all plans, the possibility of significantly improving or removing unsightly buildings through the planning system, is not frequently identified in plans. This may mean that opportunities to do so are missed.

Environmental and landscape protection

3.72   PPG7 (1997) contains detailed advice on a considerable variety of rural land designations, including National Parks [paragraph 4.5]; AONBs [paragraph 4.8]; local countryside designations such as Areas of Great Landscape Value [paragraph 4.16]; nature conservation sites [paragraph 4.12]; historic buildings [paragraph 4.13]; archaeological sites [paragraph 4.14] and development of Best and Most Versatile agricultural land [paragraph 2.17]. PPG2 (1995) contains policies for Green Belts. Plans were examined for their coverage of these policies and for whether they clearly reflected the hierarchy of designations.

3.73   All the plans contain policies relating to landscape and environmental protection, accurately reflected national policy, in that nationally and internationally important designations are given strong protection. However, almost half of the plans do not provide a clear hierarchy of protection distinguishing between national statutory and local non-statutory designations. Accordingly, the lower importance of local countryside designations compared to national statutory designations is not always clear.

3.74   Policies for development on Best and Most Versatile (BMV) agricultural land are generally very strict, mirroring PPG7, sometimes prohibiting development altogether where loss would be irreversible (e.g. Maidstone and Eastleigh). Following the research phase of this study paragraphs 2.17 and 2.18 of PPG7 were replaced in March 2001 with paragraphs clarifying the policy for BMV agricultural land in the light of the Rural White Paper (2000) and the Government's Draft Soil Strategy (2001).

Tourism and recreation

3.75   PPG7 (1997) contains guidance on tourism and recreation. It advises that tourism *"needs to develop in a way which draws on the character of the countryside and does not destroy the very asset on which its popularity depends"* and that *"a wide variety of tourist developments, in terms of nature and scale, can be acceptable in the right location"* [paragraph 3.12]. It goes on to add that *"Increasing opportunities for people to enjoy the countryside for sport and recreation provides new uses of land in the countryside and is an important source of income and employment"* [paragraph 3.13].

3.76   Both pre and post-1997 plans contain policies for rural tourism, sport and recreation, though few explicitly link these activities to farm diversification – exceptions include Ribble Valley, Stratford on Avon and Wychavon. Where the role of tourism and recreation in diversification is mentioned, it is typically in relation to conversion of buildings to tourist accommodation. The attitude towards tourism and recreation is generally positive, subject to conditions. Conditions typically include that the activities be small-scale, accessible and in keeping with the character and amenity of the rural area.

3.77   Tourism is a very significant element of farm diversification, so clearer policy (both nationally and locally) on the role of farm diversification in overall tourism development would be beneficial.

VARIATION IN POLICY BY AGE OF PLAN AND ACROSS DIFFERENT TYPES OF RURAL AREA

3.78   Separately the local plans were analysed to assess if there was any correlation between types of policy for farm diversification and category of LPA (ie urban fringe, accessible rural, and remote rural). The same analysis could not be conducted on structure plans as they frequently cover more than one category of rural district.

3.79   The primary finding is that the general variability in policies across all types of rural area over-shadows differences relating to category of local authority, with the exception of the National Parks, as noted below. Also, the difference between pre- and post-1997 policies, is more pronounced than that relating to category of LPA.

3.80   Of the remote rural areas, the plans of the three sample National Parks stand out as having both more sophisticated and co-ordinated policies for rural and farm diversification. The suite of policies from the Exmoor Local Plan for building re-use set out in **Box 3.2** is a good example. In other plans for remote rural areas, farm diversification is not always addressed and policies tend to be relatively brief, though not particularly restrictive in outlook.

3.81   In accessible rural areas, the pre-1997 plans contained little addressing rural diversification and particularly farm diversification. Post-1997 plans are noticeably fuller, reflecting much of PPG7's content but with some important exceptions, such as not always explicitly addressing farm diversification, not always favouring the commercial re-use of buildings over residential re-use, and very rarely reflecting local social and economic needs.

3.82   Pre-1997 plans in urban fringe areas only occasionally mentioned farm diversification. Their policies for rural diversification and the re-use of farm buildings, whilst reflecting some of the elements of PPG7, are often more restrictive than the national guidance. Post-1997 plan policies more closely reflect PPG7 but do not explicitly cover farm diversification in every case, and also fail to reflect local social and economic needs.

3.83   Thus, policies in accessible rural and urban fringe areas tend to be fuller in addressing rural and farm diversification, particularly those in post-1997 plans. There are probably two reasons for this. First, that PPG7's influence has lead to fuller policies in later plans, and second that urban fringe and, to a lesser extent, accessible rural areas, have experienced greater development pressure with their proximity to urban areas, encouraging fuller policies as a response. This finding is less significant, however, than the general variation in policy across LPAs.

3.84   Overall, it is clear that despite considerable variation, post-1997 policies are generally fuller and more frequently address farm diversification, reflecting the influence of PPG7 (1997). It is also clear that no plan fully takes-up PPG7's guidance and that most plans lack significant elements of it.

POLICY HIERARCHY

3.85   The influence of RPG policies on structure plans and thence to local plans, was also investigated. As the older extant RPGs contain only light coverage of farm diversification development, there is little follow through to development plans. The more recent extant RPGs and the draft versions of those under review all date from 1998 as the earliest. In consequence, they are generally too recent to have influenced structure plans, let alone local plans.

3.86   Similarly, in the case of structure plans, the majority of structure plans examined post-date their respective local plans. However, in the case of eight local plans the relationship with an earlier structure plan could be analysed. The primary finding from this is that plan policies are very variable. In this context, clear relationships between structure plan and local plan policies are difficult to discern. In general, most local plans contain policies which are notably more developed than their related structure plan policies, including in one case the specific coverage of farm diversification where this was missing from the structure plan. In two cases the policies are little different, and in one case the local plan policies are less detailed than the structure plan policies.

3.87   Overall, therefore, there appears only to be a weak relationship between structure plan policies and those within the constituent local plans, although a clearer relationship would obviously be beneficial in increasing clarity.

THE VIEWS OF DEVELOPMENT PLAN OFFICERS

3.88   Development plan officers from all 21 sample LPAs were asked about their plans and policies (County Councils were not visited). Where their comments related to specific policies they are included above. Their more general comments are examined below.

General consistency of policies with PPG7

3.89   Local plan officers were asked about the consistency of their plan policies with PPG7. Nine planning officers (42%) felt that although PPG7 (1997) had come relatively late in the production of their development plan, its key guidance on farm diversification had been incorporated. Exmoor (1997) qualified this view, stating that their policies must also be seen in the context of Section 4 of PPG7, *Special considerations in designated areas*, which sets the particular policy context for National Parks.

3.90   Ellesmere Port and Neston suggested that there is an awkward tension between PPG7 policies for farm diversification and PPG2 policies for Green Belts.

3.91   **More restrictive policies than PPG7:** 52% (11 out off the 21 sample LPAs) felt that their policies were in some way more restrictive than PPG7. Development pressure in the countryside around towns was cited as one reason for more restrictive policies by a number of authorities. Wychavon (accessible rural) and East Lindsey (remote rural) felt their policies placed greater importance on environmental rather than economic or social considerations. It was also suggested that PPG13 (1974)'s application to rural areas resulted in such a bias.

3.92   Five LPAs commented that Green Belts, AONBs and Heritage Coasts led to a more restrictive approach to farm diversification. For example, Wealden (accessible rural) felt that their policies are slightly more restrictive than advocated by PPG7, especially concerning residential conversions. This was thought to be justified by the strong development pressure, especially for residential conversions, spurred by proximity to London, and the need to protect environmental quality (the District lies largely within the High Weald AONB). However, Ribble Valley (remote rural covering the Forest of Bowland AONB) stressed that the MAFF Forest of Bowland Upland Experiment, which is promoting integrated rural development, has resolved the apparent conflict between environmental conservation and farm diversification. This initiative, through Integrated Farm Appraisals and other activities, has developed a close understanding of the social, economic and environmental needs of the locality. In consequence, it is able to direct farmers towards forms of diversification appropriate to the local area and thus more likely to receive planning permission. This underlines the benefits of understanding local economic and social needs.

3.93   All three NPAs stressed that their status in terms of conserving a national landscape resource, placed some restrictions on farm diversification, although this had to be seen in the context of their other duty to foster the social and economic well-being of their communities. Specifically, Exmoor and the Peak District commented that there were certain areas of the National Park where development was strictly controlled. North York Moors stated that the conversion of modern buildings was only considered where it complemented existing activities in the Park and improved the appearance of the building. Similarly, Exmoor gives greater emphasis to the re-use of 'traditional' buildings because of their better landscape fit. They also place stronger restrictions on the re-use of buildings in the open countryside as opposed to those in farmyards and settlements, an issue which they felt is not adequately addressed in PPG7 at present. Nevertheless, the NPAs have essentially similar approval rates to other remote rural areas (discussed in Chapter 5). This indicates perhaps, that with a focus on integrating social and economic needs with conservation objectives, and with fuller policies for farm diversification (as they have), a relatively restrictive environmental context need not frustrate farm diversification development.

3.94   **Less restrictive policies than PPG7:** Only six LPAs considered aspects of their policies to be less restrictive than PPG7. Warwick (urban fringe) and Stratford (accessible rural) acknowledged that their policies did not seek to restrict residential re-use in favour of commercial re-use. Ribble Valley (remote rural) and West Lancashire (accessible rural) also noted that their approach to residential conversions was more flexible, reflecting over-supply of holiday accommodation and strong pressure for residential conversions. The lack of demand for commercial conversions due to low unemployment and high levels of commuting, also made commercial re-use hard to insist on.

3.95   Berwick on Tweed (remote rural) identified a less restrictive approach generally. Despite a strong emphasis on environmental conservation they recognised that economic development is essential for such environmental conservation to take place. Thus they are flexible in striking a balance between conservation and development and are very sympathetic to diversification.

3.96   West Lancashire stated that they specifically favour food processing as an important additional source of farm income.

3.97   **Similar policies to PPG7:** Four LPAs commented that their policies were essentially no more or less restrictive than PPG7. Sedgemoor commented that they have treated PPG7 as a starting point and added local interpretation.

3.98   Overall, the officers' views of their plan were similar to the conclusions reached through the plan analysis conducted through this study. Specifically, both the officers' views and the plan analysis indicate that:

●   Where plans depart from the guidance in PPG7 (1997), policies are usually more restrictive. Reasons for this greater restriction are often environmental – specifically the influence of designated landscapes, Green Belt, and the desire to reduce car travel, as expressed in PPG13 (1994). Development pressure around towns was also identified by planning officers.

●   In some cases plans fail to include relevant policies, especially policies for farm diversification.

Flexibility of policies

3.99 Local plan officers were asked whether their policies had sufficient flexibility to be able to respond to the wide range of circumstances presented by farm diversification. The majority (16) felt that this was the case, either because the policies were positively worded or because they were criteria-based – providing a consistent framework within which individual circumstances could be accommodated. But five local plan officers felt that their policies were relatively inflexible because of the use of rigid criteria.

3.100 Through these discussions, it was noted that flexibility should not be at the expense of consistency and should be carefully exercised to prevent abuse of the planning system. It was also noted that flexibility needed to be exercised within important constraints set down in the plan – such as landscape conservation in designated landscapes. In the case of the Peak District and Exmoor National Parks, it was noted that this flexibility was contingent on evidence of a firm link between the farm diversification activity and the farm business (para 3.43).

3.101 In summary, most local plan officers and development control officers (Chapter 4) judged that their policies for farm diversification were applied with reasonable flexibility. Criteria-based policies were seen to bring consistency while allowing the circumstances of individual applications to be addressed, although in a few cases rigid criteria where seen to constrain flexibility.

Policy modifications: results of the Local Plan Inquiry

3.102 Local plan officers were asked how their plans had been modified at local plan inquiry relative to the guidance in PPG7 (1997). Seven reported changes, as a result of the local plan inquiry, to bring policies into line with those of PPG7. These changes included: making rural diversification policies less restrictive (Wychavon, 1998), prioritising the economic re-use of farm buildings (Maidstone, 1997), and removing the requirement for re-used buildings to have 'architectural merit' (Eastleigh,1997). Wealden (1998) reported that they had resisted pressure at the local plan inquiry to remove their policy's preference for economic re-use of buildings, before the publication of PPG7 (1997) and thus had been vindicated when the revised PPG was issued. The remainder reported no significant alterations to their farm diversification policies as a result of the local plan inquiry.

3.103 Nevertheless, the timing of different local plan inquiries relative to PPG7 (1997), has led to contradictions between plans produced at different times. For example, the BaNES (1997) inquiry led to the addition that farm diversification should be *functionally related* to agriculture, whilst Harrogate (2000) was required to remove the requirement for farm diversification to be *complementary and ancillary* to the main farm business. Similarly, Basingstoke and Deane (1996) removed the preference for economic over residential re-use whilst several more recent plans have been required to insert such a policy.

3.104 In the future, with both more up to date and fuller RPG in place and with PPG7 (1997), as amended, well established, the types of discrepancy noted above should be less frequent.

Changes in policy with plan review

3.105   From the interviews with local plan officers, it appears that most LPAs intend to make changes to their farm diversification policies as part of current or future plan review. Suggested changes included:

- seeking closer conformity to PPG7

- making policies for farm diversification better linked to those for the rural economy

- more explicit and supportive policies for farm diversification

- a clearer distinction between on and off-farm diversification

- better reflection of local variations and greater recognition of economic and social needs[9]

- a more community-based plan[10]

- greater support for economic building re-use

- more positive policies for the re-use of modern buildings

- a clearer definition of acceptable small employment uses

- better co-ordination with the rural strategy (where in place).

3.106   The introduction of stronger policies for sustainable development was also reported by one authority.

3.107   Other proposed policy modifications which may be less in line with PPG7 included:

- relaxing restrictions on residential re-use of buildings in recognition of high demand, relative to the low demand for employment re-use (two LPAs)

- a desire to restrict retail development in the open countryside

- increased restrictions on tourist accommodation to reduce the potential for these being used as permanent dwellings (Berwick on Tweed). Conversely Eastleigh wishes to promote more tourism-related farm diversification but is unsure if there is an adequate market.

3.108   Despite the view of most local plan officers, that their policies for farm diversification reasonably reflected PPG7 (1997), many foresee considerable amendments when their plan is next reviewed. Officers expect to pick up more of the elements of PPG7's guidance,

---

[9] At the Planners Workshops conducted as part of this study, Cotswold District (not one of the sample LPAs) reported that the review of the local plan will concentrate on the different types of rural area within the District and will be closely linked with the strategy for local economic development. Thus it is anticipated that farm diversification policies, amongst others, will set different priorities for different parts of the District.

[10] Wealden would like their plan to be more community-based but fear that this will be contrary to the desire of the Government Office for the South East to see more concise local plans supported by SPG.

including clarifying and enlarging their policies for farm diversification, and better reflecting local circumstances in these policies (although this is unlikely to be informed by a full appraisal of local economic and social needs (para 3.33). Where policies are developed to reflect local circumstances, it was noted that this might result in policies departing from PPG7 (1997) in some way.

3.109 These suggested changes are in line with the analysis of local plan policies described above, which has identified a frequent lack of detail on farm diversification within current local plans.

SUPPLEMENTARY PLANNING GUIDANCE

3.110 As part of the local plan review, an assessment was also made of Supplementary Planning Guidance (SPG) relating to farm diversification. Eleven of the 21 authorities had no relevant SPG. Five had design guidance for barn conversions and two had guidance that expressed a preference for commercial over residential re-use of rural buildings. Maidstone has SPG for the conversion of rural buildings which goes beyond design guidance and also addresses the new use of the building. Harrogate and North York Moors NPA are covered by the guidance produced by North Yorkshire County Council *A Planning Guide to Farm Diversification in North Yorkshire* (considered further in Chapter 6), although North York Moors NPA also propose to produce their own SPG on farm diversification.

3.111 The use of SPG for farm diversification was supported by development plan officers but with reservations. The desirability of conveying information about planning policy and procedures for farm diversification in a more 'digestible' form to farmers and their advisors was strongly supported. But it was recognised that SPG may not be the most appropriate means of doing this as it is both costly and time-consuming to produce. It may also be too slow to address the current problems of agriculture. It was suggested therefore that advice, which is less a formal element of local planning policy, and thus easier to produce, may be more appropriate.

IN SUMMARY

Plan content
- **Regional Planning Guidance:** Older RPG was widely criticised by local plan officers for its weak coverage of rural issues. PPG11 *Regional Planning* (2000), which gives significantly more advice on the coverage of rural issues, is new. Nevertheless, even before its introduction, more recent RPGs have given significantly greater coverage of rural issues. Most articulate a strategy for rural diversification, although not all directly address farm diversification. These provide context for policies at the structure and local plan level.

- **Structure plan policies:** As would be expected, structure plan policies were less detailed than those in local plans. The majority of structure plans set out policies for the diversification of the rural economy and the re-use of rural buildings, but only half specifically addressed farm diversification or expressed a preference for the commercial re-use of rural buildings. Although structure plans cannot be expected to be detailed, this lack of important elements of rural planning policy is significant, particularly as the majority of the structure plans examined post-date PPG7 (1997).

- **Local plans:** The most prominent feature of local plan policies is their considerable variation, which makes picking clear trends, either by age of plan, or types of rural area, difficult.

- Most local plans mention **sustainable development**, although economic and social considerations are sometimes placed behind those relating to the environment. All plans cover building design and appearance, environmental and landscape protection and tourism and recreation, although approaches are variable.

- PPG7's support for **economic development** in rural areas, focused in and around existing settlements, is well represented, although pre-1997 plans tend to be more restrictive of rural employment development, and especially the erection of new buildings in the open countryside.

- Only 54% of local plans explicitly address **farm diversification**. The detail of farm diversification policy is better represented in post-1997 plans, though the coverage in these plans is by no means comprehensive and no plan addresses all the issues raised in PPG7.

- Where local plans cover **National Parks, AONBs and Green Belts**, they contain stricter policies for development within them, including farm diversification. The National Park policies for rural and farm diversification are noteworthy though, for being generally more detailed and co-ordinated than policies in other local plans.

- Most plans post-date PPG13 (1994) and thus reflect its desire to **reduce the need to travel** by private car, but the tension between this and farm diversification in relatively isolated and inaccessible locations is rarely reconciled.

- Few plans link rural diversification policies to an assessment of **economic or social needs**. Although some officers identified work that had been done in this area, no authority had undertaken an assessment of the type encouraged by PPG7 (1997). Thus few plans show a clear and comprehensive tailoring of policies to local circumstances. Although some authorities indicated an intention to produce policies which better reflect local circumstances at plan review, none were intending to base such policies on an assessment of local social and economic needs as PPG7 (1997) encourages.

- Particular characteristics of local plan policies for farm diversification are that some policies are more restrictive than PPG7's generally supportive approach, often requiring compliance with other policies in the plan, seeking attachment to a working farm, or trying to ensure that farm diversification does nor result in the fragmentation of the holding.

- All plans address the **re-use of rural buildings** and most address the main criteria set out in PPG7 (1997). However, the issues of size of buildings and their cumulative impact, and mention of registers of rural buildings for re-use, are rare within local plan policies. Clear disparities emerged in policies for the commercial re-use of rural buildings. Many pre- and post-1997 plans reflect some preference for commercial over residential re-use but some older plans fail to make this important distinction and one more recent plan goes so far as to explain why the PPG7 guidance has been rejected.

Plan policies by age of plan

- Overall the considerable variation in policy between plans significantly obscures variation between pre- and post-1997 plans. However, policy for rural economic development and the re-use of rural buildings saw relatively little change in PPG7 (1997) and thus local plan policies for these two areas are reasonably full in both pre- and post-1997 plans. PPG7 (1997) added considerably to policy for farm diversification. Thus farm diversification is addressed more frequently in post-1997 plans but five such plans still fail to cover it. Thus policies are generally less detailed than PPG7 (1997) suggests. Where policies for rural and farm diversification and the re-use of farm buildings depart from PPG7's advice they are often more restrictive in some aspect.

Differences by LPA category

- Age of plan has a significantly greater influence on policy content than category of LPA (urban fringe, accessible rural, and remote rural). The main difference is that, with the exception of the National Parks, urban fringe and accessible rural plans tend to contain more detailed policies on rural and farm diversification compared to remote rural areas and also tend to be more restrictive.

Plan hierarchy

- It is too early to be able to trace the influence of the newer RPG in development plans. Many structure plans also currently post-date their local plans making a similar analysis impossible. In the few cases where the structure plan preceded the local plan, fuller structure plan policies generally produce fuller local plan policies, though this, again, is variable.

Views of local plan officers

- Most development plan officers felt their policies were broadly satisfactory and in line with national guidance, although the majority were anticipating changes at plan review to incorporate more of the detail of PPG7. However, some authorities are considering significant departures from PPG7, especially concerning relaxing their policies on the residential re-use of rural buildings.

- All officers reported the strong support of their LPA for rural and farm diversification where it is obviously supporting agriculture, accurately reflecting the analysis of the local plans. Officers noted that a less restrictive approach may be adopted where diversification activities are clearly linked to a working farm. Most regarded their policies as flexible, aided by their positive stance and use of criteria.

- Plans which had undergone modifications following the publication of PPG7 (1997) had generally been amended to bring them into line with PPG7 – making policies less restrictive and prioritising economic re-use of farm buildings over residential re-use.

Supplementary planning guidance (SPG)

- The use of supplementary planning guidance for farm diversification is rare (other than for design issues).

3.112 **Overall,** both PPG7 (1997) and PPG11 (2000) have considerably increased guidance on rural and farm diversification, though the extent to which this has been reflected in development plans is variable. Planning officers generally supported PPG7 and there was little suggestion of any significant problems with the guidance. However, from RPG to local plans it is clear that not all of the issues identified in national guidance on rural and farm diversification are fully addressed. It is also clear that there is only limited knowledge of local social and economic issues in rural areas. Thus the development of policies from the regional to the local level, articulating the requirements for rural and farm diversification, are rare. That the full guidance of PPG7 (1997) is not reflected in the majority of development plans is important, as opportunities for more detailed policies which take a pro-active role in farm diversification may be being overlooked.

CHAPTER 4

Development control process adopted for farm diversification applications

4.1   This Chapter sets out the process by which planning applications are submitted for farm diversification schemes (based on the database developed from the planning registers; the telephone survey of farmers; and the postal questionnaire of applicants), and the means by which they are determined by LPAs (based on the discussions with development control (DC) officers). The subsequent Chapter considers the various outcomes from the application process.

4.2   Traditionally there has been little contact between the farming community and LPAs, not least because the majority of farming activities operate outside the planning system. However, this situation is changing with farm diversification and a range of other pro-active initiatives (under the ERDP and the structural funds) which are requiring and encouraging stronger links to be forged between LPAs and farmers. (These links are returned to at the end of this Chapter).

MAKING A PLANNING APPLICATION

4.3   The following section outlines the process followed by applicants in submitting a planning application for farm diversification.

Applicant type

4.4   From the planning register database it appears that across our sample LPAs (for those applications where this information was recorded) over 80% of applicants were farmers and/or landowners. This figure is confirmed by the farmer telephone survey (**Figure 4.1**) which identified that nearly all respondents who had undertaken or were considering a planning application for farm diversification were owner-occupiers with, significantly, very few tenants identified. The problems associated with diversification for a tenant farmer are highlighted by case study 9, where the investment made by the tenant in the diversification of the farm buildings would have reverted to the landlord after 10 years (paras 2.21 – 2.24).

Figure 4.1: Applicant type

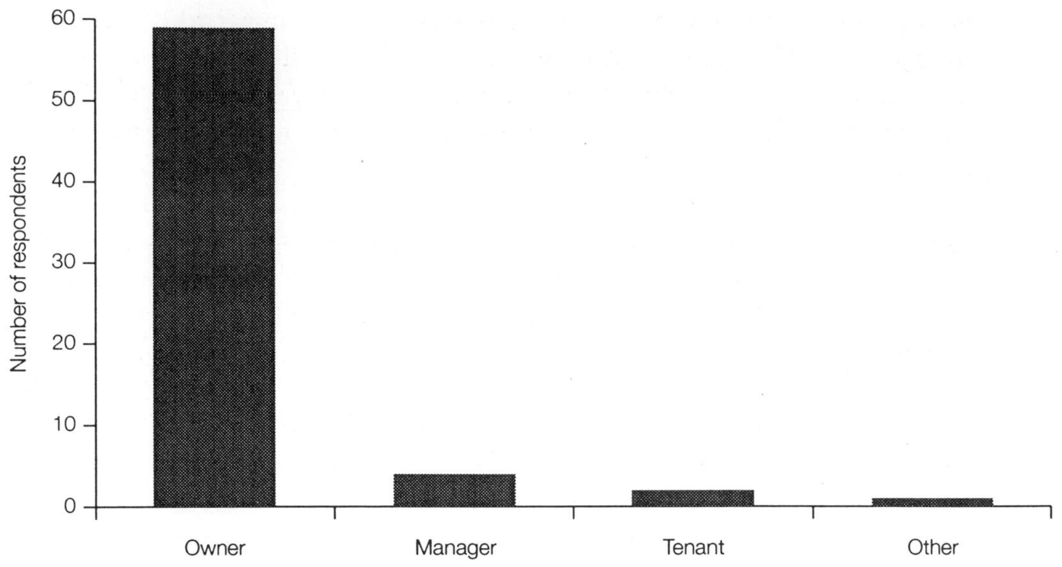

Help sought by applicants in making a planning application for farm diversification

4.5 In making a planning application, applicants for farm diversification may seek both outside advice and engage an architect or agent to assist in the preparation of the application or to make the application on their behalf.

4.6 **Seeking professional advice prior to an application:** From the farmer telephone survey and the postal questionnaire of applicants, it appears that prior to making a planning application for a diversification activity, most applicants seek advice, most commonly from a planning consultant (**Table 4.1**). The telephone survey also indicates the role of friends and neighbours in providing advice.

Table 4.1: Professional advice sought by applicants

Source of advice	Telephone survey (sample 67)		Postal questionnaire (sample 181)	
	No. of applications	%	No. of applications	%
Planning consultant	16	25%	88	47%
Land agent/surveyor	9	14%	25	13%
Non-professional (friend)	8	13%	3	2%
NFU/CLA	7	11%	10	5%
Architect	6	10%	19	10%
Other (1)	14	22%	13	7%
None	3	5%	17	9%
No answer	0	–	14	8%
Total	**63**	**100%**	**189**	**100%**

NB. Totals may not be the same as the sample size, either because applicants failed to answer the question or because they sought advice from more than one party.

(1) This included other forms of paid professional advice eg a golf course architect; unpaid professional advice eg from friends who were lawyers; builders; business advisors; British Horse Society; advice from Parish and Local Councillors; and advice from other members of the family.

4.7 **Advice from ward councillors prior to making an application:** Discussions with local councillors as part of this study, indicated that potential applicants sometimes seek advice from their elected representative before formally approaching the LPA. This situation tends to occur when applicants already know their ward councillor, having either met them informally or having sought advice on other issues. Many councillors felt that they had a more localised understanding of the problems and concerns facing farmers than the planning officers.

4.8 **Advice from development control (DC) officers prior to making an application:** From the postal questionnaire and telephone survey, it appears that over 80% of applicants for farm diversification seek some form of advice from the LPA prior to submitting a planning application for farm diversification (this figure was 87% in the postal questionnaire; and 85% in the telephone survey). In both cases the sample is only those farmers who have gone on to make a planning application. However, from the case studies, it is evident that some applicants are unaware that this opportunity is available or, where a professional advisor 'knows the ropes', this advice may be thought unnecessary (case studies 3 and 11 – see **Appendix 8**). The latter point was confirmed by DC officers who noted that many local agents are well aware of local policies and only approach the LPA on more complex issues.

4.9 According to the postal questionnaire, over 90% of these contacts were with a DC officer, although from the telephone survey it appears that just over half of the contacts were with a DC officer, and a further 13% were with the highways officer (**Table 4.2**). In the majority of cases this contact was considered helpful.

Table 4.2: Source and helpfulness of advice from the local authority

Source of advice	Number of applicants		% found helpful
Planning officer	31	(57%)	74%
Conservation officer	4	(7%)	100%
Farm/Agricultural Liaison officer	1	(2%)	100%
Highways officer	7	(12%)	86%
Unspecified	4	(7%)	50%
Other	4	(7%)	50%
None	4	(7%)	–
Total	**55**	**(100%)**	–

NB. Sample size = 55
Source: Telephone survey

4.10 From the postal questionnaire it appears that in most cases this advice was substantial in that it either involved a site visit (40% of cases) or a meeting (31% of cases) – **Table 4.3.** This is supported by the telephone survey which indicates that 85% of applicants who had contacted the LPA had a site meeting at the farm[11] as part of the pre-application advice received from the LPA.

[11] This figure needs to be treated with some caution because of the small sample size ie 29 applicants had had a site meeting out of the 35 applicants that had contacted the LPA.

Table 4.3: Method of contact with the LPA

Method of contact	No. of applicants	% of total returns (181)
Site meeting	72	40%
Phone conversation	66	36%
Meeting	57	31%
Letter exchange	41	23%
None	27	15%
No answer	16	9%
Total	**279**	–

NB. Applicants may have made more than one type of contact
Source: Postal questionnaire

4.11 **Responsibility for submitting the planning application:** From both the postal questionnaire and the telephone survey, it appears that roughly 60% – 65% of applicants for farm diversification had used a professional to submit an application on their behalf (usually a planning consultant, architect or land agent/surveyor), with roughly 40% of applicants submitting their own application. From the case studies it appears that professional assistance is valued: *"invaluable in terms of complying with building regulations etc."*, *"we could never have negotiated the grant system without professional help"*. The value of professional advice was confirmed at the farmers' workshops (Chapter 6), although there were one or two instances in the case studies where this professional assistance was considered unhelpful. This primarily related to situations where the advisor had expressed confidence in gaining planning permission but the application was subsequently refused.

4.12 **Continuing contact with the LPA after submitting the planning application:** From the telephone survey it appears that the majority of applicants who had contacted the LPA prior to submitting an application, continued this contact through to determination. Again, this contact was primarily with a DC officer, although a highways officer was also sometimes involved. From the telephone survey, it appears that this contact was considered less helpful than that given at the pre-application stage, with some applicants commenting that the advice was *"contradictory"* to that provided previously (as identified in case study 1), or *" the LPA were flexing their muscles"*. At this stage, 50% of contacts with officers were considered helpful, compared to 74% at the pre-application stage (**Table 4.2**).

4.13 The clear message is that the majority of planning applications for farm diversification have the benefit of external advice, both from professional advisors and from the LPA, although a few applicants are unaware that they can seek such advice – a point worth stressing in any future guidance.

THE PROCESS ADOPTED BY THE LPA IN DEALING WITH INDIVIDUAL PLANNING APPLICATIONS

Pre-application advice

4.14 From discussions with DC officers it is evident that there is a growing awareness of the needs of farming. This arises from the introduction of the notification procedures for agricultural developments; the increasing number of agricultural developments requiring planning permission; and, in particular, from recent government advice and national press coverage of the issues facing farming, now greatly heightened by the Foot and Mouth epidemic. Nevertheless, for the majority of DC officers a farm diversification enquiry will still be a relative novelty representing, on average, only 1–2.5% of their annual case load (para 5.5). It therefore takes time for officers to become aware of all the issues that may be relevant, especially as the range in types of development and types of diversification activity can be so great (para 1.12). Every application, therefore, is seen as different, the possible exception being building re-use for tourism accommodation, for which large numbers of applications have been received in remote rural areas.

4.15   **Availability of advice:** Every local authority visited as part of this study indicated a willingness to undertake pre-application discussions with applicants for farm diversification – there is no evidence from either the postal questionnaire or the telephone survey that this opportunity was ever denied an applicant. However, from discussions with land agents who are working in other local authority areas outside this sample, it is evident that a few LPAs have a policy of not engaging in an interchange with a potential applicant until a planning application has been submitted[12]. It should not be assumed therefore that all farmers across the country receive the pre-application advice that they require.

4.16   **Officer responsible:** Within the sample LPAs methods for dealing with pre-application enquiries vary. Several authorities operate a duty rota system to ensure that an officer is always available, or available at certain times, to give planning advice (on anything). One or two hold occasional planning clinics for a half-day or evening, when officers are available to potential applicants. These meetings will rarely be just for farm diversification but will more often be for applicants in general. In the case of Harrogate, such meetings are held at different locations around the District to increase access to planning advice across a relatively large rural area. Other authorities have one officer who specialises in farm diversification advice and applications. This is rarely a formalised role but one that develops through the experience of a particular officer, as in Basingstoke and Deane and Maidstone. Equally, where DC officers work in area teams, some teams may build up more expertise, simply because their area receives more farm diversification applications, and they will become the point of reference for such applications.

4.17   **Type of guidance sought:** From this study no details were collected on the type of guidance and advice sought by applicants prior to making an application. But from a parallel study undertaken in early 2001 in Breckland District Council, for the Countryside Agency[13], DC officers commented that farmers are increasingly approaching the LPA before they have any plans for diversification, simply to find out what is likely to be acceptable in planning terms. This can place officers in a difficult position. Planning officers must remain impartial. In consequence, they are unable to give any categorical assurance of what might receive planning permission, especially in circumstances where the applicant is not providing any form of clear proposal. This may be frustrating for would-be applicants who are looking for clarity, but equally it is to misunderstand the role of planning.

4.18   **Information given:** In terms of information supplied by officers in response to initial enquiries, the most common approach is to provide potential applicants and their agents with copies of relevant planning policies (as in case study 4). The majority of officers interviewed were aware of the DOE Good Practice Guide *Planning for Rural Diversification*

---

[12] This devise is used to help the LPA determine the majority of their planning applications within an eight week period by ensuring that officer time is not diverted from the task of processing and determining planning applications that have already been received.

[13] LUC and Kernon Countryside Consultants, *The Planning System and Sustainable Farm Diversification in the N&l MI Area 2001*, for the Countryside Agency

(1995) and the DOE/MAFF/WO document *A Farmer's Guide to the Planning System* (1996), although few authorities actually use either in their discussions with farmers (or at any other time) as they are seen to be dated. In consequence, a number of LPAs are now producing their own guidance with the aim of stimulating thoughts about diversification options, helping farmers make best use of the planning system, and encouraging prospective applicants to develop some initial thoughts or outline proposals before approaching the LPA (to overcome the problems identified in para 4.17 above). Examples are the comprehensive *Planning Guide to Farm Diversification in North Yorkshire* (para 6.42); guidance being prepared by Hampshire County Council in liaison with its Districts; and draft 10-page guidance – *A Guide to Farm Diversification* – which has been produced on behalf of the Norfolk Arable Land Management Initiative for all farmers in Breckland District, and in future will be given to all those making initial enquiries. In Harrogate, a pro-forma has been developed for potential applicants for building conversions and re-use, to help identify the type of advice needed by the applicant.

4.19 Initial enquiries to the LPA will frequently be followed up by further advice and potentially a site meeting where specific proposals are being discussed (para 4.10). Where appropriate, the DC officer will involve others in pre-application discussions, in particular the Highways Authority, as illustrated by case studies 1 and 9 (**Appendix 8**) and the farmer telephone survey.

4.20 Generally officers felt that pre-application discussions were useful and led to a higher standard of planning application. This view is borne out by the farmer telephone survey which revealed a largely positive response to this liaison from would-be applicants (**Table 4.2**). Pre-application discussions were also given strong support at the workshops held with planning officers. A clear concern though, was the potential implications of the Government's 'Best Value' regime. Currently pre-application advice is offered as a free service. Under Best Value the outreach activities of LPAs may be judged strictly in financial terms, with emphasis on speed and efficiency rather than quality of advice and the suitability of subsequent development, with either pre-application advice no longer available, or only available subject to a charge. This would be unfortunate for a service that is highly regarded by applicants.

4.21 It is a strong view from the DC officers interviewed during this study that in the vast majority of cases, positive advice from planning officers given at the pre-application stage leads to the submission of a planning application.

4.22 Overall, it appears that while DC officers want to provide pre-application advice to potential applicants, there are few formalised systems in place for doing so, and planning officers only build up experience on farming matters in an ad hoc fashion (this is perhaps not surprising given the small proportion of farm diversification applications relative to the total DC case load (para. 4.14)).

Advice and consultation on submitted applications

4.23 **Recording of pre-application advice:** One of the concerns of farmers about the planning system is the apparent inconsistency between views expressed by the LPA during pre-application discussions and those provided by the case officer after the application has been made (para 4.12). This highlights the importance of having a recording system for pre-application enquiries. Of the sample LPAs, few reported having a formal recording system. The authorities with a system tended to rely on a single file for all enquiries, or to break these down into parishes. Some authorities keep details electronically. Most authorities sought to ensure that the officer responsible for pre-application advice dealt with any subsequent application. However, this was generally achieved on an ad hoc basis. This general lack of recording of pre-application discussions is highlighted by the fact that, while over 85% of applicants had some form of contact with the LPA before submitting a planning application, records of these discussions were only found on the case files in 10% of cases.

4.24 **Site visits:** LPA case officers will visit all application sites on receipt of the application. They do not normally contact the applicant prior to these visits because of the need to fit a number of visits into the day and the resource implications of arranging meetings. Exceptions are made where applicants specifically request to be present at an officer's site visit; where access is required to a secure building or site; or where there is a need to discuss an aspect of the application with the applicant.

4.25 **Consultees:** A number of consultees are regularly consulted to provide views on submitted applications for farm diversification. Highways officers/engineers are invariably consulted by the DC officer on all applications involving farm diversification, and may be involved in post-application discussions with the applicant, as in case studies 3 and 8 (**Appendix 8**). The local authority conservation officer will be involved where applications involve a Listed Building or Conservation Area and the county archaeologist may also be consulted. The local authority ecologist will often be involved where the application raises issues relating to nature conservation eg where buildings may house protected species such as bats and barn owls. Another frequent consultee, where available, is the county land agent or occasionally, where not available, an external specialist agricultural consultant may be contacted. The Environment Agency is also regularly consulted.

4.26 In Stratford, since 1993, every application for farm diversification has been referred to the District's economic development officer for advice on the economic merits of the application. This advice is passed both to the planners and the applicant. In this way the LPA has been able to take a broader view of applications, seeking to maximise both the land use and the economic benefits they might provide, and the applicant has received a co-ordinated response to their proposal on two crucial issues. This approach has been regarded as successful by both parties, as highlighted in case study 5 where advice from an economic development officer was received during pre-application discussions.

4.27 To summarise, the lack of a method for co-ordinating pre-application advice can potentially lead to inconsistency subsequently in the planning process. Other important comments on an application from consultees may raise points not previously considered. This may add to the apparent inconsistency in comments made at the pre and post-application stages and highlights the importance of farmers understanding the planning process and the sequence in which comments will be made.

Quality of planning applications and the impact of planning fees

4.28 **Quality of applications:** The quality of submitted applications caused concern in some authorities, whilst others felt that standards were generally adequate. In many cases, planning officers indicated that the higher quality applications were submitted either for larger-scale development or by larger estates. Officers felt that pre-application discussions and the use of professional agents in the preparation and submission of applications (at least 60% of cases) helped improve the standard of submitted applications.

4.29   Applications for smaller schemes submitted by an individual farmer tended to be of a lower quality and did not always include all the required information. However, there was little indication that the quality of applications led to an increase in refusal rates. Some authorities, such as Harrogate, indicated a willingness to advise an applicant on how to revise a scheme, even to the extent of sketching alternative proposals. Most officers expressed an awareness of the problems for smaller scale farmers in preparing planning applications and a willingness to both provide guidance and negotiate necessary improvements. This is tempered with a need to be consistent and fair in the treatment of all applicants.

4.30   **Farm plans:** Within the sample LPAs very few farm plans have been received in support of a farm diversification application, even in those authorities which favour their use in local plan policies (para 3.45). From discussions with land agents it is clear that farmers are concerned about the potential resource implications of plan preparation. Yet, looking beyond the scope of this research, it is evident that considerable effort is currently being focused on farm business planning and Integrated Farm Appraisals:

● Under the Small Business Service launched in October 2000, farmers can receive an initial health check of their business and an Action Plan from which they will then be signposted to other sources of advice and help

● In the MAFF Upland Experimental areas and in many of the Countryside Agency's Land Management Initiatives (including the High Weald, Severn Vyrnwy, and North York Moors) Integrated Farm Appraisals have or are being undertaken, linking environmental, economic and community needs in the future development of individual farms.

Much of the information set out in Farm Action Plans, Business Plans and Integrated Farm Appraisals, is the same or similar to that which might be presented in a farm plan in support of a planning application. There is therefore a need to see the extent to which these emerging approaches, designed to assist a farmer in planning the future of the farm business, can be used to support planning applications, in ways that avoid a duplication of effort.

4.31   **Planning fees:** These are set nationally. They range from £95 for minor alterations, £190 for change of use and small-scale development and rise in increments of £190 thereafter, proportionate to floor or site area. For the 213 applications on which details were recorded during the planning register review, over 76% of applicants paid a fee of £190 (or the equivalent rate in earlier years). Eighteen applicants paid £95 or equivalent and a further 19 applicants paid less than £400. Only ten applications required a fee of £500-£1000, with a further three applications generating a fee of over £1000.

4.32   Discussions with planning officers indicated that they had not received significant adverse feedback on fee levels. This view was confirmed by the workshops for both farmers and planners, neither of which raised fees as a major concern. It is clear from studying the case studies (**Appendix 8**) that the cost of implementing permissions is generally far in excess of the application fee. The cost, for example, of implementing a wild flower nursery in case study 7 would have been £20,000 and in case study 9 building conversion and refurbishment was estimated as in excess of £45,000.

4.33   In general, it appears that planning fees and the quality of planning applications for farm diversification are not key concerns. Larger and more complex applications are mostly prepared by professional advisors and for small schemes planning officers are usually prepared to provide guidance. To-date very few farm plans have been produced in support of applications for farm diversification, but other emerging farm planning tools might be developed to provide the required supporting information without duplicating effort.

Delegated powers

4.34 Although DC officers estimated that between 65-85% of farm diversification applications were dealt with under delegated powers, the planning register review (para 5.63) confirms that in reality roughly 40% are dealt with under delegated powers, with 60% determined by committee. The main reason for this is that many LPAs have no delegated powers to determine applications on which an objection had been received, and many farm diversification applications were noted to generate at least one objection, often from the Highways Authority. Two other common reasons for taking an application to committee were that the proposals were contrary to policy, or following a request from a councillor.

4.35 All DC officers interviewed felt that committee members usually supported officer recommendations. A common response though, was that, if anything, members were more likely to take a sympathetic view, taking account of individual circumstances, and occasionally approving applications where the officer recommendation was for refusal. One remote rural LPA noted that this outcome was more frequent with farm-related applications than other types of development. Elected members interviewed recognised the need for farmers to develop alternative sources of income and some felt that countryside and landscape designations could be applied too rigidly in situations where working farms were seeking to develop. The support of members is illustrated by case studies 6 and 9. Here refusal was recommended on highway grounds but the committee members felt that the additional traffic would be minimal and therefore approved the application subject to highway conditions.

4.36 In case study 6 (change of use to craft workshops and retail), the applicant had the opportunity of addressing the planning committee in person. The planning committee in turn was able to ask questions. The applicant felt that this was very helpful in that it allowed him to address any objections in person.

4.37 As explored further in Chapter 5 (paras 5.63 – 5.67), the fairly high percentage of applications for farm diversification determined by committee does not appear to affect overall approval rates, although it does inevitably slow down the approval process.

Decision-making

4.38 In accordance with the Town and Country Planning Act 1990 (Section 54A), DC officers reported that they rely, in the first instance, on the policies in the development plan and other material considerations, when recommending determinations for farm diversification applications. Where there are no specific policies on farm diversification (Chapter 3), reference is made to those policies of most relevance which, depending on the nature of the application, will include those relating to the rural economy, building re-use, environmental conservation and highways issues. In addition, where PPGs either post-date the development plan, or when the policies of the development plan are not as full as those set out in the PPGs, officers will give additional weight to the latter. Not all DC officers interviewed though, clearly indicated that they refer to PPG7 (1997) when determining farm diversification applications.

4.39 Although criteria-based policies for farm diversification bring greater clarity to the planning process, it is clear that all LPAs seek to positively support farm diversification so long as the proposal is not in significant conflict with the policies in the local plan. Nevertheless, discussions with DC officers revealed a number of key issues that arise in relation to farm diversification proposals. These are closely interrelated and are:

- Conflict between positive policies for rural and farm diversification (PPG7, 1997) and policies seeking to **reduce traffic movements** (PPG13, 1994).

- Potential conflicts between diversification policies and policies for **landscape designations**, such as AONBs and Heritage Coasts.

- Conflict with **Green Belt policies** in urban fringe authorities. This is borne out by the appeals analysis where, of the 19 appeals examined in detail, eight were in the Green Belt and of these, five were dismissed with reference to Green Belt policy.

- The **scale and expansion of use** relating to farm diversification.

- The **relationship of the proposal to a working farm unit**. DC officers expressed confusion as to whether national support for farm diversification related to all development on existing and former farms, or primarily to situations where the diversification activity directly contributes to the continued economic viability of a working farm unit.

- The **design and materials** used in building conversions and new build associated with farm diversification, which are normally addressed through conditions.

4.40 **Traffic and highways**: DC officers identified a clear conflict between the policies of PPG7 encouraging farm diversification and those of PPG13 (1994) which sought (prior to revision in March 2001) to reduce the need to travel by discouraging development in relatively isolated locations (paras 3.61 – 3.67). This tension is reflected in local plan policies.

4.41 Traffic and highways have been one of the key reasons for refusal of farm diversification applications. This is confirmed by the case studies and the review of appeals where, in five out of the 12 case studies and in seven out of the 19 appeals examined, traffic was identified as a key issue. From the planning registers it appears that where traffic was raised as a key issue, the approval rate dropped from an overall average of 83% to 74%, a difference of 9%. The reasons for refusal are equally divided between (para 5.40):

- highway safety issues raised by the Highways Authority, relating to the capacity of the local road network and the creation of road hazards; and

- traffic generation and potential conflicts with the guidance in PPG13 (1994).

The appeals raise a third issue, namely the loss of visual amenity with increased traffic movements (noted in the case of two of the appeals).

4.42   Discussions with DC officers indicated that they work with highways officers to try and overcome highway safety issues[14] – a particular problem being the frequent difficulty of meeting modern highway standards on country lanes. Furthermore, in remote rural areas, officer recommendations in line with objections from highway engineers may be overturned by members (as illustrated by case studies 6 and 9).

4.43   With regard to the policy tension between PPG7 and PPG13 (1994), DC officers have often dealt with this by the simple expedient of favouring the supportive guidance in PPG7 for farm diversification while setting aside PPG13's aims, especially in remote rural areas. The main exception has been development likely to generate significant amounts of traffic, which are frequently refused. In remote rural areas it is generally accepted that the car is the main means of transport and the most sustainable approach will be to provide a scatter of small-scale economic developments to match the scattered nature of population distribution.

4.44   **Scale of developments:** DC officers are concerned about the increasing size of buildings coming forward for re-use, and the lack of policy guidance, nationally and within their own plans, on this issue. This is seen as a particular issue in Green Belts and AONBs. The two specific issues raised by large buildings are:

●   their size which, in prominent locations, can detract from the landscape and impinge on the open character of Green Belts

●   the increased intensity of use and the resultant storage, car parking needs and traffic generation which may result as a consequence of the re-use.

Where the building(s) are very large and where the re-use will result in significant intensification of use, applications may be refused, especially within AONBs and Green Belts, as indicated in case study 11 and appeal 7.

4.45   DC officers are particularly concerned about intensive livestock units (eg pig, chicken and calf rearing units) which can come forward for re-use. These units tend to be economically vulnerable, with many business failures resulting from salmonella, BSE, and the 1999/2000 slump in pork prices. Where these units come forward for re-use in the urban fringe, their floor area can compete with sites and areas identified for employment use in the local plan (as illustrated by appeal 7). A further planning issue is that these modern intensive livestock rearing units will often have provided the justification for an agricultural workers dwelling. If the agricultural use ceases, this justification no longer applies.

4.46   **Relationship to a working farm unit:** LPAs are often keen to see a clear relationship between a diversification activity and its support for a farm business, and so will frequently be more receptive to applications on a working farm. Although the case studies have been chosen to illustrate different types of diversification activity (**Appendix 8**), they nonetheless indicate the differences in attitude of planners to:

●   diversification activities connected to a working farm, where the contribution to an agricultural unit is self-evident; and

[14] As identified with reference to the highway design requirements set by DoE's Design Bulletin 32 *Residential Roads and Footpaths* (1992), local versions of this guidance or the Highway's Agency's Design Manual for Roads and Bridges (1999).

- developments occurring on small-holdings in the urban fringe, and on land and in buildings that have been severed from an active farm, where the support of an agricultural business may not be clear cut.

4.47   Thus for the four larger working farms in the case studies, ranging from an 81 hectare upland sheep farm to a 283 hectare mixed farm in middle England, all had had a good experience with the planning system: *"The local authority advice was very helpful, had no problems and were generally surprised with the ease and speed of negotiating the planning process"*; *"The planning officers advice was very helpful..... We were generally happy with the process"*. This compares to the cases where the application related to an urban fringe small-holding, a non-farmed unit or buildings, and enterprises that were not contributing to the finances of the farm. Here applicants tended to be less happy about the planning system: *"Didn't contact the local authority before making the planning application because of problems in the past"* (the site has been the subject of a series of planning applications only some of which had been successful); *"Generally unhappy with the planning process – felt the LPA was unreasonable and not particularly consistent in its decision-making."*

4.48   In summary, policy conflicts (in terms of PPG7 and PPG13) combined, sometimes, with a lack of clear local plan policies on scale of development and linkage (or otherwise) to a working farm, reduce clarity for DC officers and applicants. Officers and members seek to reconcile conflicting policy and cope with gaps in policy when determining individual applications. But further clarity on these issues, both at the national level (as now provided with regard to mode of travel with the 2001 revision of PPG13) and in local plans, would be welcomed by DC officers. This could potentially be provided by a national definition of sustainable farm diversification discussed further in Chapter 7.

Conditions

4.49   With the wide range in types of application for farm diversification, few standard conditions are used, other than those relating to design and use of materials in building conversions. Key issues raised by DC officers with regard to conditions were:

- *Tying building to land/farm unit:* Approximately half the sample authorities seek (at least sometimes) to tie diversification activities to the land of the farm (primarily urban fringe and accessible rural LPAs), although most of these commented that a Section 106 agreement[15], rather than conditions, was the most appropriate way to achieve this. Interestingly, this potential control over wider farming activities was not reflected strongly through analysis of the planning register details (paras 5.52 – 5.55).

- *Removal of agricultural permitted development rights:* The majority of sample LPAs remove agricultural permitted development rights in some circumstances. Despite this, many officers expressed caution about the use of such a condition. For example, Ellesmere Port and Neston, like other urban fringe authorities, stated that they were more likely to refuse planning permission if this was a key issue. The removal of permitted development rights was also found to only a limited extent in the planning register review (para 5.52).

---

[15] Section 106 agreements under the Town and Country Planning Act 1990, allow a legal agreement to be made between an applicant and the LPA. The fundamental basis for the use of legal agreements is that planning permission cannot be bought or sold but that the agreement may allow development to proceed where it might otherwise be refused. Government advice on the use of legal agreements sets out similar tests to those relevant to the application of planning conditions.

- *Traffic generation:* Whilst many authorities seek appropriate controls over traffic, it was generally considered unenforceable to restrict numbers of vehicle movements. Control tended to be sought through conditions over hours of operation, delivery together with routing agreements, and number of parking spaces provided (which also relates to landscape impacts).

- *Improvements to appearance:* In most cases, required improvements would be sought through negotiations prior to the determination of an application, rather than through subsequent conditions. Some conditions covering issues such as materials and landscaping were common.

- *Personal/temporary permissions:* The majority of authorities sought to avoid personal and temporary permissions. In cases where a farmer would be making a significant financial investment, several officers commented that a temporary permission would be unfair and reduce the likelihood of the scheme proceeding, as indicated in case study 7. Others, particularly in urban fringe authorities, stated that due to the number of retrospective applications it was often easy to judge actual impact and so temporary permissions were not relevant. Personal permissions, where they were used, tended to be applied to potentially disturbing uses carried out by a farmer in close proximity to the farmhouse, such that if the farmhouse changed hands, the permission would no longer be valid.

4.50   Where there has been on-going contact between the applicant and the LPA, the conditions will often be discussed with the applicant prior to determination, as in case study 6. Here the applicant felt that *"the outcome of the application and the conditions were reasonable, largely because everything had been negotiated previously and therefore the conditions that were imposed were expected."* However, applicants are often not contacted specifically about conditions, as illustrated by case study 8 where the applicant was surprised at the subsequent highway condition. On the other hand, Section 106 agreements will usually be discussed with the applicant prior to determination, unless it is introduced at committee as a way of avoiding a refusal (para 5.66).

4.51   The telephone survey of farmers indicated little opposition by applicants to conditions imposed, although some applicants indicated that planners did not fully understand the specific circumstances of their application. For example, in some cases existing, farm-related, traffic movements were thought to be higher than those that would be generated through a new activity.

Monitoring and enforcement

4.52   Resource constraints within LPAs means that there is only limited monitoring of planning consents and conditions (for any type of development). Some LPAs, such as Exmoor NPA, have dedicated monitoring officers. Many others rely on an informal monitoring system, for instance, the case officers may visit if they are passing the site. A few authorities rely on a computer system to inform case officers of the commencement of development, whilst others rely on building control officers for this information.

4.53   Some authorities, such as Wealden and North Norfolk, actively monitor conditions. This monitoring process can take the form of visiting the site and sending written reminders to applicants (e.g. on the need to submit landscaping details within a specified period). Monitoring is a time consuming process, but those LPAs that are pro-active see their actions as avoiding the greater resource input required by enforcement action. Member support and willingness to maintain staffing levels is crucial to successful monitoring.

4.54 Enforcement action is also constrained by resources. Most authorities find it easier to remove resources and staff from those actions which the authority undertakes of its own accord, such as enforcement, than services such as development control that follow directly from the submission of applications. At the farmers' workshops the lack of enforcement action, unless third party objections were raised, was welcomed by the farming community. In most cases, authorities prefer to request retrospective applications for those developments which they may approve in order to regularise the position. Maidstone is a good example. Officers here felt that an extremely high proportion of their farm diversification applications were retrospective and arose from enforcement investigations. (This high percentage of retrospective applications in urban fringe locations has been picked up in previous studies, eg LUC, 1995).

FORMING LINKS WITH THE FARMING COMMUNITY

4.55 As picked up in para 4.2 above, there is generally no formalised system within LPAs to help planning officers develop an understanding of farming (or vice versa). Nevertheless, communication between the farming community and LPAs is now being improved through a number of mechanisms.

Agricultural liaison officers

4.56 Agricultural liaison officers have been in place for some years within National Park Authorities (NPA) forming part of their Farming and Countryside Service or similar. Traditionally the role of these officers has been to administer and advise the farming community about the conservation grants available from the NPA, and more recently to promote and apply national agri-environment schemes, such as Countryside Stewardship. They have also traditionally played a key role in administering the notification procedure for agricultural permitted development rights but are now increasingly involved in giving advice on farm diversification. To the farming community they have been the accessible face of the NPA, providing a ready point of contact, making themselves available through farm visits etc.

4.57 Outside National Parks, the nearest equivalent to these liaison officers has been provided by county and district Countryside Management Services (CMS) which, amongst other activities, have promoted conservation management on farms. Many of these services are now either disappearing (with local authority resource cuts) or are developing as independent trusts. Where they still exist, some are developing a strong rural economic business role. For example, on the Isle of Wight, Island 2000 (the CMS Trust) is promoting development of rural business opportunities that reflect and support the distinctive characteristics of the Island. Separately, new agricultural advisory posts have and are being created under projects aimed at delivering integrated rural development, such as the Forest of Bowland and Bodmin Moor Upland Experiments, and activities in The Marches 5b area. Within Objective 1 areas, similar posts are also being created at county level. For example, in Cornwall there are three farm facilitators (funded through Objective 1) responsible to the Cornwall Agricultural Council[16] who are based at the County Council and help farmers

[16] Representing all aspects of agriculture, horticulture, food and other land-based industries in Cornwall and Isles of Scilly.

obtain funding, business advice etc. Similarly, in Somerset, which lies outside Objective 1, an agricultural advisor has been appointed by each of the District Councils (co-ordinated at county-level) to signpost farmers to other services and sources of advice. Prior to the outbreak of Foot and Mouth disease, such coverage was, however, the exception rather than the rule.

4.58   Importantly, in the context of this study, these posts have no formal link to the planning functions of LPAs. Indeed, planning officers noted that it may be inappropriate for such officers to give planning advice, as there is a risk that this could conflict with that of qualified planning officers. One step in forging more positive liaison with planning is being made by North York Moors NPA, where funding is being sought for an officer to provide a link between farm advice and the specific requirements of development control (see also para 4.62).

Agricultural fora

4.59   For a number of years some county councils have administered Rural or Countryside Fora (for example, Hampshire, Hertfordshire, Bedfordshire and Warwickshire), many of which have agricultural sub- or working groups. County councils may also engage farmers through economic fora, for example, the Hampshire Economic Partnership has a Rural Group which includes farming members and works to maximise the assets of the County's rural economy. In Somerset the County Council runs the 'Agriculture in Somerset' roundtable. It is less usual for such fora to operate at district level, although a few authorities, such as Harrogate, have regular forum group meetings to discuss issues relating to rural areas and farming. In a few cases LPAs have taken a more pro-active role in dealing with the current problems facing farming. In the case of Stratford, for example, the authority set up a series of workshops over autumn 2000 with farmers and their advisors to debate the issues surrounding farm diversification and the planning system. In the aftermath of Foot and Mouth many more such fora are likely to emerge.

Economic and business advice

4.60   Nearly all local authorities have economic development officers. Although traditionally strongly urban-based, many are now taking an increasing interest in farming issues. A key role is to develop economic development strategies for their district. As part of these, a number of economic development officers interviewed are commissioning rural economic surveys. BaNES, for example, is about to undertake a survey of farms, investigating the potential for economic re-use of agricultural buildings. Invest in East Sussex is undertaking an audit of all farms to assess the availability of buildings for conversion, and Basingstoke and Deane is currently developing a Rural Property Register where farmers can place available buildings. However, as noted in the previous Chapter (para 3.57), to date little of this work has been used to influence local plan policies, although it does help raise awareness of agricultural issues.

4.61   At a day-to-day level economic development officers are now giving more advice to farmers. In Caradon, for example, the economic development officer indicated that he now receives about two farm diversification enquiries per week, compared to only two enquiries in the whole of 1997. The Caradon officer is also regularly informed by development control colleagues of proposals that may be eligible for redundant building grants, while the Stratford economic development officer is consulted on all farm diversification planning applications (para 4.26).

4.62   In a few instances more concerted attempts are being made to ensure that farmers can gain planning and business advice under one roof, as a 'first-stop shop' advisory service on farm diversification. Again, best practice is focused in the National Parks. In the Peak District NPA business advice to farmers is available through the Farming and Countryside Service and is used as a filter on problematic schemes, and to improve the business quality of proposals before they are submitted for planning approval. Similarly, in the North York Moors, Whitby Business Development Agency is in the process of making an officer available to give business advice from the North York Moors NPA offices. The National Park will be providing free office accommodation allowing farmers to seek advice from both the Business Development Agency and planning advice from National Park officers under one roof. In addition to providing a more convenient and user-friendly service for potential applicants, the arrangement should permit closer interaction between the relevant officers.

4.63   The longer history within NPAs of assisting farming and farm diversification recognises the pivotal role which farming has, and continues to play, in the local economy, social structure and management of the landscape in these areas. The proportionally greater economic importance of farm diversification in these remote rural areas, compared to areas closer to centres of population, is highlighted by the statistics on numbers of planning applications for farm diversification explored in the next Chapter (para 5.7).

IN SUMMARY

Process followed by applicants

- Landowners are overwhelmingly the main applicants for farm diversification activities. Although not a planning issue, tenants find it hard to justify significant financial investment without a permanent interest in the land.

- 90%-95% of applicants seek some form of professional advice before submitting a planning application for farm diversification. Over 80% contact their LPA at this stage.

- 60% – 65% of applications are made on behalf of applicants by professional advisors with roughly 40% of applicants submitting their own application.

Advice from LPAs

- There are indications that farmers are increasingly contacting LPAs to find out what type of diversification they should undertake to gain planning permission, before developing any diversification proposals. This can place planning officers in a difficult position as they should remain impartial at all times.

- In response, a few LPAs are producing or supporting local farmer guides to diversification and the planning system to help farmers through the initial steps of developing a farm diversification proposal. Current national guidance on farm diversification and the planning system is seen as outdated.

- For those farmers who go on to make a planning application for farm diversification, approximately 85% currently seek advice from the LPA before submitting the application. In the majority of cases this contact is with a DC officer and over 70% of this advice involves a site visit, and/or face to face meeting – in other words, this advice is substantial. This advice is thought helpful by applicants and is supported by planning officers as a means of improving the quality of planning applications received. There is concern amongst planning officers though, that this advice will be curtailed by the Government's Best Value regime.

- Generally, within LPAs there are few formalised systems in place to provide planning advice to farmers and planning officers only build up experience on farming matters in an ad hoc fashion. This is not surprising as farm diversification applications, on average, make up no more than 2.5% of all planning applications received by LPAs.

- To try and provide more co-ordinated advice to farmers on farm diversification, a number of National Parks are developing First Stop Shop facilities for farmers, providing planning and business advice under one roof. Other LPAs are now involving economic development officers in advising farmers on individual applications for farm diversification. But this more comprehensive approach to advice-giving is the exception rather than the rule.

- The majority of applicants who contact the LPA before making a planning application continue this contact after submission of the application. From a limited sample, it appears that applicants find advice given at this stage less helpful as it may be contradictory to earlier advice given, sometimes reflecting comments received from statutory and other consultees. This potential lack of consistency is not helped by generally poor recording by LPAs of pre-application discussions with would-be applicants.

Planning applications
- The cost of planning fees is not a key concern amongst the farming community.

- The quality of applications submitted for smaller scale farm diversification schemes is slightly below standard, but there is little indication from officers that this affects approval rates and authorities generally appear willing to negotiate improvements, rather than refuse where a scheme is otherwise acceptable.

- Farm plans are currently very rarely used in support of a planning application for farm diversification. Yet considerable effort is now being focused on farm business planning and Integrated Farm Appraisals. There is therefore a need to assess the extent to which these emerging approaches, designed to assist a farmer in planning the future of the farm business, can be used in support of planning applications in ways that avoid duplication of effort.

- 40% of farm diversification applications are dealt with under delegated powers and 60% are determined by committee. Whilst this may not affect the outcome, particularly given the willingness of some members to approve schemes despite planning objections, it undoubtedly delays the decision.

- Both members and officers appear to have considerable sympathy with farmers wishing to diversify and will seek to positively support farm diversification applications as long as the proposal is not in significant conflict with the local plan policies.

- Key issues for DC officers when reviewing planning applications are: traffic and highways; landscape designations; Green Belt; the size of modern farm buildings now coming forward for re-use, and the relationship of the application to a working farm unit. Further clarity on these points both at the national level (as now provided in the review of PPG13 (2001) on transport issues) and in local plans, would be welcomed by DC officers. This could be provided in the form of a national definition of sustainable farm diversification which can then be interpreted at the local level.

Forming links with the farming community

- Communication between the farming community and LPAs is now being developed in some areas through a number of mechanisms including agricultural fora and agricultural liaison officers. These are best developed in National Parks where there is a longer history of assisting farming and farm diversification. This recognises the pivotal role that farming plays in the local economy, social structure and management of the landscape in these areas.

CHAPTER 5

Results of the planning register review

5.1 A major element of this study involved gathering information on planning applications for farm diversification submitted between February 1997 and February 2000, from the planning registers of each of the 21 sample LPAs. This Chapter sets out the detailed findings from analysis of the resulting database. Details of the database structure are included as **Appendix 6.** Where appropriate, this Chapter also refers to the postal questionnaire of applicants and farmer workshops.

NUMBER AND TYPE OF FARM DIVERSIFICATION APPLICATIONS

5.2 A total of 1397 applications for farm diversification activities were submitted across the 21 sample LPAs over the three years February 1997 – February 2000, ranging from 15 in BaNES to 162 in Stratford (**Table 5.1**). This is equivalent to between five and 54 applications per year per authority. The total figures demonstrate that strict conservation designations do not hold back diversification applications, with North York Moors and the Peak District National Parks being in the top four LPAs in terms of the number of applications received for farm diversification.

Table 5.1: Number of applications for farm diversification by LPA category

Urban fringe		Accessible rural		Remote rural	
LPA	No. of applications	LPA	No. of applications	LPA	No. of applications
Bath and NE Somerset	15	Basingstoke and Deane	62	Berwick on Tweed	22
Blaby	25	Harrogate	60	Caradon	23
Eastleigh	27	Sedgemoor	44	East Lindsey	41
Ellsmere Port and Neston	21	Stratford on Avon	162	Exmoor National Park	53
Maidstone	70	Wealden	89	North Norfolk	128
Warwick	71	West Lancashire	80	North York Moors National Park	139
		Wychavon	102	Peak District National Park	125
				Ribble Valley	38
Total	**229**		**599**		**569**
Average	**38**		**86**		**71**

Source: Planning Register details for the three years February 1997 – February 2000

5.3 **Applications by LPA category:** On their own the total numbers of diversification applications by LPA category are potentially misleading, in that they do not take account of population density or the geographical extent of the local authority area concerned (unfortunately statistics are not readily available on numbers of farms per LPA area). **Appendix 7** provides information on the number of applications, approval rates, population size and geographical area of each LPA.

5.4 Most of the sample LPAs received between three and 10 farm diversification applications per 10,000 head of population and an average of 1.8 applications for farm diversification per 1000 hectares. But looking more closely at the different LPA categories, important distinctions emerge. Urban fringe areas received the least number of farm diversification applications per head of population (reflecting the significantly greater urban population densities in these areas), but received the greatest number of such applications per 1000 hectares (**Table 5.2**). This reflects the larger number of small-holdings and the greater development pressure close to urban areas. By comparison, in remote rural areas there are more farm diversification applications per head of population, reflecting a more rural and dispersed population, but only 35% of the number of applications per 1000 hectares when compared to urban fringe authorities. Surprisingly, given the larger overall numbers of diversification applications in National Parks, the number per 1000 hectares is, on average, 42% of that in urban fringe areas, reflecting the very large areas of upland moorland with no development at all.

Table 5.2: Number of applications for farm diversification by LPA population and area

LPA category	Applications per 1000 ha. Average	Applications per 10,000 pop. Average
Urban fringe	2.0 applications	3.4 applications
Accessible rural	1.3 applications	7.5 applications
Remote rural	0.6 application	21.8 applications
Overall average	1.3 applications	11.8 applications

Source: Planning register details and the Municipal Year Book 1997 – Volume 2. Newman Books

5.5 **Number of farm diversification applications relative to the total number of planning applications received:** Across the sample LPAs studied, farm diversification planning applications tend to make up only a small proportion of the total number of planning applications submitted. Typically they account for between 1-2.5% of applications determined (average 1.5%) but with higher rates in the National Parks (para. 5.7). In Maidstone, for example, 1907 planning applications were determined in the year ending 31 March 2000. Assuming an even spread of farm diversification applications recorded over the three-year period in this study, only about 1.2% of Maidstone's decisions related to farm diversification. The lowest figure (0.2%) was recorded in BaNES (urban fringe).

5.6 Clear differences emerge between urban fringe, accessible rural and remote rural areas. Proportionately, farm diversification proposals become more significant moving from urban fringe to remote rural areas and, with odd exceptions, LPAs within each category are similar. The average number of farm diversification decisions as a percentage of all planning decisions within each category is shown in **Table 5.3**.

Table 5.3: Farm diversification decisions as a percentage of all planning decisions

LPA category	Total farm diversification decisions recorded (Feb. 1997-Feb 2000)	Average per year	Total decisions taken by LPA type (Year ending 31 March 2000)[17]	Average recorded farm diversification decisions as % of decisions taken in year ending 31 March 2000
Urban fringe	210	70	8071	0.9%
Accessible rural	526	175	12456	1.4%
Remote rural	523	174	7661	2.3%
Totals/averages	**1259**	**140**	**28188**	**1.5%**

Sources: Planning register details and DTLR website – www.dtlr.gov.uk

5.7   The three National Parks are the only areas in the sample in which the proportion of farm diversification decisions are significantly higher (average 5% of all planning decisions). The greatest proportion is within North York Moors National Park, where 649 planning applications were determined in the year ending 31 March 2000, of which farm diversification proposals accounted for 7.1% of decisions. Figures of 5.1% and 4.7% apply to Exmoor and the Peak District National Parks respectively.

5.8   Overall, therefore, there appears to be a clear difference in the pattern of farm diversification activity between urban fringe and remote rural areas, with activity in accessible rural areas lying between the two. Urban fringe areas are characterised by strong development pressure. They receive three times as many applications for farm diversification per unit area (compared to remote rural areas) but farm diversification applications make up only 0.9% of all planning applications determined by these LPAs. On the other hand, remote rural areas receive over six times the number of farm diversification applications per head of population (compared to urban fringe areas), with these applications making up a significantly higher proportion of all planning decisions. These figures highlight that in terms of density of development, farm diversification is most common in the urban fringe but contributes more to the economy of remote rural areas, where it makes up a greater percentage of all development.

Types of diversification activity[18]

5.9   In this study, as in previous studies[19], tourism (494 applications) was the most common type of diversification activity overall, making up 31% of all farm diversification applications

[17] Source: DTLR website – www.dtlr.gov.uk

[18] Through this Chapter the sample size for subsequent figures on diversification activities, types of development, conditions, reasons for refusal etc will vary from the total number of applications (1397) recorded. This is because of the fairly frequent inclusion of more than one category within a single application. For instance, an application may be made for both a craft workshop and farm shop, or within one application, seek a change of use and extension to an existing building. Totals will also vary dependant on whether data are drawn from the full sample or a sub sample and the number of LPAs where this information was available on the case files.

[19] LUC et al (1995) Planning Controls over Agricultural and Forestry Developments and Rural Building Conversions. Report prepared on behalf of DoE. HMSO
Elson, M. & McDonald, R.(1995) Planning for Rural Diversification. Report prepared on behalf of DoE. HMSO
University of the West of England (2000) Rural Diversification in Farm Buildings: An investigation into the relationship between the re-use of farm buildings and the planning system. Report prepared on behalf of the Planning Officers Society.

(**Figure 5.1**). These were concentrated in the remote rural and, to a lesser extent, accessible rural areas. Tourism applications were focussed particularly in the National Parks – North York Moors NP (95 tourism applications) and Peak District NP (80 tourism applications). This dominance of tourism applications in remote rural areas is also exemplified by a recent study undertaken for Cornwall County Council looking at *Planning Rural Employment in Cornwall* (Atlantic Consultants, 2000) which noted that the vast majority of farm building re-use applications in the County were for tourism. Equestrian activities (269 applications – 17%), storage (165 – 10%), offices (159 – 10%), and manufacturing/industry (130 – 8%) were the other most common farm diversification proposals.

Figure 5.1: Number of planning applications by diversification activity across all LPAs

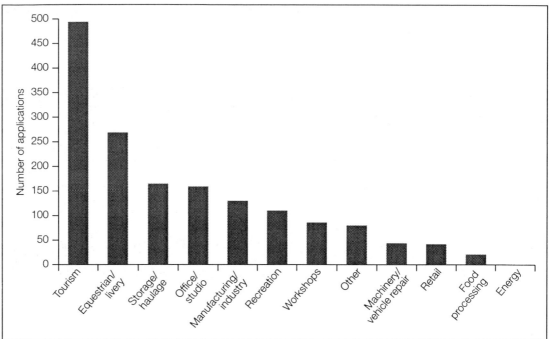

5.10   **Figure 5.2** and **Table 5.4** indicate the breakdown of diversification activities by category of local authority. The pattern that emerges is that the nature of diversification activities is generally very similar within urban fringe and accessible rural areas, with a very similar proportion of recreation, workshop, manufacturing, storage, and office use in both categories of LPA. The main difference is that in urban fringe areas equestrian activities make up 30% of the total, compared to 17% in accessible rural areas. A notable characteristic of both areas is the generally low level of activity in food processing and farm shops (although farm shops may have been established without planning permission where they are only selling produce from the farm).

5.11   In contrast, as already noted, remote rural areas are characterised by a very heavy reliance on tourism activity which makes up 53% of all farm diversification activities in these areas. This is followed by equestrian activities which make up nearly 11% of the remote rural total, and storage and recreation, each at 6%. Beyond these, no other activity makes up more than 5% of the total.

5.12   This clear contrast between accessible and more remote rural areas indicates the importance of accessibility to urban areas in determining the types of diversification activity that are pursued. Recreation and equestrian uses will clearly require a substantial customer base, while industrial and commercial uses, depending on their nature, may require access to suppliers, labour markets, and specific skills within the workforce.

5.13   Leaving aside farm tourism activities, many of which are of a very high quality, the general impression gained from reading all the case files is not one of quality and innovative diversification, although there are obviously notable exceptions. Perhaps surprisingly, food processing and other methods of adding value to farm produce are still very unusual, making up no more than 1.6% of diversification applications across all the LPA categories. Thus, reality does not currently match the vision of farm diversification painted by the Rural White Paper and the ERDP, or the Government's Task Force for the Hills. This state of affairs is hardly surprising, as many farmers have been forced into diversification as a reaction to declining incomes and have not had the benefit of training and business advice – this is the challenge for the schemes which have now been introduced under the ERDP and the *Action Plan for Farming* (Chapter 2).

Table 5.4: Applications by type of diversification activity

a	Tourism	Equestrian	Storage	Office
Urban fringe	39 (15%)	78 (30%)	37 (14%)	31 (12%)
Accessible rural	128 (18%)	123 (17%)	89 (12%)	100 (14%)
Remote rural	327 (53%)	68 (11%)	39 (6%)	28 (5%)
Total	**494**	**269**	**165**	**159**

b	Manufacturing/ industry	Recreation	Workshops	Retail
Urban fringe	25 (10%)	21 (8%)	9 (3%)	6 (2%)
Accessible rural	83 (12%)	53 (7%)	44 (6%)	20 (3%)
Remote rural	22 (4%)	36 (6%)	33 (5%)	16 (3%)
Total	**130**	**110**	**86**	**42**

c	Machinery/ vehicle repair	Food processing	Energy	Other (see note)
Urban fringe	7 (3%)	1 (0%)	0 (0%)	9 (3%)
Accessible rural	21 (3%)	10 (2%)	0 (0%)	44 (6%)
Remote rural	16 (3%)	10 (2%)	1 (0%)	27 (4%)
Total	**44**	**21**	**1**	**80**

Sample size = 1601. Percentage figures relate to each category of local authority (100% is total number of applications within that category of authority). Totals: urban fringe = 263; accessible rural = 715; remote rural = 623 each.

'Other' includes kennels, catteries and other pet related uses, animal burial, wildlife conservation, fisheries, health facilities, nursery and child minding facilities and helicopter and aircraft uses.

Source: Planning Register details

Types of diversification development

5.14 More than half the applications recorded involved the re-use of existing buildings (**Figure 5.3**), although these were concentrated in the accessible and remote rural authorities. The majority of the remaining applications fell into the categories of new building or change of use of land.

5.15 **Table 5.5** provides more detail on the types of diversification development. Significantly it demonstrates the much higher proportion of applications for new build in urban fringe areas compared to other areas where building re-use predominates. This is potentially surprising recognising that a good proportion of urban fringe areas have a Green Belt designation. Nevertheless, this is likely to relate to the strong emphasis on equestrian developments in the urban fringe (para 5.10), with these activities frequently starting on bare land plots resulting from earlier land fragmentation. In some cases it may also reflect a lack of more traditional agricultural buildings available for re-use. From previous studies (LUC, 1995) and interviews with planning officers during this study, it appears that the majority of traditional buildings available for re-use in urban fringe areas had already been converted to residential accommodation by the beginning of the 1990s.

Figure 5.2: Diversification activity by authority type

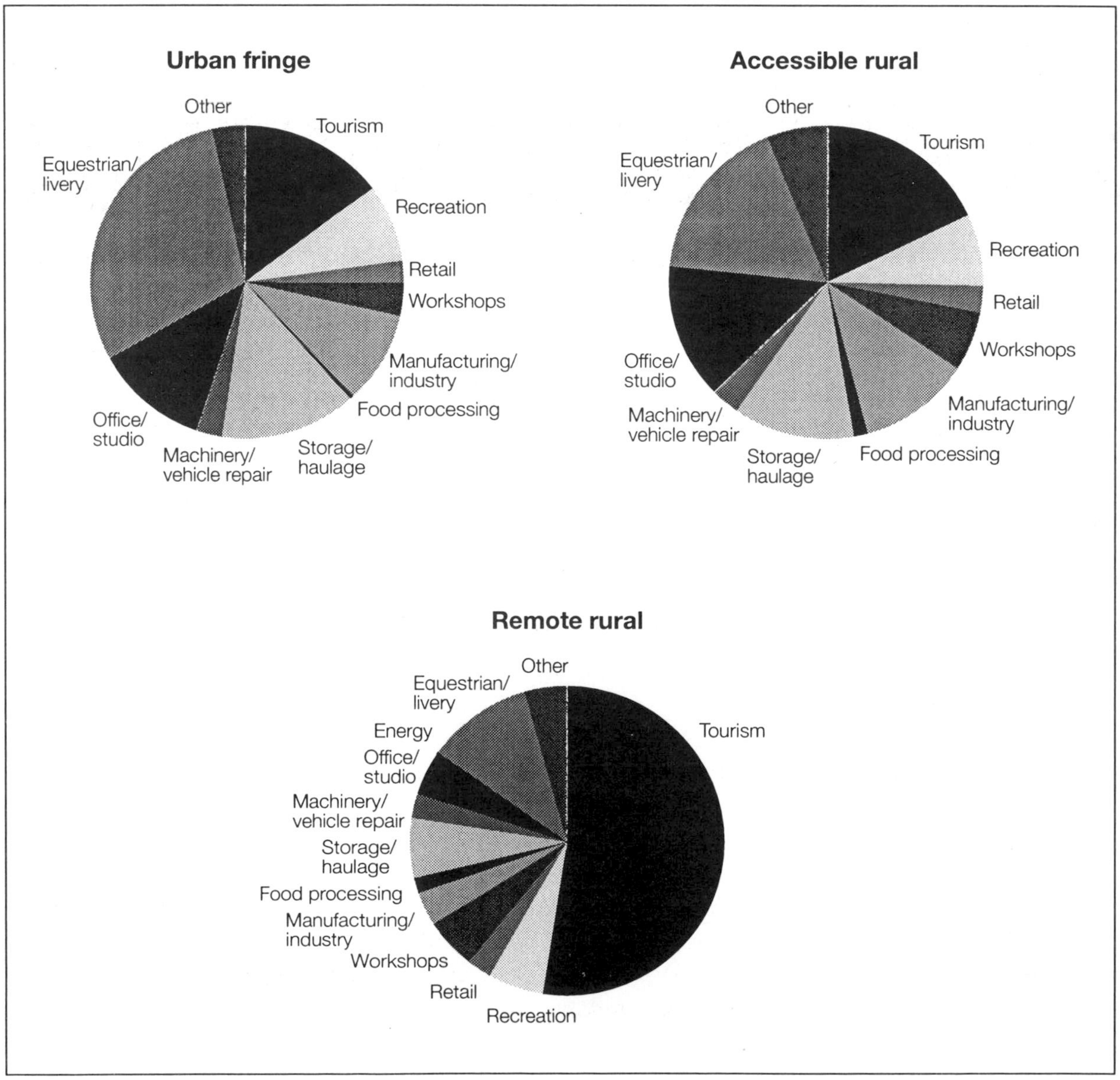

Figure 5.3: Number of applications by type of development

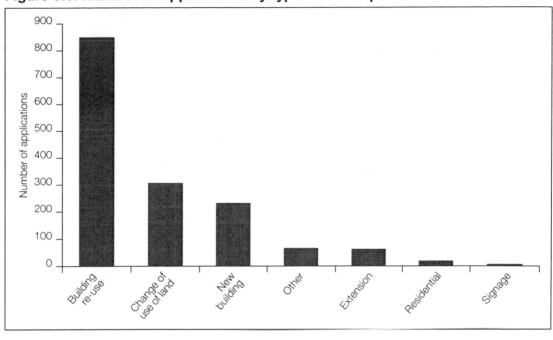

Residential = residential use in support of a diversification activity.

Table 5.5: Type of development by type of local authority

	New building	Building extension	Building re-use	Change of use of land	Ancillary residential	Signs	Other	Total
Urban fringe	68 (27%)	11 (4%)	93 (37%)	70 (28%)	5 (2%)	3 (1%)	3 (1%)	253 (100%)
Accessible rural	82 (13%)	24 (4%)	379 (57%)	145 (22%)	10 (2%)	3 (0%)	12 (2%)	655 (100%)
Remote rural	83 (14%)	28 (5%)	379 (62%)	93 (16%)	5 (1%)	2 (0%)	11 (2%)	601 (100%)
Total	**233**	**63**	**851**	**308**	**20**	**8**	**26**	**1509**

Sample size = 1509. Percentage figures relate to each category of local authority (100% is total number of applications within that category of authority).

Source: Planning Register details

Incidence of diversification development on working farms

5.16   Through this study, information was sought on the relationship of diversification applications with a farm unit. In particular:

●   whether the farm was still involved in some form of agricultural production (a working farm); and

●   if the development was located in a farmstead, whether that farmstead was still used for agricultural purposes (an active farmstead), or whether it was a redundant farmstead no longer involved in agricultural production. This may be because it had been sold away from the farm, or because, with farm amalgamations and rationalisation, it was now surplus to agricultural requirements.

5.17 From the case files it was often not possible to define the nature of the farming activity, although it was usually possible to identify the nature of the farmstead (where relevant). From this analysis it appears that, across all types of rural area, between 55% and 70%[20] of farm diversification activities are occurring within an active farmstead, with approximately 20% occurring within a redundant farmstead. The remaining developments are occurring on open land or within isolated buildings.

APPROVAL RATES FOR ALL APPLICATIONS

5.18 Across the full sample, for those applications for farm diversification on which a decision has been recorded (excluding withdrawals and those with no decision yet), 1039 out of 1259 were approved (83%). This approval rate compares to the national average approval rate for all planning applications in England in 1999/2000 of 88% or just over 90% for minor developments (excluding dwellings)[21]. However, there are clear differences in approval rates for farm diversification between different categories of LPA. Urban fringe authorities have an average approval rate of 68%. The average approval rate for accessible rural authorities is 84%, while for remote rural authorities it is 87% (**Table 5.6**). This differential was picked up at the farmer workshops where LPAs in remote rural areas were seen as having a more positive attitude to farm diversification compared to those in the urban fringe, where overall development pressure is greater. **Appendix 7** provides a breakdown of decisions by each individual authority.

Table 5.6: Total applications and approval rates

	Total applications	Approved	Refused	Withdrawn	No decision
Urban fringe	229	143 (68%)	67 (32%)	8	11
Accessible rural	599	439 (84%)	87 (16%)	66	7
Remote rural	569	457 (87%)	66 (13%)	26	20
Total	**1397**	**1039 (83%)**	**220 (17%)**	**100**	**38**

Sample size = 1397. Percentage figures relate to applications that have been approved or refused only. For example, the 68% approval rate in the urban fringe represents 143 applications approved from a total of 210 approved or refused.

Source: Planning Register details

5.19 One hundred planning applications (7%) from the total of 1397, were withdrawn. These withdrawals were heavily concentrated in the accessible rural authorities (66 applications). Only eight applications were withdrawn in the urban fringe authorities where planning officers identified a high level of retrospective applications, often as a result of unauthorised activities such as building re-use for car repairs. Where a use already exists, it cannot be in the applicant's interest to withdraw their application, as they will be left with a continuing unauthorised activity.

5.20 **Comparisons with previous studies:** These approval rates closely reflect the findings of other studies. The LUC (1995) study of rural building re-use identified an average approval

[20] Based on a sample size of 298 applications

[21] Minor developments are those where the floor area to be developed does not exceed 1000 square metres or the site is under 1 hectare.

rate across England and Wales of 80% for the re-use of buildings for economic purposes. As in this study, there was a difference between urban fringe areas with an approval rate of between 53% and 79%, and remote rural areas with a high percentage of tourism applications and approval rates in excess of 80%. Similarly, the recently completed study of *Rural Diversification in Farm Buildings,* undertaken for the Planning Officers' Society (2000), identified an overall approval rate across three counties of 74%, with a breakdown by county[22] as follows:

Table 5.7: Approval rates by County for the economic re-use of buildings

County	Applications	Approved	Refused	Withdrawn
Essex	251	174 (70%)	51 (20%)	26 (10%)
Shropshire	56	51 (91%)	4 (7%)	1 (2%)
Somerset	39	30 (77%)	8 (21%)	1 (2%)

Source: Shorten et al (2000) Rural Diversification in Farm Buildings: An investigation into the re-use of farm buildings and the planning system

5.21   The above table demonstrates the same pattern of approvals between remote rural and more accessible areas, with Shropshire Districts (remote rural) having an average approval rate of 91% compared to the urban-influenced areas of Essex with an average approval rate of 70%. The high approval rate in remote rural areas is further exemplified by the study of *Planning and Rural Employment in Cornwall* (Atlantic Consultants, 2000) which identified that 95% of applications for tourism re-use of buildings are approved within Cornwall.

Approval rates by type of diversification activity

5.22   **Figure 5.4,** indicates the total number of approvals and refusals by diversification activity.

Figure 5.4: Total number of approvals by diversification activity

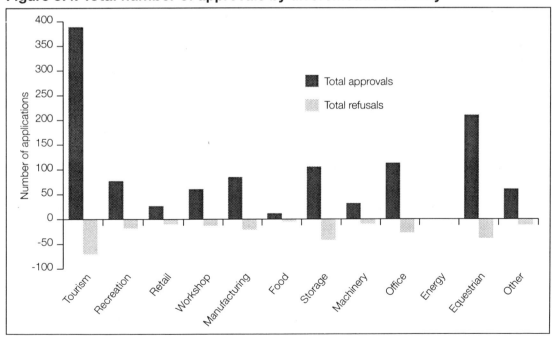

[22] Note: this is based on a sample of LPAs within each County as follows: Essex – Colchester BC, Braintree BC, Maldon BC; Shropshire – North Shropshire DC, Shrewsbury and Atcham BC, South Shropshire DC; Somerset – Sedgemoor DC, Taunton Deane DC.

In terms of the percentage approval rate, the highest approval rates are for tourism activities (85% approved) closely followed by equestrian activities at 84% approved. Other activities with approval rates between 81% and 83% are workshops, recreation and offices. Lower approval rates (although the sample size is considerably smaller) relate to vehicle repair (78%), and food processing and retail, both at 75%. The lowest approval rate overall (71%) relates to storage which may be associated with HGV movements.

5.23   In line with the overall approval rates by LPA category, urban fringe areas have the lowest approval rates for most individual diversification activities (**Table 5.8**). But some clear variations emerge. Tourism and equestrian activities have lower approval rates in the urban fringe than the average for all LPA categories, standing at 57% and 70% respectively. Conversely (although the sample is very small) the approval rate for workshops and manufacturing in the urban fringe (86%) is higher than the overall average, possibly reflecting that many of these application are retrospective (para 5.19).

5.24   Approval rates in accessible rural areas generally follow the averages noted in para 5.22. In remote rural areas very high approval rates are evident for tourism (88%) and equestrian (92%). Perhaps surprisingly, the approval rates for storage are much higher in remote rural areas (83%) compared to urban fringe areas (54%). This almost certainly reflects differences in storage activity, with distribution activities dominating in the urban fringe (illustrated by the example appeals) and with storage activities associated with tourism more characteristic of remote rural areas (for example, the storage of caravans and the over-wintering of boats in coastal locations).

Table 5.8: Numbers of approvals and approval rates by type of diversification activity

a	Tourism	Equestrian	Office	Storage
Urban fringe	20 (57%)	52 (70%)	21 (70%)	19 (54%)
Accessible rural	96 (84%)	112 (89%)	71 (84%)	57 (74%)
Remote rural	273 (88%)	58 (92%)	21 (84%)	30 (83%)
Total	**389**	**222**	**113**	**106**

b	Manufacturing/ industry	Recreation	Workshops	Machinery/ vehicle repair
Urban fringe	19 (86%)	14 (70%)	6 (86%)	5 (71%)
Accessible rural	53 (80%)	37 (84%)	32 (82%)	16 (80%)
Remote rural	13 (72%)	26 (84%)	23 (82%)	11 (79%)
Total	**85**	**77**	**61**	**32**

c	Retail	Food processing	Energy	Other
Urban fringe	2 (40%)	0 (0%)	-	7 (71%)
Accessible rural	13 (77%)	6 (86%)	-	41 (83%)
Remote rural	12 (86%)	6 (75%)	-	22 (88%)
Total	**27**	**12**	**-**	**70**

Sample size =1404. Percentage figures show the percentage of applications for that activity within that type of LPA that are approved.

Source: Planning Register details

Approval rates by development type

5.25 **Figure 5.5** shows the total number of approvals and refusals by type of development. In terms of percentage approval rates, the highest rates overall relate to building re-use and extensions, both with approval rates of 86%, whereas approval rates for new buildings and change of use of land stand at 79% and 74% respectively. **Table 5.9** shows this breakdown relative to the LPA categories. The same pattern is evident across the local authority categories but with significantly lower approval rates within the urban fringe for new building (possibly relating to Green Belt issues), building re-use, and change of use of land. The significant difference in approval rates for building re-use between remote rural areas (90% approved) and the urban fringe (73% approved), almost certainly reflects the nature of the building stock, with a wide range of traditional vernacular buildings still available for re-use in remote rural areas but with most activity in urban fringe areas now relating to more modern agricultural buildings (para 5.15).

Figure 5.5: Total number of approvals by development type

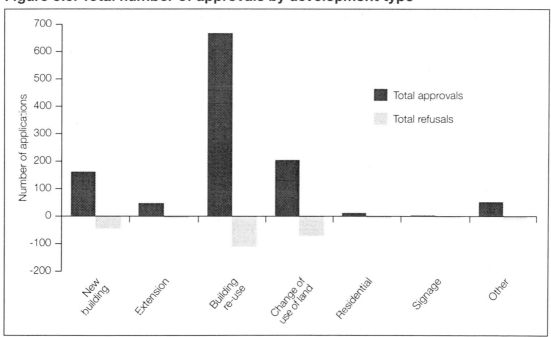

Table 5.9: Approval rates by development type

	New building	Building extension	Building re-use	Change of use of land	Ancillary residential	Signage	Other
Urban fringe	41 (67%)	9 (90%)	62 (73%)	38 (57%)	3 (60%)	1 (50%)	3 (100%)
Accessible rural	63 (89%)	19 (90%)	282 (85%)	102 (80%)	6 (60%)	1 (33%)	8 (80%)
Remote rural	58 (78%)	20 (80%)	324 (90%)	64 (79%)	3 (60%)	2 (100%)	41 (84%)

Sample size =1404. Percentage figures show the percentage of applications for that activity within that type of LPA that are approved.

Source: Planning Register details

Approval rates by size of building

5.26 As noted in Chapter 4, one of the key concerns of some DC officers is the size of some modern agricultural buildings coming forward for re-use as part of diversification proposals (paras. 4.44 – 4.45). These concerns relate to the landscape impacts of such buildings and the potential intensification of use and traffic generation which may result. An analysis has therefore been made of the approval rates relating to older (and usually smaller) farm buildings compared to those associated with modern (and usually larger) farm buildings. As is evident from **Table 5.10**, there is a notable difference in approval rates between these two building types. On average, 28% of modern buildings were refused for a diversification re-use compared to an average of only 13% for traditional buildings. This differential was also noted at the farmer workshops.

5.27 Interestingly, the refusal rates for modern buildings are significantly higher in urban fringe and accessible rural areas (averaging 33%) compared to remote rural areas (15%). This reflects the higher refusal rates all round within accessible rural areas, and the greater concern about intensification of use within areas suffering from development pressure. It may also reflect the entirely separate point of LPAs seeking to control the abuse of agricultural Permitted Development Rights [PPG7 paragraph 3.7], especially in urban fringe areas.

Table 5.10: Approval rates by type of building

Category of LPA	Modern buildings		Traditional buildings	
	Approved	Refused	Approved	Refused
Urban fringe Approval/Refusal rate	17 68%	8 32%	17 77%	5 23%
Accessible rural Approval/Refusal rate	22 67%	11 33%	36 88%	5 12%
Remote rural Approval/Refusal rate	17 85%	3 15%	69 89%	9 11%
Total Approval/Refusal rate	56 72%	22 28%	122 87%	19 13%

Sample size = 219. Figures show the percentage of applications approved/refused for that building type within that category of LPA.

Source: Planning Register details based on sub sample of 20 applications per LPA

Approval rates in Green Belts and other designated areas

5.28   Approval rates within Green Belts are 12% below the average found for all farm diversification applications, representing the lowest approval rate of any designation. This approval rate is similar to that for urban fringe locations more generally (68% approved in the urban fringe: 71% approved in Green Belts). Where applications were refused within Green Belts the most common reasons for refusal were: inappropriate development in the countryside and adverse landscape or visual impacts (ie., issues relating to PPG7 advice more generally, rather than specific Green Belt considerations). However, in 50% of these cases, specific mention was also made of the need to maintain the open aspect of the Green Belt (an issue relating to PPG2 *Green Belts*). Similarly, in six out of nine appeals in a Green Belt, the inspector raised the appropriateness of development in the Green Belt as a key issue (**Appendix 9**).

5.29   In AONBs, approval rates are approximately 7% below the average for all farm diversification applications. But within local non-statutory landscape designations, the approval rate of 83% is exactly the same as the average approval rate for all farm diversification applications, suggesting that local landscape designations do not restrict farm diversification activities as much as has been suggested in previous studies (eg Elson, 1995).

5.30   Other planning designations also do not seem to lead to a higher refusal rate. Approval rates in National Parks closely match the average for remote rural authorities (86% approved in National Parks: 87% approved in remote rural areas) and exceed the average approval rate for all farm diversification applications by 3%. This high rate of approval may partly reflect the dominance of tourism applications which generally have low impact, and the higher quality vernacular building stock. It may also reflect a long-standing appreciation within the NPAs of the critical role of farming in the local economy and in the maintenance of the landscape.

5.31   The approval rates for applications involving Listed Buildings and Conservation Areas are also over 80% as indicated in **Table 5.11**. For the other land and conservation designations excluded from the Table, such as Ramsar sites and Sites of Special Scientific Interest, the numbers of applications affecting such sites were so small as to make meaningful analysis impossible. Significantly, in no case was Best and Most Versatile (BMV) agricultural land identified as a reason for refusal.

Table 5.11: Approval rates by key land and conservation designations

	Total applications	Total decisions	Approved	Refused
National Park	317	300	259 (86%)	41 (14%)
Listed Buildings	35	31	26 (84%)	5 (16%)
Local landscape designation	31	29	24 (83%)	5 (17%)
Conservation Areas	22	20	16 (80%)	4 (20%)
AONB	44	42	32 (76%)	10 (24%)
Green Belt	46	41	29 (71%)	12 (29%)
Totals	**495**	**463**	**386**	**77**

Sample size = 495

The approval and refusal rates shown above exclude applications that have been withdrawn or remain undetermined and therefore will not add up to the figure in the total applications column.

Source: Planning Register details based on sub sample of 20 applications per LPA.

Approval rates by geographical location and relationship to an active farm

5.32   Discussions with planning officers indicated that generally diversification activities are more acceptable when they are located close to or within an existing complex of farm buildings, as opposed to being an isolated development in the open countryside (para 3.93). This is borne out by the approval rates for developments in different types of location. Thus diversification activities[23] :

- in a farmstead had an average approval rate of 86%, with little difference in approval rate between activities within redundant and active farmsteads

- in an isolated building in open countryside had an average approval rate of 67%

- on land in the open countryside had an average approval rate of 50%.

5.33   **Relationship with a working farm unit:** With regard to the relationship of diversification activities to a working farm, the postal questionnaire of applicants reveals that where a diversification activity is associated with a working farm, the approval rate is 83%. This compares to only 68% approved on farms which are no longer farmed, or in buildings, or on land which have been sold away from the holding. This underlines the emphasis that a number of LPAs have on promoting diversification activities that are clearly linked to a farm business (paras 3.43, 4.46).

5.34   Nevertheless, amongst the diversification activities that have been approved and implemented, the postal questionnaire identifies that while 57% form part of an active farm business, a significant minority (30%) are no longer related to an active farm unit (**Table 5.12**). Interestingly, even on working farms, only 39% of the diversification activities are bringing additional income to the farm businesses. As illustrated by some of the case studies (**Appendix 8**), this may occur where a farm is split between family members with those no longer directly involved in the farm business developing diversification activities on the farm, but not necessarily related in any way to the farm business.

Table 5.12: Relationship between implemented permissions and an active farm unit

Type of farm	No. of implemented permissions	% of implemented permissions (87)
Working farm	50	57%
Farm no longer farmed	18	21%
Sold away from farm	8	9%
No answer	11	13%
Total	**87**	**100%**

Source: Postal questionnaire of applicants

[23] Based on a sample of 267 applications:

Impact of pre-application discussions

5.35 **Discussions with LPAs:** From a small sample in the database it appears that pre-application discussions with the LPA may contribute to a positive outcome for farm diversification activities. Of the 41 applications with a decision to date where it is known that there were pre-application discussions, 33 (81%) were approved with conditions and a further three (7%) were approved subject to a Section 106 agreement. The resulting refusal rate of only 12% is significantly lower than the average refusal rate for farm diversifications of 17% (see **Table 5.6**).

5.36 The postal questionnaire also sought details of any pre-application discussions (**Table 5.13**). Pre-application, the majority of applicants have a site meeting, meeting elsewhere or a telephone conversation with the LPA, with 75% of subsequent applications being approved. By comparison, where there was only an exchange of letters, 66% of subsequent applications were approved, and 71% were approved where there was no pre-application advice. The variations in these approval rates are relatively small but appear to substantiate the impression that detailed, face-to-face pre-application advice assists in securing planning permission. By way of contrast, pre-application advice by an exchange of letters, a relatively cursory process, appears to be less than helpful.

5.37 If anything, the value of pre-application discussions may be more important than suggested by these figures, as applicants and agents are undoubtedly more likely to seek pre-application advice on more complex or potentially controversial schemes (para 4.8).

Table 5.13: Pre-application contact with the local authority

Method of contact	Number of applications where there was pre-application contact with the LPA	Subsequent approval rate
Site meeting	72	74%
Telephone conversation	66	73%
Meeting	57	76%
Letter exchange	41	66%
None	27	71%
No answer	16	-

NB. Sample size = 279, but includes some applicants that experienced more than one method of contact with the LPA.
Source: Postal questionnaire of applicants

5.38 **Advice from agents:** Interestingly, the postal questionnaire also reveals that where an agent was used to assist in the preparation of the planning application, the refusal rate was higher (28%) compared to situations where the applicant made his/her own application (8%). The reason behind this statistic is almost certainly that external advice tends to be used in more complex cases. Nevertheless, the fact that agents less frequently engage with the LPA prior to making an application (para 4.8) may have something to do with this. Furthermore, through the case studies there is clear evidence of some agents, especially those from a property development background, misadvising their client.

5.39 In summary, in remote rural areas approval rates for farm diversification are 19% higher than in urban fringe areas, with particularly high approval rates for tourism and equestrian uses, of 88% and 92% respectively. These approval rates serve to highlight the recognised link between farm diversification and support for the rural economy in these remote rural areas. It also potentially highlights the low environmental impact of the majority of diversification activities proposed, assisted by a remaining stock of vernacular farm buildings suitable for conversion. On the other hand, in more accessible areas, the stronger development pressures, patterns of land fragmentation, combined with more frequent proposals involving modern agricultural buildings, and the issues of scale and increased intensity of use that this raises, are reflected in lower approval rates. Approval rates may also be influenced in these areas by Green Belt and AONB designations, although local landscape designations do not appear to affect decisions.

Reasons for refusal

5.40 The reasons given for refusal of farm diversification proposals reflect the above picture, with many refusals relating to more than one issue. From the planning registers it appears that the most common reasons for refusal relate to:

- landscape and visual impact (62% of applications refused)[24]

- development inappropriate in the countryside (52% of applications refused)

- traffic and highways (51% of applications refused) with reasons for refusal equally divided between highway safety and traffic generation issues

- not appropriate in the Green Belt/AONB (33% of applications refused)

- likely intensification/cumulative impact (14% of applications refused)

- impacts on neighbours (14% of applications refused)

- question over the structural soundness of the building being converted (14% of refusals)

- noise generation (10% of refusals)

All other reasons for refusal related to less than 10% of the sample.

5.41 These issues broadly reflect the policies in local plans for farm diversification (paras. 3.41 – 3.47). The considerable emphasis on *development inappropriate in the countryside* reflects the exceptional nature of farm diversification, in that it often necessarily involves development outside settlements requiring DC officers to reconcile the national policy of strictly controlling development in the open countryside (para 3.14), with policies in support of farm diversification. This reconciliation is made all the more difficult where plans require farm diversification to have conformity with all or some other policies in the plan (para 3.43).

5.42 Reasons for refusal relating to traffic and highways, Green Belt, and intensification of use, closely mirror the key issues raised by DC officers with regard to the practical implementation of farm diversification policy (paras 4.40 – 4.45).

---

[24] Based on a sample of 81 applications that had been refused.
Source planning register details.

5.43   Having analysed reasons for refusal both by type of diversification activity and by type of development, no clear patterns emerge from this study. This suggests that it is more often the nature of specific impacts, rather than type of development or type of activity, that trigger a refusal. It also underlines the point made by DC officers that no two farm diversification applications are the same.

Local plan policies and refusal rates

5.44   From this study it is clear that no direct correlation can be made between the nature of local plan policies and refusal rates. At a very crude level, leaving aside the National Parks, the local plan policies within remote rural areas are often the most general in nature, frequently with no criteria and often only partially reflecting the policies in PPG7 (para 3.80). Yet it is in these areas that the highest approval rates are experienced. The reality is that the local plan policies and approval rates are strongly driven by the nature of development pressure that the authority is under and the overall appropriateness of applications that come forward. The key to local plan policies, and the determinations that flow from them, is that they are able to differentiate and encourage beneficial farm diversification and control those forms of diversification that will not bring local benefits. This is a level of sophistication that has yet to be achieved, partly because farmers have to-date, received little guidance on the development of sustainable farm diversification options (para 5.13) and partly because local plan policies have not generally been informed by an understanding of local social and economic needs. (paras 3.30 – 3.34).

CONDITIONS AND PROCESS

Conditions

5.45   Where farm diversification applications are approved conditions are frequently imposed. The most common conditions relate to:

- design and materials (57% of approvals)[25]

- landscaping and screening (46% of approvals)

- restrictions on activities (43% of approvals)

- restrictions on car parking (35% of approvals)

- limit hours of working (25% of approvals)

- traffic/access issues (21% of approvals)

- occupancy restrictions (19% of approvals)

- removal of Part 2 PDRs (18% of approvals)

[25]All figures in this list are based on a sample of 265 applications that were approved. Source: Planning Register details

- limit to the use of external spaces (17% of approvals)

- removal of Part 6 PDRs (12% of approvals)

All other conditions are applied in less than 10% of the sample.

5.46 These conditions are imposed in a wide range of circumstances and across all LPA categories. From discussions with DC officers they are often used to make up for a lack of information on these aspects in submitted planning applications. They also reflect the general concern with highway and traffic issues (paras. 4.40 – 4.43).

5.47 **Conditions by diversification development: (Table 5.14)**. Generally the predominance of conditions covering landscaping and materials is reflected across all development types. Restrictions on operating hours, occupation and noise/sound-proofing appear to be particularly applied to building re-use proposals. Conditions applied to the limited number of ancillary residential accommodation proposals, generally seek to control occupation and remove permitted development rights.

5.48 **Conditions by diversification activity: (Table 5.15)**. Aside from standard planning concerns, tourist activities receive a high proportion of conditions seeking to control activities and occupation. These controls, such as preventing occupation for several weeks during the winter period, are designed to prevent the formation of freestanding residential accommodation in the countryside.

5.49 Conditions restricting use, hours of operation and controlling internal and external space are frequently applied to commercial developments, such as workshops and offices. Other than this, there are no very obvious relationships between type of condition and type of activity.

5.50 A wide range of other fairly standard planning concerns, such as drainage issues, and storage of oil and chemicals, are also frequently addressed by condition. These were picked up under the 'Other' category in the database and are not shown in the tables below.

Table 5.14: Frequency and type of conditions applied by type of development

Conditions	Development type						
	New building	Building extension	Building re-use	Change of use of land	Ancillary residential	Signage	Other
No. of employees	-	-	2	-	-	-	-
Parking	5	6	93	15	4	1	1
Access/traffic	7	-	39	14	-	1	1
Design/materials	22	9	152	20	6	1	6
Restriction on future expansion	1	-	4	1	-	-	-
Landscaping	23	4	83	41	3	2	3
Restrictions on activities/use	13	4	102	23	1	1	7
Limits on operating hours	3	-	55	20	1	1	1
Limits on use of internal space	-	-	7	-	-	-	-
Limits on use of external space	3	-	41	11	-	-	-
Noise/sound proofing	2	-	15	3	-	-	1
Occupational restrictions	4	4	46	8	3	-	1
Removal of Part 2 PDRs	-	1	46	6	3	1	-
Removal of Part 6 PDRs	-	1	29	4	2	-	-
Personal permission	-	-	12	4	-	-	-
Tying approval to the land of the holding	1	1	7	-	-	-	1
Improve the appearance of an existing building	1	1	2	1	-	-	-

Sample size = 265.

Source: Planning register details

5.51   DC officers commented in discussion that it is very difficult to control future expansion through conditions and this is reflected in the low number of conditions of this type. It may be that conditions on parking numbers are used to control expansion but this was not obvious from the case files. As noted previously, DC officers also believe it is difficult to control traffic generation through conditions, although restrictions on hours of working and parking may be used for this purpose (para 4.49).

Table 5.15: Frequency and type of conditions applied by diversification activity

Conditions	1	2	3	4	5	6	7	8	9	10	11	12
No. of employees	1	-	-	-	-	-	-	-	1	-	-	-
Parking	25	4	4	9	25	1	12	2	36	-	11	10
Access/traffic	17	8	-	2	14	1	5	3	12	-	6	4
Design/materials	75	7	3	9	33	3	18	1	43	-	-	-
Restriction on future expansion	2	1	-	1	1	-	1	-	3	-	-	-
Landscaping	29	14	3	7	26	2	24	5	28	-	25	11
Restrictions on activities/use	28	9	4	14	24	4	27	4	30	-	20	6
Limits on operating hours	1	7	1	6	22	1	19	6	21	-	4	11
Limits on use of internal space	-	-	-	-	4	-	1	2	4	-	-	-
Limits on use of external space	3	3	-	5	18	-	18	3	19	-	1	4
Noise/sound proofing	1	3	-	3	9	-	4	2	5	-	2	-
Occupational restrictions	40	2	-	2	1	-	2	1	2	-	5	3
Removal of Part 2 PDRs	15	1	1	4	12	1	9	1	13	-	3	2
Removal of Part 6 PDRs	6	1	0	2	12	-	7	1	10	-	2	2
Personal permission	1	1	2	2	4	-	2	1	1	-	2	4
Tying approval to the land of the holding	4	1	-	-	-	-	-	-	-	-	3	-
Improve the appearance of an existing building	-	-	1	2	-	-	-	-	-	-	2	-

Sample size = 330.
Source: Planning register details

1= Tourism
2 = Recreation
3 = Retail
4 = Workshops
5 = Manufacturing
6 = Food processing
7 = Storage/haulage
8 = Machinery repair
9 = Offices
10 = Energy
11= Equestrian
12= Other

5.52   With regard to the specific factors identified in PPG7 (1997) Annex G *Re-use and adaptation of rural building*, as being potentially controllable by conditions/Section 106 agreements (para 3.49), the following trends were identified:

- Removal of agricultural permitted development rights by condition [PPG7 paragraph G8] was used in 12% of farm diversification approvals (para 4.49).

- Tying of the diversification activity to the remainder of the holding was only applied as a condition in seven instances [PPG7 paragraph G9]. This accords with the limited usage of Section 106 agreements for the same purpose (paras 5.54 – 5.55). The reasons for this limited use appear to be twofold: (a) the difficulty of enforcing such a condition, in terms of monitoring land sales, and (b) a sensitivity by LPAs to farmers' concerns that such a condition or Section 106 agreement could impose significant restrictions on inheritance if a farm would otherwise be divided amongst the children.

5.53   Personal conditions also do not feature to any great extent within this sample. However, it has been noted that in Cornwall there are more temporary and personal permissions for farm diversification activities than for other types of planning permission granted (Atlantic Consultants, 2000). The reason for this has been to enable small-scale employment development to take place in rural areas where rigid adherence to other local plan policies might otherwise have precluded it.

Section 106 agreements

5.54   As noted above, PPG7 Annex G, supports the possible use of agreements under Section 106 of the Town and Country Planning Act 1990 to tie a re-used farm building to the rest of the holding, in order to prevent fragmentation. Government advice on the use of legal agreements[26] sets out similar tests to those relevant to the application of planning conditions. The fundamental basis for the use of legal agreements is that planning permission cannot be bought or sold, but that they may allow development to proceed that would otherwise be refused.

5.55   From this research it appears that the use of legal agreements to tie buildings to the land, or for any other purpose, was extremely limited over the three year period investigated. In total S106 agreements were only used in 26 out of 1397 planning applications. Furthermore their use was limited to six LPAs out of a total of 21 – all urban fringe and accessible rural areas under significant development pressure. In these cases legal agreements were seen as one way of ensuring that the economic benefits that would be derived from the diversification activity were ploughed back into the farm unit.

5.56   The other main use of legal agreements has been to:

- control occupancy, either of holiday accommodation or of residential development provided in support of a diversification application;

- to control traffic movements or seek highway improvements.

5.57   One potential concern regarding S106 agreements is the cost to applicants of preparing the necessary legal document. Wealden has a standard agreement so that the costs to applicants is limited.

[26]Circular 1/97 – Planning Obligations, Department of the Environment, January 1997.

Appeals

5.58   From the planning register search, the 1397 planning applications led to 52 subsequent appeals. Of these, 28 (61%) were dismissed and 18 (39%) were allowed. Nationally, a similar proportion (36%) of planning appeals was allowed in 1999 – 2000[27]. From the planning register details, a further two appeals were withdrawn and the remaining four have no decision yet.

5.59   **Table 5.16** shows the breakdown of these appeals by diversification activity, comparing the total number of appeals relative to the total number of applications for the diversification activity. The table shows that for most activities the appeal rate is broadly consistent with the number of applications received. A lower proportion of appeals are submitted on tourism and equestrian applications, undoubtedly reflecting the high approval rate and general acceptability of such schemes (other than in urban fringe areas). The activities that seem to generate a higher level of appeals are the commercial and industrial uses (workshops, vehicle repair, storage and offices). From the sample appeals examined in more detail, the main issues here appear to be traffic generation and appropriateness of these activities within a countryside setting.

Table 5.16 Appeals and total applications by type of diversification activity

a	Tourism	Recreation	Retail	Workshops
Appeals	10 (2%)	5 (5%)	2 (5%)	7 (8%)
Applications	494	110	42	86

b	Manufacturing/ industry	Food processing	Storage	Machinery/ vehicle repair
Appeals	5 (4%)	-	10 (6%)	3 (7%)
Applications	130	21	165	44

c	Offices	Energy	Equestrian	Other
Appeals	12 (8%)	-	6 (2%)	2 (3%)
Applications	159	1	269	80

Sample size = 62 (appeals) and 1601 (applications). Percentage figures show the proportion of appeals in relation to the total number of applications for that activity. The total figures for appeals and applications are higher than those given in paragraph 5.58 because some include more than one diversification activity.

Source: Planning Register details

5.60   In terms of development type, 54% of the appeals relate to building re-use and a further 27% to change of use of land.

5.61   Additional information on the number of farm diversification appeals across England between February 1997 and February 2000 was gathered with the help of the Planning Inspectorate. In total 300 potentially related to farm diversification. From these, 19 appeals were reviewed in more detail, of which 12 have been written up (**Appendix 9**). These were

[27] Source: Planning Inspectorate website (www.planning-inspectorate.gov.uk)

chosen to give a broad range of activities, locations and types of development. Approval rates are therefore not meaningful for these appeals.

5.62   The key issues identified by the inspectors for these appeals related to Green Belt designation (8 appeals), landscape impact (6 appeals); traffic and highways (5 appeals), and the appropriateness of development in the countryside (3 appeals). From these appeals it is evident that the inspectors were reflecting the current guidance in PPG7 – being supportive of farm diversification so long as it could be reconciled with other policy areas, and seeking controls through conditions where appropriate. A noticeable feature of those that were allowed was the imposition of conditions restricting the use to a particular use class or diversification activity.

Committee and delegated decisions

5.63   Through the review of case files, information was recorded on whether applications were determined by committee or the decision was delegated to officers. **Table 5.17** indicates the dominance of committee decisions, both in total and across the three authority categories, for farm diversification proposals. On average, 60% of farm diversification activities go to committee, while 40% are dealt with under delegated powers, although in remote rural areas the split is more even, with 55% of applications determined at committee, perhaps because of the lesser number of objections raised in these areas.

Table 5.17: Committee and delegated decisions by authority type

Type of local authority	Committee decisions	Delegated decisions	Total
Urban fringe	43	30	73
Accessible rural	163	95	258
Remote rural	67	54	121
Total	**273**	**179**	**452**
% of total	60%	40%	100%

Sample size = 452.

Source: Planning register details based on the sub- sample of 20 applications per LPA

5.64   Looking at development type, it appears that some types of development are more likely to go to committee than others (**Table 5.18**). Only 55% of new building applications are reported to committee, compared with 62% for both building re-use applications and changes of land use. This may be because a high percentage of new development relates to equestrian activities (para 5.15), a significant proportion of which are delegated (para 5.65). Again, it may also indicate that it is the nature of the impact that is considered to be more important than the type of development.

Table 5.18: Committee/delegated decisions by development type

a	Building re-use	Change of use of land	New building	Building extension
Committee	187	67	32	11
Delegated	115	42	26	5
Total	**302**	**109**	**58**	**16**
% reported to Committee	62%	62%	55%	69%

b	Ancillary residential	Signage	Other	Total
Committee	7	1	11	316
Delegated	2	2	3	195
Total	**9**	**3**	**14**	**511**
% reported to Committee	78%	33%	79%	62%

Sample size = 511. The sample size is higher than that for Table 5.17 as some decisions cover more than one development type.

Source: Planning register details based on the sub sample of 20 applications per LPA

5.65   Variations also occur according to diversification activity (**Table 5.19**). For most activities, between 57-65% of applications are reported to committee. The activities that are most frequently delegated are equestrian and workshop uses. The activities that are most frequently reported to committee are storage and distribution. This probably reflects traffic concerns and the more common use of larger buildings for storage (paras 4.40 – 4.44). Other activities that are generally determined by committee are recreation and retail uses. These again probably reflect traffic generation concerns and, in the case of recreation, the use of extensive areas of land. For retail uses an issue may be the importance attached to PPG6 *Town Centres and Retail Development* (1996) with its emphasis on controlling 'out of town' shopping.

Table 5.19: Committee/delegated decisions by diversification activity

a	Tourism	Equestrian	Office	Storage
Committee	77	46	49	51
Delegated	47	43	32	21
Total	**124**	**89**	**81**	**72**
Percentage to Committee	62%	52%	61%	71%

b	Manufacturing/ industry	Recreation	Workshops	Retail
Committee	38	26	11	10
Delegated	27	12	12	5
Total	**65**	**38**	**23**	**15**
Percentage to Committee	59%	68%	48%	67%

c	Machinery/ vehicle repair	Food processing	Energy	Other
Committee	9	4	-	16
Delegated	5	3	-	15
Total	**14**	**7**	**-**	**31**
Percentage to Committee	64%	57%	-	52%

Sample size = 559.

Source: Planning Register details based on the sub sample of 20 applications per LPA

5.66 Only rare occurrences were picked up of planning committees overturning an officer recommendation. Of the applications on which an officer recommendation was recorded, only five were refused following a positive officer recommendation and nine were approved following a recommendation for refusal. In a few cases committee decisions incorporated agreements under Section 106 of the Town and Country Planning Act 1990, or excluded them contrary to officer advice. Overall, from the review of case files there was little indication that elected members go against their officers' advice, although the case studies have indicated situations where elected members have overturned the advice of highways officers (para 4.42).

5.67 Table 5.20 below compares the approval rates for the three authority categories against the method of determination. Overall, the figures indicate a higher approval rate for delegated decisions (85%), compared to committee decisions (77%), reflecting the less controversial nature of applications dealt with under delegated powers. The exception to this pattern occurs in urban fringe authorities, where the committee approval rate is higher. This may reflect the stricter planning policies of urban fringe authorities and the desire of officers to uphold these in the face of considerable development pressure.

Table 5.20: Committee/delegated approval and refusal rates by authority category

Category of LPA	Committee approvals	Committee refusals	Delegated approvals	Delegated refusals
Urban fringe	30 (70%)	13 (30%)	19 (63%)	11 (37%)
Accessible rural	130 (81%)	30 (19%)	71 (89%)	9 (11%)
Remote rural	62 (78%)	18 (23%)	52 (91%)	5 (9%)
Total	**222** (78%)	**61** (22%)	**142** (85%)	**25** (15%)

NB. Sample size = 450

Source: Planning Register details based on the sub sample of 20 applications per LPA

Timescale for decision

5.68 The Government's target is that 80% of planning applications should be determined within eight weeks. As part of this study information was gathered on decision times for farm diversification applications. For the 843 applications with a recorded timescale, only 33% were determined within eight weeks. A further 28% were determined within 8-13 weeks. In handling farm diversification applications none of the sample LPAs achieved the Government's overall 80% target. The nearest was one NPA which determined 63% in eight weeks, and the lowest was an LPA in the accessible rural category that determined only 7% of farm diversification applications in eight weeks. As would be expected, applications reported to committee took longer to determine than delegated decisions.

5.69 No clear patterns emerge between different categories of LPA, other than that remote rural authorities, on average, have slightly faster determination times (**Table 5.21**) with rates in NPAs being similar to remote authorities more generally. Nor is there any evidence of a correlation between determination time and approval rates, number of diversification applications, total number of planning applications or the nature of farm diversification policies. This leads to the conclusion that determination times are primarily driven by the overall priorities within individual authorities.

Table 5.21: Number of determinations for farm diversification falling into each time band

LPA category	Determination time			Totals
	< 8 weeks	8 – 13 weeks	13+ weeks	
Urban fringe	60 (39%)	46 (30%)	47 (31%)	**153** (100%)
Accessible rural	113 (25%)	129 (28%)	211 (47%)	**453** (100%)
Remote rural	106 (45%)	57 (24%)	74 (31%)	**237** (100%)
All sample LPAs	279 (33%)	232 (28%)	332 (39%)	**843** (100%)

Sample size = 843. For some authorities, records of timescale for determination were difficult to obtain.
Source: Planning register details

5.70 **Comparison with other national data:** For comparison, the average determination rate for all planning applications across England, over the same three year period, was 62-63% within eight weeks.[28] This is nearly twice the average determination rate of 33% for farm diversification applications in the sample LPAs.

[28] Source: DTLR website – www.dtlr.gov.uk

5.71   Looking at different types of application, nationally 26% of major developments were determined in eight weeks. The equivalent figure was 54% for minor developments and 51% for change of use. Farm diversification can fall into any of these three categories but even so, the average determination rate of 33% uncovered by this study is significantly slower than for the latter two categories.

5.72   Based on the DETR league table[29] of determination rates for all planning applications by LPA for the year ending 30 September 1997, it appears that the average placing of the sample LPAs is 200 out of a total of 296 LPAs. This indicates that the sample LPAs were generally below average in speed of determination, suggesting that the slow rate for farm diversification applications may also be reflected across other application types. Nevertheless, by comparing the average determination rate for all applications with the determination rate for farm diversification, it is clear that the determination rates for farm diversification are particularly slow, even within this relatively slow set of authorities.

5.73   **Determination times by activity**: As indicated in **Table 5.22** there is little clear pattern in determination times by type of diversification activity. The only activity which appears to have a generally faster determination time is equestrian developments which, as noted in para 5.65, are more frequently determined under delegated powers. It is noticeable from the table that most activities have a spread of determination times across the three time bands. This again suggests that it is the nature of the impact rather than the type of activity which is more important in determining the decision timescale.

---

[29] Comparative performance of local planning authorities in deciding planning applications – Year ending 30 September 1997, Planning Inspectorate website

Table 5.22: Determination time by activity

Diversification activity	< 8 wks	8-13 wks	13+ wks	Total
Tourism	89 (35%)	66 (26%)	103 (40%)	258
Recreation	23 (38%)	18 (30%)	20 (32%)	61
Retail	6 (30%)	6 (30%)	8 (40%)	20
Workshop	15 (31%)	9 (18%)	25 (51%)	49
Manufacturing	12 (13%)	28 (29%)	56 (58%)	96
Food	3 (33%)	2 (22%)	4 (44%)	9
Storage	27 (26%)	29 (28%)	48 (46%)	104
Machinery	3 (14%)	8 (36%)	11 (50%)	22
Office	29 (24%)	37 (31%)	54 (45%)	120
Equestrian	82 (43%)	50 (26%)	58 (31%)	190
Other	15 (33%)	11 (24%)	20 (44%)	46
Total	**304**	**264**	**407**	**975**

NB: Sample size=843. The sample size varies from the totals as some applications cover more than one diversification activity.

Source: Planning register details

5.74 It is important to note though, that determination time alone is a poor measure of the service provided by LPAs, or of the quality of the development that may result. Nevertheless, it can be very frustrating to applicants when the development of a new business is held up significantly because of the time taken in determining the application.

IN SUMMARY

Planning applications for farm diversification

- There appears to be a clear difference in the pattern of farm diversification activities between the urban fringe and more remote rural areas. Remote rural areas have over six times the number of applications for farm diversification per head of population, compared to urban fringe areas, highlighting the importance of farm diversification to the rural economy. Conversely, urban fringe areas receive three times as many farm diversification applications per unit area, highlighting the greater development pressure in these areas. In both cases, accessible rural areas lie between these two extremes.

- On average farm diversification applications make up only 1.5% of all planning applications determined per year by the sample LPAs. In urban fringe areas the average is 0.9% (highlighting the overall greater number of applications in urban fringe areas). Moving away from the urban influence the proportion of farm diversification applications increases. Highest proportions, ranging from 4.7% – 7.1% were found in the National Parks.

- Tourism is by far the most common farm diversification activity (31% overall). In remote rural areas it makes up 53% of all applications for farm diversification. Equestrian-related proposals are also common (17% overall), particularly in the urban fringe (30%). The overall proportion of the other most common activities is storage/haulage and offices both at 10%, and manufacturing/industry at 8%. These latter activities form a small proportion in remote rural areas (5% – 6%) but make up between 10% and 14% in more accessible areas.

- Aside from tourism, the quality and innovation of farm diversification activities seen in the study are limited. Food processing and retail only make up between 2% and 3% of all applications for farm diversification and there was only one application relating to energy (excluding wind farms). Reality therefore currently falls well short of the aspirations of the Rural White Paper and the ERDP.

- Building re-use forms the most frequent development type for farm diversification, followed by change of use of land and new build, with the highest proportion of these latter two types found in urban fringe areas.

Approval rates
- The average approval rate for farm diversification applications is 83%. This compares with a national average approval rate for all planning applications of 88% or just over 90% for minor developments.

- There is a gradation in approval rates for farm diversification between urban fringe and remote rural areas. Urban fringe areas have an average approval rate of 68% for farm diversification; the figure in accessible rural areas is 84% approved; while in remote rural areas 87% of applications are approved.

- The highest approval rates for farm diversification overall relate to tourism and equestrian activities (85% and 84% approved respectively). These figures rise to 88% and 92% respectively in remote rural areas. The lowest approval rate overall relates to storage and haulage at 71%.

- For building re-use, a significantly higher proportion of modern buildings are refused (average 28%) compared to traditional buildings (average 13%). This pattern is particularly strong in accessible rural and urban fringe areas where, on average, 33% of modern buildings are refused, compared to remote rural areas (15% refused).

- Approval rates in Green Belts (71%) are similar to those in other urban fringe areas (68% approved) but 11% below the overall average approval rate for farm diversification. In AONBs the approval rate is 7% below the overall average but local landscape designations do not appear to affect approval rates and in National Parks the approval rate is 3% above the overall average.

- 83% of applications are approved where the application relates to a working farm holding while only 68% are approved when the development has no relationship to a working farm. Even on working farms, only 39% of the diversification activities are bringing additional income to the farm business.

- The most common reasons for the refusal of farm diversification activities are: landscape and visual impact (62% of refusals); development inappropriate in the countryside (52%); traffic and highways (51%); and not appropriate in the Green belt/AONB (33%). Overall, there are no clear patterns in the reasons for refusal, suggesting that it is the nature of specific impacts, rather than the type of development or type of activity, that trigger a refusal.

- Pre-application discussions may have a positive impact upon approval rates, although the evidence is not strong.

Application process
- The most frequently applied conditions to farm diversification relate to: design and materials (57% of approvals); landscape and screening (46%); restrictions on activities (43%); restrictions on car parking (35%); limits on hours of working (25%); and traffic and highways issues (21%).

- Conditions are not often used to control agricultural permitted development rights, and Section 106 agreements to tie the diversification activity to the farm holding are relatively rare.

- Within this sample, the number of appeals for farm diversification that were allowed is similar to the national average for all appeals. Diversification activities that most frequently go to appeal were workshops (8% of all applications of this type); offices (8%); machinery and vehicular repair (7%); and storage (6%).

- 60% of farm diversification applications go to committee for determination compared to 40% dealt with under delegated powers. Activities which are more regularly dealt with under delegated powers are equestrian and workshops, whereas storage and haulage will most frequently go to committee.

- Overall there is a higher approval rate for delegated decisions (85%), compared to committee decisions (77%) but this simply reflects the less controversial nature of applications determined under delegated powers, as it is rare for planning committees to overturn the recommendations of their officers. Where committees do go against the officer recommendation, the more usual result will be approval of an application recommended for refusal.

- Determination times are particularly slow for farm diversification applications with, on average, only 33% determined in eight weeks within the sample LPAs. This may reflect potential conflict with a number of key planning concerns, such as countryside/landscape protection and highways issues.

CHAPTER 6

Perceptions and opportunities

6.1   The previous Chapters have focused on the policies, process and outcomes relating to farm diversification applications and approvals. This Chapter takes a slightly different standpoint and explores the perceptions of the planning process as seen by applicants and their advisors. At the end of the Chapter, it also explores the views of planners and other officers within the LPAs, as expressed at the three planning workshops.

6.2   The Chapter draws on a range of different sources:

- The postal questionnaire sent to applicants in the 21 sample LPAs (420 questionnaires sent, with a return of 181).

- The telephone survey of farmers drawn from three districts – Maidstone (urban fringe); Stratford (accessible rural); and North York Moors (remote rural). 554 farmers were contacted (of whom 183 were consistently unavailable; 92 refused to take part; 212 had no experience of the planning system; and 67 completed the questionnaire) (Appendix 4).

- Three 'stakeholder workshops', one within each of the sample districts named above, for agricultural advisors and representatives, including land agents and CLA and NFU representatives.

- Three 'farmer workshops' for farmers who had experience of farm diversification and the planning system identified from the telephone survey. The aim was to have eight to 12 attendees at each workshop, although in the case of North York Moors, only two farmers were eventually able to attend.

6.3   The telephone survey and the subsequent stakeholder and farmer workshops were conducted by the Royal Agricultural College Enterprise. All work was undertaken in autumn 2000, well before the Foot and Mouth epidemic. In all the above cases, the aim was to understand the experience of farmers and their advisors when taking farm diversification proposals through the planning system.

6.4   Separately, once the data had been collected for this study, the preliminary findings were introduced at three planning workshops. These involved an invited audience of local authority planners and others working with farm diversification and the planning system, such as economic development advisors, county land agents and representatives of the Regional Development Agencies. This occurred at three venues in London, Bristol and Manchester. The objective of these workshops was to enable further development of the findings.

REASONS FOR NOT DIVERSIFYING

6.5   A range of previous studies have looked at the key barriers to farm diversification. In the 1999 NFU study *Farming Economy 1999: Routes to Prosperity for UK Agriculture*, the most significant reason given for diversifying was to raise income. Equally lack of resources was identified as the key deterrent. Other reasons given were: lack of labour (28%); lack of physical resources (22%); planning restrictions (17%); and tenancy restrictions (4%).

6.6   According to the farmer workshops conducted as part of this study, key factors that influence the likelihood of diversifying are:

- *a general reluctance by farmers to consider non-agricultural enterprises:* Diversification was perceived as a sign of failure in the core agricultural enterprise, bringing about a loss of control over the whole business, through the intrusion of outside activities and perhaps people. It was suggested that it would break the cohesion between home and workplace;

- *lack of a risk-taker mentality amongst farmers:* This poses problems when most diversification options require capital investment;

- *tenancy arrangements:* As identified in Chapter 2, tenancy arrangements can place restrictions on the tenant, inhibiting diversification, even where there is a strong desire to do so;

- *reliance on other members of the farming family to take on management of the diversification activity:* Tourism uses are popular because the management role can be taken by other members of the farmer's family – frequently the farmer's wife. There may be less willingness to consider non-agricultural diversification activities where the main effort would be required by the farmer, rather than another member of the family.

6.7   It was also noted at the planning workshops that in some areas the market for diversification activities, especially farm tourism, is now saturated and any further developments in these areas is likely to threaten the viability of existing diversified businesses. This concern re-enforces the view expressed in Chapter 2 (para 2.25) that farm diversification is not a panacea for agriculture.

The planning system

6.8   As indicated in Chapter 2 (para 2.20), there has been concern in recent studies that farmers are sometimes discouraged from making planning applications for farm diversification by the attitude of LPAs. As noted above, the NFU found that planning was a deterrent in 17% of cases.

6.9   From the telephone survey conducted by the Royal Agricultural College Enterprise (RACE) as part of this study, only a very small number of farmers were identified who felt that the planning system was a major barrier to beginning a farm diversification enterprise. Based on their professional knowledge, RACE believe that if farmers had felt that there was a significant issue, especially if it had affected them individually, it is likely that they would have wanted to express an opinion. However, of the 368 farmers spoken to (212 of whom had no experience of the planning system) only three said that they had not pursued a diversification enterprise that they had been considering[30]. Of these three, only one related this to planning.

6.10   From the postal questionnaire of applicants, out of the sample of 181 returns, only three applications had been withdrawn, of which only one related to the negative attitude of the LPA. In addition, from the stakeholder and farmer workshops there was little evidence to suggest that any pre-application discussions with the LPA produced a totally negative or unhelpful response (see also para 4.21).

6.11   From other studies and from discussions with land agents, it appears that the view that planning can put off would-be diversifiers may at least in part relate to:

- The broader definition that farmers will often give to farm diversification compared to that described in PPG7. Farmers may, for example, classify the sale of land for housing or industrial development as part of a diversification package. This is a controversial area of planning, and one on which planners would be very cautious about expressing any opinion without the full facts, unless the land was zoned for development in the development plan.

- The nature of the initial approach made to the planning authority. As noted from a study in Breckland (para 4.17) farmers are increasingly approaching LPAs to gain general advice on what might be acceptable in planning terms. Enquiries of this nature can place officers in a difficult position, as they must remain impartial. In some cases such impartiality could be seen as unhelpful.

6.12   The findings of this study suggest therefore that planning is not a major deterrent to farm diversification, although a much larger sample would be required to categorically prove this point. Nevertheless, many farmers contacted through this study did identify very considerable problems with the planning process which they felt could be improved to encourage farm diversification. These are discussed below.

Satisfaction rating with the planning process

6.13   Both the telephone survey and the postal questionnaire sought opinions on the planning process and farm diversification, The final section of the telephone survey asked for general comments on the LPA and the interviewees' dealings with them. Of the 58 respondents who made a comment, 18 (35%) said they found the LPA helpful, or that they had had a positive experience. The comment was often made that the situation was made better if the authorities were involved in the early stages, or if a third party was used in the approaches to the LPA. The remaining 65% identified some areas of concern. In the postal questionnaire[31], 19% of respondents gave no comment, 25% reported a positive experience of the system, 20% a satisfactory experience and 36% a negative experience, as shown in **Table 6.1**.

---

[30] The survey, however, was not designed to disprove that planning puts off potential applicants from pursuing a diversification activity. A very much larger sample size would be required to prove this point.

[31] Responses to the questionnaire were entirely by self-selection. 33 responses were received from applicants whose planning application had been refused (18% of the total responses). This reflects the average refusal rate for farm diversification applications of 17% identified through this study (Table 5.6).

Table 6.1: The views of applicants on the planning system

Response (1)	Number (2)	% of Total Returns (181)
Very Positive	11	6
Positive	35	19
Satisfactory/Indifferent/Fair	36	20
Negative	47	26
Very Negative	18	10
No Comment or Contact	34	19
Total	**181**	**100%**

Source: Postal questionnaire of applicants

Sample size; 181 responses

(1)The comments of the respondents were grouped by the strength of their views on the planning system.

(2) For those responses expressing a positive view of the planning system 95% of applications were approved. 80% of applications were approved for those expressing a satisfactory view whereas, for those expressing a negative view, only 64% of applications were approved. It may not be surprising, therefore, that those with more negative views of the planning system are also those who have had their applications refused.

6.14   Typical responses in the postal questionnaire from those who had had a positive experience of the planning system included:

"Very reasonable. Time from application to final decision was within expectations. Site visits were helpful." (Source: postal questionnaire)

"Very good, important to have good architect, detailed drawings, discussion with planning authority before making application." (Source: postal questionnaire)

"Good – some advice was offered and some compromises reached." (Source: postal questionnaire)

6.15   A strong feature of these comments is their particular support for liaison with the LPA. This is reflected in similar comments from the telephone survey, as illustrated below:

"Have been involved several times, have always consulted planning officers at earliest stage. Liked to be asked for advice, will stop you going down blind alley and will offer alternative ideas/solutions." (Source: telephone survey)

6.16   In these cases a constructive relationship with the LPA seems to have led to satisfaction with the system, even where negotiation resulted in amendments to the original scheme. The comments highlight the value of dialogue between the applicant and the LPA. On the other hand, where applicants have had their application refused there is often a view that planning officers are not prepared to understand the individual circumstances of the applicant and offer little co-operation. Typical responses from this group taken from the postal questionnaire include:

"Inflexible. Rigid adherence to inappropriate standards. The application of which inevitably led to refusal. No regard to special circumstances thus stifling attempt at diversification." (Source: postal questionnaire)

"Both myself and my family were shocked by the way I was treated. The council/planning officers I dealt with were patronising, rude, evasive and had no knowledge of what they dictated. Did not give me any help. Was told not to waste my time and money." (Source: postal questionnaire)

"In a word, shocking! There was little interest, a degree of scepticism and ultimately little co-operation." (Source: postal questionnaire)

6.17   These views are similarly reflected in the responses to the telephone survey:

"Planners are sticking to the book/don't help through the process. Natural reaction is NO until you ask, then they start to think – not flexible enough." (Source: telephone survey).

PROBLEMS IDENTIFIED BY THOSE CONSULTED

6.18   From the comments received through the different surveys and workshops conducted as part of this study, some clear themes emerge regarding the areas where there is dissatisfaction with the planning system, either real or perceived. These themes are grouped under the two broad headings of 'Planning policy' and 'Planning process'.

Planning policy

6.19   From both the stakeholder workshops and the farmer workshops the key issues with regard to planning policy were identified as:

- The continuing urban bias of development plans and the general lack of a comprehensive policy framework for the future of the countryside.

- The failure to adopt the positive stand of PPG7 for farm diversification in development plans – often because such plans pre-date PPG7 (1997).

- The potential contradiction in plans between policies supportive of farm diversification and those supportive of environmental conservation.

- The tension between the support for farm diversification in PPG7 (1997) and the emphasis on reducing the need to travel by car in PPG 13 (1994). This point was also picked up in some of the responses to the postal questionnaire, for example:

"Local plan policies must reflect PPG's which in turn should be realistic, particularly in relation to lack of public transport in rural areas and inevitably less than ideal highway standards (e.g. road widths). There must be some flexibility in approach." (Source: postal questionnaire)

- The apparent significant increase in areas covered by local protective designations.

6.20   From the results of other aspects of this study, reported in earlier Chapters, a number of the above points are borne out. The frequent lack of vision for the countryside was reflected at the planners workshops (considered at the end of this Chapter). It was also reflected in the review of development plans – while plans may be supportive of economic farm diversification, this can be constrained if there is no clear understanding of the needs that the plan is addressing (para 3.34). From the plan review, 46% of plans made no specific mention of farm diversification (para 3.47) and there can be apparent contradictions between farm diversification policies and other policies in local plans, especially where there is a reliance on general policies (para 3.43). Until the revision of PPG13 in March 2001 there was evident tension between PPG7 and PPG13 which continues to be reflected in many of the local plan policies (para 3.66). This tension was recognised by both local plan and development control officers. The one point that the data collected through this study does not directly support is the comment on local designations. Whilst this study cannot comment on the growth in local designations, the results of development control decisions do not indicate that these designations are standing in the way of appropriate farm diversification (para 5.29).

Planning process

6.21   A considerable range of problems were identified with the planning process. These have been grouped under the following headings:

- lack of understanding of the needs of modern agriculture

- inconsistency in advice and support

- time taken

- the role of councillors

- the cursory treatment of applications

6.22   **Lack of understanding of the needs of modern agriculture:** From the farmer workshops there was a view that LPAs simply see farm diversification as an urban intrusion into the countryside and lack sympathy with the need to develop a more broadly based rural economy. This point is illustrated by comments made in the postal questionnaire. For example:

"The planning authority is totally against any plans or projects which we put forward. We feel they are not interested in getting involved in the unavoidable change in the farming environment. We also feel they do not have the necessary experience." (Source: postal questionnaire)

6.23   From this research it appears that most planning officers **are** sympathetic to the needs of agriculture. However, they may lack a sound understanding of agriculture simply because agricultural planning issues only form a very small part of their overall workload and because the variety of different circumstances mean that it is difficult to develop a standard response (para 4.14). It may also be hindered by the ad hoc way that DC officers build up an experience of farming matters within individual LPAs (para 4.16).

6.24   **Inconsistency in advice and support:** At the farmer and stakeholder workshops, while there was strong support for planning advice from the LPA, there were concerns about the consistency of that advice. The key comments made were:

- Where contact has been made with the LPA there can be inconsistency between the advice given by different officers, for example, between planning officers and highway officers and between different officers over time. In particular, there was a strong feeling that younger planning officers were not prepared to comment and, on balance, contact with them seemed to suggest potential difficulties rather than to convey a feeling of optimism.

- The support for farm diversification proposals is usually qualified, especially in relation to highway issues and the interpretation that is put on PPG13. In particular, highway constraints are seen as inflexible, often appearing to ignore the existing use of the farmstead by large vehicles in support of the agricultural business.

- At the pre-application stage, planning officers seem to be prepared to identify relevant issues and policies, but often fail to take a pro-active role once an application has been submitted and, if approached, may not be particularly informative, often taking a neutral stance.

6.25 These comments raise a number of issues. The potential for inconsistency of advice has been picked up in other aspects of this research, partly as noted above, because of the relatively ad hoc way in which farm diversification applications are dealt with within LPAs, and partly because of a lack of recording of pre-application advice (para 4.23). Leaving aside the issues associated with PPG13, the problem of meeting rigid highway standards on narrow country lanes is a key problem also recognised by DC officers, but one that is not easily addressed without accepting a significant reduction in highway standards in rural areas (para 4.42).

6.26 The lack of a pro-active response from planners to individual applications no doubt reflects the severe resource constraints within LPAs. Nevertheless, from discussions with DC officers, there appeared to be a willingness to help farmers with planning applications (para 4.29), although it is clear that conditions are often not discussed with applicants (para 4.50). The impartial role that planners are required to assume may appear unhelpful (para 4.17) but is an aspect that could potentially be better explained to would-be applicants in terms of the help and advice that planning officers can and cannot provide.

6.27 The points raised also highlight a broader issue. Some local plans fail to address the exceptional (in terms of its location) nature of farm diversification and, therefore, the approach which should be taken to reconcile support for sustainable farm diversification schemes with transport and countryside protection policies. These are complex matters that need to be weighed in the determination of individual applications. This may explain (although not excuse) views that planning officers appear inflexible and uncertain.

6.28 A separate but related issue raised in the responses to the postal questionnaire is the perceived inconsistency in determination decisions. For example:

"Refusal extremely short sighted. Change of use could only improve existing area. Other alteration in close proximity approved." (Source: postal questionnaire)

6.29 This highlights the importance of having clear policies against which applications can be judged and making the reasons for refusal clear to the applicant. If policies have changed since previous approvals, this should also be made clear to the applicant.

6.30 **Time taken:** From the telephone survey there were a number of comments on the long time taken for farm diversification applications to be determined:

"They have been very positive although very slow." (Source: telephone survey)

"Matter of speed. Trying to swim through treacle, go around and around." (Source: telephone survey)

"Very slow." (Source: telephone survey)

6.31   This is a point that was also raised by case studies 2 and 4 and has been confirmed by review of the planning register details, with only 33% of all farm diversification applications within the sample, determined within eight weeks (paras 5.68 – 5.74). Time taken is a problem for applicants but again underlines the range of issues that need to be considered in individual circumstances. There is obviously a need to try and speed up this process, although the quality of the decision should not be sacrificed for the sake of speed, especially if this leads to a greater number of refusals.

6.32   **The role of councillors:** From the postal questionnaire a number of views were expressed about the role of committees in the determination of applications for farm diversification. On the one hand, there was a view that councillors may be more sympathetic to the needs of individual farmers compared to officers, or at least more willing to listen to personal circumstances. For example, comments were made in the postal questionnaire:

"(Officers) indifferent or downright discouraging. Took a lot of work and lobbying councillors to overturn officers' recommendation." (Source: postal questionnaire)

"The planning officers initially were against the application until the intervention of a councillor of our acquaintance." (Source: postal questionnaire)

6.33   On the other hand, the view was also expressed in the responses to the postal questionnaire that councillors tended to be less supportive than their officers to farm diversification applications:

"Planning officers largely very helpful – almost all our applications (6-7) recommended for approval by officers – most refused/ delayed by councillors – one went to appeal which was granted with costs!" (Source: postal questionnaire)

"An understanding, sensitive and realistic attitude was forthcoming from the planning officer. Unfortunately, the elected members were insensitive and unhelpful, particularly at local level. Whilst policies appear to promote and encourage diversification, any excuse seems to be found (particularly by members) to avoid implementing the policies." (Source: postal questionnaire)

6.34   An apparent conflict in view between officers and members can obviously be confusing to applicants. Nevertheless, from the review of case files and from discussions with planning officers and elected members within the sample LPAs, it appears that this is a relatively rare occurrence. Where it does occur, it appears that on balance, councillors are more sympathetic to farm diversification than their policies potentially allow (para 5.66).

6.35   In the farmer workshops a few comments were also made on the role of Parish Councils as statutory consultees. The view was expressed that they may often raise objections to diversification proposals. For example:

"Parish Councils are negative and should not be given any greater powers in the decision-making process." (Source: farmer workshops)

6.36   Similarly, there was a view from one or two comments in the postal questionnaire responses that representations from other objectors can stand in the way of farm diversification proposals:

"The LPA lost its nerve when it was confronted by an orchestrated campaign of objection from a minority group of local representatives." (Source: postal questionnaire)

6.37   The role of Parish Councils as a statutory consultee and the influence of objectors is an area where insufficient data was collected from the case files to enable comment in this report. This may be an area that requires further investigation.

6.38   **Cursory treatment of consultees:** Finally, there was a view that often farm diversification applications are only given cursory examination by planning officers with insufficient attention paid to the relevant issues. This view was specifically raised in one or two cases in the postal questionnaire:

"My view is that they (who they are I don't know) took the money, then turned it down without much thought." (Source: postal questionnaire)

"Our views were shock and amazement at the refusal. It only took three days for the inspector to come to her decision, we expected not to hear for three months, very hasty!" (Source: postal questionnaire)

6.39   It is not known if these applications were discussed with the LPA at the pre-application stage or whether they accorded with local plan policies. It is difficult therefore to draw conclusions. However, at the very least, it does underline the importance of ensuring that applicants understand the reasons for refusal.

6.40   Overall, these perceptions support the findings of this study with regard to local plan policies (Chapter 3). They also highlight general support for liaison between the applicant and the LPA during the planning process – it is where there has not been liaison that adverse comments more often seem to arise. Nevertheless, clear issues come through from the comments made:

- The need for greater clarity in the determination process, ensuring that applicants are aware throughout of the relevant policy areas and criteria against which individual applications are being assessed.

- The need for greater consistency in the advice given to applicants through the planning process.

- The need to speed up the determination process for farm diversification.

- The need for greater understanding of farming needs and the aspirations of the Rural White Paper and the ERDP amongst DC officers.

- The need for greater understanding of the planning system amongst the farming community and the areas in which it can and cannot provide help and assistance to applicants.

(The report returns to these issues in Chapter 7)

POTENTIAL WAYS FORWARD IDENTIFIED BY CONSULTEES

6.41 In response to the types of concern noted above, the various workshops held as part of this research came up with some clear recommendations on how the planning system could be improved to assist with farm diversification. These recommendations divide into two: those relating to planning policy identified at the planning workshops, and those relating to the planning process identified at the farmer/stakeholder workshops.

Planning policy (the Planning Workshops)
6.42 The key recommendations identified by the planning workshops were:

1. **A vision for farm diversification at the local level:** Policies for farm diversification in local plans should be based on a vision of what is trying to be achieved in the locality, for whom and why. Such a vision should draw on a clear understanding of local economic and social, as well as environmental, circumstances of the LPA area. This was seen as an important mechanism for addressing the different issues relating to farm and rural diversification in different areas of countryside, for example, between the more accessible and remote areas within a single LPA. However, whether LPAs would have the resources to support such a detailed approach was raised more than once.

2. **Clarification of the policy stand on large modern buildings and those developments no longer attached to a working farm:** The need for further clarification at the national level on large scale developments (paras. 3.56, 4.44 – 4.45) and the potential differentiation between those farm diversification applications relating to a working farm and those separated from a working farm (paras 3.43, 4.46 – 4.47) was identified. This reflects concerns raised both by local plan officers and DC officers. It was considered that LPAs might develop guidance on the differing issues raised by different types of holding, such as hobby farms, small-holdings, horticultural enterprises and larger working farms.

3. **Further review of the use of farm plans:** It was recognised that little use has been made of farm plans to-date in the context of planning. Yet where major changes are anticipated, it was identified that farm plans could help clarify how the proposals related to the remainder of the farm.

Planning process (Stakeholder/Farmer Workshops)
6.43 At the stakeholder/farmer workshops recommendations focused on developing a better interface between LPAs and the farming community and built on initiatives that have been tried in a few LPAs:

1. **Rural fora** should be considered, embracing the range of stakeholder interests. Where there is real commitment to their effective operation such fora can provide an effective basis for helping to define realistic policies which reflect local priorities.

2   There should be **better liaison within LPAs** between different departments and sections, for instance, between planners and economic development officers, ensuring that an understanding of local economic circumstances is reflected in local plan policies and in the determination of individual planning applications.

3.   There should be **regular liaison meetings between LPAs and representatives of the farming community** – making planners more aware of the issues facing farming and helping the farming community understand the planning issues and the policies that might be applied to farm diversification applications.

4.   Methods need to be put in place to **make planning more accessible to the farming community**. Options identified which are not mutually exclusive were:

- the holding of Planning Clinics offering free planning advice to potential applicants

- the development of first stop shops for farmers where planning advice can be given alongside advice on grants and business planning

- the appointment of agricultural liaison officers or equivalent to provide the bridge between the LPA and the farming community, although as identified elsewhere, it may be inappropriate for them to give planning advice unless they form part of the planning department

- the preparation of written guidance, such as the recently published North Yorkshire Diversification Guide.

Box 6.1: A planning guide to farm diversification in North Yorkshire

This guide is a free, 40-page booklet. It was published in November 2000 by North Yorkshire County Council following concern that planning was providing insufficient support for farm diversification. Its production was partly funded by Yorkshire Forward, the Regional Development Agency, and it has been supported by the seven local authorities and two National Parks of the County. It provides a comprehensive but simple guide to the planning system and how it works for farm diversification, the general issues to be addressed by such development and specific guidance on a range of potential diversification activities, from agricultural contracting to camping barns.

The idea for the guidance arose out of the Agriculture Group of the County Council, which is a group of farmers and their representatives (including the CLA and NFU), brought together from time to time to look at specific issues such as farm diversification. The County Council, the District Councils and the National Park Authorities are considering whether to adopt the guide as Supplementary Planning Guidance.

IN SUMMARY

- Key factors identified by the farmer workshops as preventing farmers from diversifying were: a reluctance on the part of farmers to consider a non-agricultural enterprise; lack of a risk-taker mentality amongst farmers; tenancy arrangements; and reliance on other members of the family.

- The findings of the telephone survey of farmers and postal questionnaire of applicants are that planning is not a major deterrent to the development of farm diversification proposals, although a very large sample would be required to categorically resolve this point.

- From the postal questionnaire 45% of applicants reported a positive experience of the planning system compared to 36% who had had a negative experience. From the telephone survey the comparative figures are 35% and 65%.

- Areas of planning policy which were identified as a particular concern by the farmer and stakeholder workshops were: the frequent urban bias of development plans; the lack of emphasis on farm diversification in older plans; and the contradictions in plans between different policies.

- Aspects of the planning process that were identified for criticism by the farmer workshops, telephone survey and postal questionnaire were: the lack of understanding amongst planners of the needs of modern agriculture; inconsistency in advice and support provided by LPAs; the time taken in determination; the role of councillors and sometimes parish councils; and the sometimes cursory treatment of applications for farm diversification.

- Key areas of improvement identified by the planning workshops were in the development of a vision for farm diversification at the local level; clarification of the policy stand on diversification involving large modern agricultural buildings and those developments no longer attached to a working farm; and review of the use of farm plans in support of planning applications for farm diversification.

- Key recommendations identified by the farmer and stakeholder workshops related to the use of rural fora; better liaison within LPAs; regular liaison meetings between LPAs and representatives of the farming community; and methods for making planning more accessible to the farming community.

CHAPTER 7

Conclusions and best practice

ROBUSTNESS OF FINDINGS

7.1 For this research a considerable body of information has been collected and analysed, based on a sample of 21 LPAs spread across urban fringe, accessible rural and remote rural areas in England. The policies of 14 RPG documents, 16 structure plans and 24 local plans were examined. Information on the 1397 farm diversification planning applications made within the sample LPAs over the last three years was gathered and more detailed information was added through 181 questionnaire returns from a sample of 420 applicants. From this sample 12 individual case studies were examined. In addition, 554 farmers were contacted by telephone of which 67 provided information for the research. Sixteen national organisations were consulted along with relevant local authority officers (dealing with local plans, development control and economic development) and members within each of the 21 sample authorities. These interviews were backed by workshops with planners; with advisors and representatives of the farming community; and with farmers who have considered farm diversification in some form.

7.2 This comprises the fullest investigation of the relationship between farm diversification and the planning system for some time and can be assumed to be representative of the wider situation in England. In this respect the research is similar in scope to previous work on rural planning policies and development control decisions for both the former DoE (1995, two studies) and the former Rural Development Commission (RDC) (1998), which gathered less information whilst addressing broader issues.

Meeting the aims of the study

7.3 As summarised in turn below, this fact-finding research has addressed the aims of the study, namely:

1. The extent to which national planning policy guidance set out in PPG7 for farm diversification (prior to the amendment in March 2001) is reflected in development plan policies

2. The extent to which national planning policy guidance (PPG7) is reflected in development control decisions

3. The operation of the planning system and identification of problem areas

4. The extent to which LPAs currently take a pro-active approach to farm diversification.

7.4 It has also addressed the issues set out in the brief (para 1.4). The only aspect raised that has not been directly addressed has been the comparison of farm diversification approval

rates with those of other rural developments (outside settlements). This would have required significant additional data gathering. Instead farm diversification approval rates have been compared with national data on all planning approvals.

CONCLUSIONS

7.5   In line with the previous conclusions of the seminar hosted by Nick Raynsford in May 2000 (para 2.10), the findings of this research have not suggested that there are any significant problems with the national planning guidance for farm diversification, as set out in PPG7 (1997). Nevertheless, a range of issues about the operation of the planning system is raised. These are identified in (3) below.

(1)   PPG7 guidance on farm diversification in Regional Planning Guidance and development plans

7.6   **Diversification of the rural economy:** Overall, the strong support for diversification of the rural economy in PPG7 (1997) is addressed in all the more recent Regional Planning Guidance (RPG) (para 3.8) and is well reflected in the majority of structure and local plans reviewed, both pre and post-1997 (para 3.29).

7.7   **Farm diversification:** Explicit mention is also made of farm diversification in 60% of the more recent RPG documents. Nevertheless, only 50% of the structure plans and 54% of the local plans reviewed, included specific policies on farm diversification. Of the local plans with no specific policies on farm diversification, the majority were pre-1997 plans although, significantly, they also included 40% of post-1997 local plans (para 3.41). In local plans with policies for farm diversification, the relevant policies are largely criteria-based and typically cover landscape/visual impacts (especially in AONBs and Green Belts), traffic and access, and the operational needs of farming. Where there are no specific policies on farm diversification the expectation is that it will be addressed through more general policies on rural diversification and building re-use.

7.8   The over-riding characteristic of farm diversification policies is that of variability. Age of plan is generally a stronger determinant of policy content than category of LPA or the relationship of local plans with the relevant structure plan and RPG policies (paras 3.85 – 3.86). However, leaving aside National Parks (which have very full policies on farm diversification), there is a general pattern whereby remote rural areas have plans that do not always address farm diversification and, where it is addressed, policies tend to be brief and not particularly restrictive. This compares with the plans of accessible rural areas and the urban fringe authorities where policies on farm diversification are notably fuller and often more restrictive than the national guidance, responding to the stronger development pressures in these areas (paras 3.80, 3.83).

7.9   **Conflicting policies:** More restrictive development plan policies for farm diversification than that suggested in PPG7 most frequently relate to designated areas, in particular AONBs and Green Belts (para 3.92), and situations where development plans place greater emphasis on environmental conservation over local economic and social need. The situation can become particularly confusing where policies for farm diversification require conformity with other specified, or all other policies in the plan, which may expressly restrict development outside settlements (para 3.43). The key area of potential policy conflict, however, is that between farm diversification and the need to reduce reliance on the private car, as expressed in PPG13 (1994). No plan policies identified how this potential conflict might be addressed, leaving it to development control officers to reconcile this issue on individual applications. This particular conflict in policy should be resolved by the recent amendment to PPG13 (2001), and the revisions to local plans that should flow from this.

7.10   **Addressing local circumstances:** PPG7 [paragraph 2.9] suggests that LPAs should assess local social and economic needs to inform rural development policies. This theme is picked up in PPG11 (2000) which sets a clear requirement that RPG should provide a firm regional context for farm diversification, in both its broader economic circumstances and geographical variation. An earlier example of this thinking had already been provided by the West Midlands RPG which notes that "*authorities should, with partners, assess the specific needs and opportunities for rural diversification within different parts of their areas, having regard to the economic differences between accessible and remote rural areas*". In reality though, the majority of planning documents treat rural areas as homogeneous, failing to recognise the considerable difference in rural areas across regions and within local authority areas. None of the structure or local plans reviewed clearly demonstrated an understanding of local social and economic needs in the development of farm and rural development policies. This general lack of information on local social and economic needs is significant, in that it lessens the ability of plans to make a pro-active and integrated response to local needs, identifying and promoting those types of development suitable to different localities.

(2)   PPG7 guidance on farm diversification and development control decisions

7.11   **Types of diversification activity:** This study confirms that tourism is by far the most common farm diversification activity (31% of all applications) subject to planning controls. Equestrian (17%), storage/haulage and offices (both 10%), and manufacturing (8%) are the next most common. More innovative farm diversification applications are limited. The nature of applications indicates that, with the exception of tourism, the majority are responding to the vibrancy of the economy within surrounding urban areas, rather than adding value to land-based products or drawing from their rural location. Reality therefore currently falls well short of the aspirations of the ERDP and Rural White Paper (paras 5.11 – 5.13).

7.12   **Farm diversification by category of LPA:** The difference in farm diversification activity between different categories of local authority is pronounced (although there is considerable variety within local authority categories). Urban fringe areas receive three times the number of farm diversification applications per unit area compared to remote rural areas and, according to development control officers, a high proportion of these applications are retrospective. The significantly higher development pressure in these areas is emphasised by the higher number of planning applications overall, of which farm diversification makes up only 0.9% of all planning applications determined within these LPAs. Here equestrian activities make up the highest proportion of farm diversification applications (30%), with tourism, storage and offices making up between 12% and 15% each (paras 5.4 – 5.8).

7.13   In contrast, remote rural areas receive over six times the number of farm diversification applications per head of population compared to urban fringe areas, with these applications making up 2.3% (5% in National Parks) of all planning applications determined. This highlights the greater importance of farm diversification to the local economy in these areas, compared to more accessible areas. In these remote rural areas there is a heavy dependency on tourism which makes up over half of all applications for farm diversification, followed by equestrian development at 11%. Currently, no other diversification activity makes up more than 6% of the total in these areas. As noted by the planning workshops, a concern is the potential saturation of the farm tourism market in these remote rural areas and the lack of other diversification opportunities (para 6.7).

7.14   The pattern of farm diversification in accessible rural areas lies between that described for remote rural areas and the urban fringe, both in terms of the number of applications by area and by head of population. But in terms of the type of farm diversification activity, the situation is similar to that found in urban fringe areas (para 5.10).

7.15   **Approval rates:** From this study the average approval rate for farm diversification applications over the three years February 1997 – February 2000 was 83%, with 17% refused (excluding the 7% of all farm diversification applications that were withdrawn). This compares with a national average approval rate for all planning applications in England in 1999/2000 of 88%, and of just over 90% for minor developments (excluding dwellings)[32]. This suggests that farm diversification applications are, in general, treated favourably by the planning system although it is likely that their exceptional nature, in terms of location, (para 7.18) keeps approval rates below the average for other minor developments.

7.16   The highest approval rates for farm diversification relate to tourism (85%) and equestrian activities (84%), and the lowest approval rates to storage and haulage (71%). There is also a strong gradation across local authority categories, with an average approval rate for farm diversification activities in remote rural areas of 87%, in accessible rural areas of 84% and in the urban fringe of 68% (para 5.18).

7.17   **Approval rates in designated areas:** Approval rates for farm diversification in Green Belts (71%) are similar to those for farm diversification in the urban fringe more generally. In AONBs approval rates (76%) are approximately 7% below the average for all farm diversification applications, reflecting the stricter policies in these areas (para 7.9). However, significantly, no other designation appears to affect approval rates for farm diversification. Within local non-statutory landscape designations, the approval rate of 83% is the same as the average approval rate for all farm diversification applications and in National Parks the approval rate of 86% closely matches that for remote rural areas more generally (87%). Across the full LPA sample there were no examples of Best and Most Versatile agricultural land being raised as a reason for refusal for farm diversification (paras 5.28 – 5.31).

7.18   **Reasons for refusal:** Where applications were refused, the most common reasons given related to: landscape and visual impact (62% of applications refused); development inappropriate in the countryside (52% of refusals); traffic and highways (51% of refusals) and inappropriate development in AONBs/Green Belts (33%) (paras 5.40 – 5.43). These issues broadly reflect policies in local plans on farm diversification. The high incidence of *'development inappropriate in the countryside'* as a reason for refusal can be seen as a reflection of the exceptional nature of farm diversification, in that it often necessarily involves development outside settlements. The main considerations and concerns that development

---

[32] Minor developments are those where the floor area to be developed does not exceed 1000 square metres or the site is under 1 hectare.

control officers have in reconciling the national policy of strictly controlling development in the open countryside with policies in support of farm diversification, are also reflected in the other most common reasons for refusal.

7.19   **Conditions:** For those farm diversification applications that are approved, the most common conditions applied are: design and materials (57% of approvals), landscape and screening (46%), restrictions on activities (43%), and restrictions on car parking (35%), reflecting a similar range of concerns as those for refusals.

7.20   **Correlation between decisions and local plan policies:** Few development plans can be said to fully reflect the advice on farm diversification in PPG7, yet a high proportion of farm diversification applications are approved. In broad terms, therefore, the absence of fuller policy does not seem to be resulting in the refusal of an unduly large number of farm diversification applications. Indeed, in remote rural areas where policies were generally less detailed and less closely reflect PPG7, 87% of applications were approved, while in urban fringe areas, where policies are fuller, reflecting the higher development pressure in these areas, only 68% of applications were approved. Thus, very crudely, the lower the overall development pressure, the less the need for detailed policies and the higher the approval rate for farm diversification.

(3)   The operation of the planning system and identification of problem areas

7.21   **Operation of the planning system:** The findings of this research suggest that most farm diversification applications are adequate in terms of information provided, with at least 60% being made on behalf of clients by professional advisors. Most officers expressed an awareness of the problems for smaller-scale farmers in preparing planning applications and indicated a willingness to both provide guidance and negotiate necessary improvements (para 4.29). From this study it appears that over 85% of would-be applicants seek advice from the LPA prior to submitting a planning application, which in over 70% of cases is substantial involving a site visit or meeting. This may be followed by further dialogue once the application has been submitted. Both farmers and planners regard this dialogue as valuable with pre-application discussions appearing to improve approval rates (paras 5.35 – 5.36).

7.22   Approximately 60% of farm diversification applications are determined by LPA planning committee, with an average approval rate 8% below that of diversification applications determined by LPA officers under delegated powers. But the clear evidence of this study is that committees, when determining farm diversification applications, will follow officer recommendations and, if anything, will lean towards approving applications recommended for refusal by officers, especially where highways issues are the main stumbling block. The lower determination rate for committees, therefore, generally reflects the more complex nature of these applications, rather than any prejudice on their part. Indeed, in urban fringe areas, approval rates for farm diversification applications are lower under delegated powers than when determined by committee (paras 5.63 – 5.67). Nevertheless, the postal questionnaire does contain examples of a negative attitude on the part of some councillors towards farm diversification (para 6.33).

7.23   **Problem areas:** The research, however, has identified some problem areas in the operation and perceptions of the planning system with regard to farm diversification. These divide between those largely relating to policy and those relating to process. In terms of policy and the application of policy, the four most significant areas of concern relate to: large-scale developments; the relationship of farm diversification applications to a working farm; the potential tension between farm diversification and traffic generation, and the lack of vision for rural areas. With regard to process, problems relate to the perceptions of the planning system, the giving of advice and the time taken in determination.

Policy concerns

- **Large-scale developments:** Development control officers are concerned about the increasing size of agricultural buildings that are coming forward for re-use and the lack of policy guidance on this, both at the national level and within their own local plans (para 4.44 – 4.45). This concern relates both to the visual impact of such buildings and the potential intensification of use that could result. Of particular concern are intensive livestock units, which tend to be economically vulnerable and where the whole farm unit, including major buildings, may come forward for re-use when the agricultural business fails. This concern is reflected in the approval rates with, on average, 28% of diversification applications involving modern farm buildings being refused compared to only 13.5% in the case of traditional agricultural buildings. This refusal rate is particularly noticeable in the more accessible areas where refusal rates for modern buildings rise to 33%, reflecting a greater concern about intensification of use within areas already suffering from development pressure (paras 5.26 – 5.27). This compares with a refusal rate of only 15% for modern buildings in remote rural areas.

- **Attachment to a working farm:** Both in local plan policy and in determination, LPAs are often keen to see a clear relationship between a diversification activity and its support for a working farm, especially where large or significant new building are involved (paras 3.43, 4.46). This issue is not directly addressed in PPG7. Agricultural development and farm diversification are, as noted earlier, treated as an exception within PPG7 to the more general development constraint within the countryside. The advice in PPG7 on the use of mechanisms to tie development to the farm unit and restrict agricultural permitted development rights reflects this special status. But, in doing so, it might be argued that this aspect of national guidance (inadvertently) places constraints on the diversification of working farms without placing similar constraints on those diversification activities no longer related to an agricultural holding. Within this study, a significant minority (30%) of farm diversification applications did not relate to a working farm and, importantly, where the diversification application had been implemented only 39% were bringing additional income to the farm business (para 5.34). In both policy and practice therefore there seems to be a lack of clarity about the importance or otherwise of diversification activities linking to a working farm (para 6.42).

- **Traffic generation and farm diversification:** Traffic generation and potential conflict with the guidance in PPG13 (1994) is an issue evident in local plan policies (para 7.9). Development control officers have in the past dealt with this potential conflict by the simple expedient of favouring support for farm diversification over the objectives of PPG13, especially in remote rural areas. The main exceptions have been developments likely to generate significant amounts of traffic, which are frequently refused – where traffic is raised as a key issue approval rates drop by an overall average of 8% (para 4.40 – 4.43). The recent revision of PPG13 (March 2001) has helped resolve this conflict but there still remains the issue of meeting modern highway safety standards on country lanes without incurring significant landscape impact.

- **Lack of vision:** Lying at the heart of the above issues is a desire on the part of planners to be clear about what farm diversification should be delivering to whom and why. It is for this reason that the planning workshops pointed to the need for LPAs to have a vision for their rural areas, based on a clear understanding of local economic and social, as well as environmental, needs (para 6.42).

Process problems

- **Perceptions on the role of planning:** From this research it is evident that there is often a poor understanding of the planning system amongst farmers. In particular, there may be an expectation that planners can give categorical advice on what will and will not receive planning permission, even before any thoughts or proposals have been developed on the part of the would-be applicant. Enquiries of this nature can place planning officers in a difficult position, as they must remain impartial, particularly in their consideration of comments subsequently received from statutory consultees and other objectors. Such impartiality can be seen as unhelpful (para 6.11).

- **Understanding of farming amongst planners:** From this study it is clear that LPAs are keen to support the farming community and are sympathetic to their needs. It is also clear that pre-application discussions between applicants and the LPA are considered helpful by both parties in resolving potential issues. Nevertheless, planners may not be particularly familiar with farm diversification proposals, for a number of reasons (para 6.22 – 6.23). In urban fringe areas farm diversification applications are often difficult to distinguish from other developments, as they are frequently not related to a working farm (para 3.44). More generally, farm diversification only makes up a very small proportion (average 1.5%) of the case work of development control officers. Consequently, it takes time for officers to build up an understanding of the issues (para 4.14), especially as farm diversification involves such a wide range of developments, with no two cases being the same.

- **An ad hoc approach:** The potential lack of experience of farming issues amongst planners is exacerbated by the ad hoc approach in dealing with farm diversification within LPAs. Officers are rarely trained in diversification and agricultural issues, records of pre-application advice are frequently not retained, the lack of clarity in policy in key areas can result in unclear and inconsistent advice being given, and the general co-ordination of planning advice with other sources of support for farm diversification is poor. In combination these factors can be a significant hindrance to the positive and pro-active support of farm diversification (para 6.24).

- **Availability of guidance:** There is also little written guidance which LPAs or the farming community currently feel able to draw on. There is the DOE good practice guide for LPAs, *Planning for Rural Diversification*, which still contains useful information and advice but is in need of updating. This current lack of up to date advice should be remedied at the national level by DTLR's preparation of a revised edition of *A Farmer's Guide to the Planning System*. Very good examples of guidance are also beginning to emerge at the local level but these remain the exception rather than the rule (para 4.18) and currently most local authorities operate without the use of any written guidance, other than the policies in their local plan.

- **Best Value regime:** As already noted, the pre-application advice given by LPAs is generally welcomed by the farming community. There is concern, however, that the

Government's Best Value regime may curtail the outreach activities of LPAs, by judging activities strictly in financial terms, with emphasis on speed and efficiency rather than the quality of the advice given. Against these criteria, pre-application advice may be curtailed or stopped, or be made subject to a charge. This would be to the significant detriment of the developing relationship between farming and planning.

- **Determination times:** The final key issue is that of the time taken to determine farm diversification applications. By whatever measure used, the determination of farm diversification applications is slow (paras 5.68 – 5.74). This potentially serves to highlight the exceptional nature of farm diversification applications in terms of rural planning policy, and the lack of co-ordination and potential clarity in policy which might enable a more rapid determination time to be achieved.

(4) The extent to which LPAs currently take a pro-active approach to farm diversification

7.24 It has to be concluded from the results of this research that at present the majority of LPAs are not proactively assisting farm diversification to any great extent. The lack of full policy development and problems of advice and assistance identified above, highlight that neither in development plan policies, other publications, or in the delivery and coordination of advice to farmers, is the full potential to identify and promote farm diversification suitable to its locality being taken up. It should be stressed, though, that it was rarely found that LPAs and others involved in farm diversification are *unwilling* to extend their activities and proactively support farm diversification. Rather, and overwhelmingly, the problem is *lack of resources* to do so. There is however a range of Best Practice examples identified through this study which illustrate how a more pro-active approach might be developed. These examples are considered further below.

RECOMMENDATIONS AND BEST PRACTICE

7.25 The over-riding message that emerges through the findings of this research is the need for greater clarity of purpose in farm diversification and its role in wider rural diversification. This clarity of purpose is required at all levels: in defining the parameters under which farm diversification should operate; what it should deliver at the local level and for whose benefit, and clarity and consistency in the communication between LPAs and the farming community. It is this clarity of purpose and understanding that will enable planning to move from its currently re-active support of farm diversification to assuming a positively pro-active role.

7.26 The following recommendations, in combination, seek to assist in developing greater clarity and pick up on the issues raised above. They are considered under the three headings of national guidance; local plan policies; and implementation. It should be stressed that the emphasis of this research has been fact-finding. It has not been required to explore alternative approaches and therefore the recommendations below largely build on existing examples of good practice.

National guidance

7.27 In the policy statement issued by DETR in March 2001 clarifying PPG7 (1997), emphasis is placed on "*sustainable farm diversification projects*" (para 2.18 of this report) and the support for proposals that are "*consistent in their scale with their rural location*". These two points are re-affirmed in the case of new buildings in support of farm diversification where it is noted that these *".... may be acceptable provided that they satisfy sustainable development objectives and are of a design and scale appropriate to their rural surroundings"*.

7.28   As has been noted previously, key concerns of LPAs are the scale of buildings now coming forward for re-use, linkage or otherwise to a working farm, and issues of traffic generation.

7.29   Although difficult to formulate, a definition of sustainable farm diversification which addresses the three sustainability concerns of economy, community and environment, would go some way to addressing the more specific concerns of LPAs. Such a definition would be invaluable in enabling policy and individual decisions properly to differentiate between farm diversification that, depending on local circumstances, would assist wider rural sustainability, and that which would not. As is evident from this study, different types of diversification activity may be appropriate in different localities. Such a definition therefore, could not be overly prescriptive, but it could be much clearer about the key sustainability objectives that farm diversification should be meeting.

7.30   In turn, national guidance should clearly acknowledge that different approaches to farm diversification may be required to achieve sustainability objectives in different areas – responding to the different needs and pressures of different areas. Thus the type of farm diversification promoted in remote rural areas might not be appropriate in more accessible rural areas and vice versa.

7.31   In developing thinking on farm diversification it would also be helpful if DEFRA/DTLR gave further consideration to how the wide range of farm plans that are now being developed for a variety of purposes might be used in support of applications for farm diversification (para 4.30).

7.32   *Recommendation 1: The Government should consider the feasibility of providing a clearer, but flexible, definition of sustainable farm diversification which, amongst other things, addresses issues of scale of development and the differences between farm diversification which is and is not attached to a working farm.* Only if sustainable farm diversification is better defined, and locally interpreted in policies, can farm diversification which is beneficial to a local area be differentiated from that which is not.

7.33   *Recommendation 2: National policy guidance should clearly acknowledge that different approaches to farm diversification may be required to achieve sustainability objectives in different areas – responding to the different needs and pressures of different areas.*

7.34   *Recommendation 3: DEFRA/DTLR and the Countryside Agency at the national level, and local authorities at the more local level, should consider how the range of farm plans now being produced in support of farm business development and environmental protection, might be used in support of planning applications for farm diversification.*

Local plan policies

7.35   Based on the results of this study and the planning workshops, it is evident that there would be considerable benefit if local plan policies for farm diversification could be framed by a clear vision and objectives for the integrated development of their rural areas, including the role of rural and farm diversification within this. To be effective, such a vision and objectives should be based on a clear understanding of local social and economic, as well as environmental, needs (as already promoted by PPG7 (1997)), with local plan policies tailored to reflect these local needs. Thus policies would be based on a more systematic understanding of local needs and the clearer articulation of local requirements for farm diversification.

7.36 *Recommendation 4: LPAs should develop a clear vision for the integrated rural development of their rural areas, based on a rigorous understanding of local social and economic, as well as environmental, needs. This may require further emphasis in PPG7.* Such work should be undertaken in close liaison with the farming community and might link to the development of Community Strategies as required by the Local Government Act July 2000, Part 1.

7.37 *Recommendation 5: LPAs should have clear criteria-based policies for farm diversification which reflect local needs and which differentiate, where appropriate, between the types of diversification activity appropriate in different types of rural area. This information might be better provided as Supplementary Planning Guidance.*

7.38 *Recommendation 6: Subject to any clearer national definition of sustainable farm diversification, development plans should address the scale of development appropriate to their rural area and how (if at all) farm diversification activities should relate to a working farm.*

Best practice in local plan policies

7.39 **Surveys of local need:** As has been noted through this research, to-date resource constraints have meant that none of the local plans reviewed clearly demonstrate an understanding of local social and economic needs in the development of farm and rural development policies. However, the emerging range of integrated rural development initiatives promoted by MAFF and now DEFRA (the Forest of Bowland and Bodmin Upland Experiments) and the Countryside Agency's Land Management Initiatives (LMIs), combined with other such initiatives which are likely to be forthcoming under the ERDP and in response to the Foot and Mouth epidemic, may provide the vehicle for LPAs to work in partnership with others to identify local needs and develop a clear vision for the future. In the Forest of Bowland, through Integrated Farm Appraisals and other mechanisms, a close understanding has been developed of the social, economic and environmental needs of the locality. In consequence, farmers have been directed towards forms of diversification appropriate to the local area and thus more likely to receive planning permission (para 3.92). Other mechanisms that could serve the same purpose include AONB Management Plans, Rural Strategies and Community Strategies, so long as these give specific consideration to the future needs of farming in the locality.

7.40 **Clear criteria-based policies:** All the National Park plans reviewed have criteria-based policies. The clear focus of these plans with their requirement to foster rural social and economic well-being, alongside conservation of national landscapes, has resulted in more focused and co-ordinated planning policies for rural areas in general, and farm diversification in particular (para 3.93).

Implementation

7.41 Greater clarity of policy should assist in the development of a more pro-active approach to farm diversification. But to have effect such policies need to be supported by better communication between LPAs and the farming community. This requires better understanding of planning by the farming community, better understanding of farming amongst planners, and the giving of clear and consistent advice to farmers by LPAs. It also requires that the farming community is actively involved in the development of a vision for rural areas and the planning policies that result.

7.42 *Recommendation 7: The value of pre-application advice should be fully taken into account in any Best Value review of LPA services.*

7.43 *Recommendation 8: Within LPAs there should be consistent linking of pre- and post application advice.* Currently systems for recording pre-application discussions are weak. From this study there was no clear evidence of best practice but this is an area that needs to be addressed to ensure consistency of advice given.

7.44 *Recommendation 9: LPAs should consider training for development control officers in farm diversification, or the identification of a specialist officer to deal with inquiries and applications.* Within our sample LPAs no officers have received training in farm diversification, although in some LPAs one officer is identified to deal with these applications.

7.45 *Recommendation 10: LPAs should establish clear coordination with other bodies offering assistance and advice on farm diversification, such as DEFRA, local Economic Development Departments, the Farm Business Advisory Service and the Rural Enterprise Scheme.* This is to ensure that applicants receive co-ordinated advice, and that planning determinations are set in a clear understanding of economic opportunities.

7.46 *Recommendation 11: Local authorities, the Regional Development Agencies, DEFRA and other relevant bodies should consider establishing first stop shops where applicants can gain planning and economic development advice under one roof.* In addition to providing a more convenient and user-friendly service for potential applicants, the arrangement should encourage greater interaction between the relevant officers.

7.47 *Recommendation 12: LPAs should develop closer partnerships with the farming community through agricultural or farming fora, or regular liaison meetings between planners and the farming community.* These provide opportunities for the interchange of concerns and experience. They also provide the mechanism for involving the farming community in the development of policies for farm diversification. To-date these interchanges have tended to occur at the county level (para 4.59). But it is very important that planning officers at the district level form part of the dialogue.

7.48 *Recommendation 13: LPAs should consider producing written advice (a leaflet or similar) that explains how farm diversification applications will be dealt with and the issues that will be taken into account in their determination reflecting local circumstances.* The aim of such guidance is to ensure that by the time would-be applicants approach the LPA for planning advice they are clear on the issues that are likely to be raised.

7.49 *Recommendation 14: LPAs should take planning advice out to the farming community, perhaps through planning clinics, or the work of agricultural liaison officers, or by working with those who are already in close liaison with the farming community, for example, planning advisors operating under the Rural Enterprise Scheme.*

7.50   In making these recommendations it is realised that it would not be appropriate or practical for all LPAs to follow all the recommendations directed at them to the same degree. It will be for individual local authorities to decide the actions which are most appropriate for them depending on local circumstances. Under the ERDP, the Action Plan for Farming, the Rural White Paper and the response to Foot and Mouth Disease there are a broad range of activities being undertaken by a wide range of organisations. In many cases the actions identified above could and should be shared as part of these initiatives rather than falling to local authorities alone.

Best practice in implementation

7.51   **Co-ordination with other sources of advice:** Within this study there were still relatively few examples of development control officers co-ordinating with other advisors on farm diversification. An exception is Stratford District Council where all farm diversification planning applications are referred to the District's Economic Development Officer (para 4.26).

7.52   **First stop shop:** In a few instances more concerted attempts are being made to give more co-ordinated advice. For example, In the North York Moors, Whitby Business Development Agency is in the process of making an officer available to give business advice from the North York Moors National Park Authority offices, allowing farmers to seek advice from both the Business Development Agency and planning department under one roof.

7.53   **Written advice:** The North Yorkshire County Council publication is cited as an example of good practice (para 6.43) although shorter publications may be equally useful in alerting the farming community to relevant planning issues, such as that currently in draft form produced by the Norfolk Arable Land Management Initiative for Breckland District Council.

7.54   **Agricultural liaison:** In the National Parks, agricultural liaison officers have been very helpful in breaking down the barriers between the farming community and the planning authority. Whilst it is potentially inadvisable for these officers to give planning advice (unless they form part of the planning department) they can provide the link between planners and farmers, signposting farmers to the relevant advice. In North York Moors NPA, a link officer is being appointed to provide precisely this service (para 4.58).

POSTSCRIPT: THE FOOT AND MOUTH EPIDEMIC

7.55   The Foot and Mouth epidemic adds further dimension to the conclusions and recommendations of this research. The impacts of the epidemic and strategies for recovery are complex issues and well beyond the remit of this research. Yet the emphasis that is likely to be placed on farm diversification as a result of the epidemic needs to reflect on a number of issues.

7.56   Diversified farmers are likely to be amongst the hardest-hit by the epidemic. Although they will have been compensated for the loss of their livestock they will not have been fully compensated for the losses incurred by their diversification enterprises, especially those connected with tourism. Such farmers may be unable to sustain existing diversification enterprises and may be extremely reticent to contemplate new enterprises. At the same time the market for additional farm diversification, particularly in tourism, in those areas hardest-hit by the epidemic, may be limited. Following compensation, some farmers may be relatively cash-rich but should they be encouraged to diversify without careful assessment of the potential economic sustainability of their proposals and the potential competition that they could pose to remaining diversification activities that are seeking to recover from the effects of the epidemic?

7.57   This potentially highlights again the importance of understanding local circumstances and encouraging all parties concerned with farm diversification (both directly and indirectly) to work together in finding a solution.

BIBLIOGRAPHY

ADAS (2000) *English Agriculture: Opportunities for Change and Diversification*, report prepared for the Countryside Agency, ADAS, Wolverhampton.

Atlantic Consultants in association with LUC (2000) *Planning and Rural Employment in Cornwall*, report prepared for Cornwall County Council, Truro.

Bramley G and Smart G (1995) *Rural incomes and housing affordability*, Research Report No 20, Rural Development Commission, Salisbury.

Cabinet Office (December 1999) A Performance & Innovation Unit Report: *Rural Economies*, Stationery Office, London.

Cabinet Office (February 2000) A Performance & Innovation Unit Report: *Sharing the Nation's Prosperity – Economic, Social and Environmental Conditions in the Countryside*, Stationery Office, London.

Cabinet Office (November 2000) Better Regulation Task Force Report: *Environmental Regulations and Farmers*, Stationery Office, London.

Campaign for the Protection of Rural England (2000) *Farm diversification: planning for success*, CPRE, London.

Clement P R (1992) *The Planning System: Friend or Foe of Farm Diversification? Working Paper No 138*, School of Planning, Oxford Brookes University, Oxford.

Country Landowners Association (June 2000) Jones M, *Local Interpretation of Planning Guidance*, CLA, London.

Country Landowners Association (June 2000) Buckwell A and Harwood OHF, *Diversification in the Agricultural Let Sector*, CLA, London.

Countryside Agency (2000) *The State of the Countryside Report 2000*, Countryside Agency, Cheltenham.

Crawshaw C (2001) *Planning and the Facilitation of Sustainable Rural Development*, unpublished report prepared for the North West Development Agency by the University of Lancaster.

Deloitte Touche (2000) *Annual Farm Results*, Deloitte Touche Consulting, London.

Department of the Environment, Welsh Office, MAFF (undated) *A Farmer's Guide to the Planning System*, Previously available free from the DoE, PO Box 135, Bradford, West Yorkshire.

Department of the Environment (1992) *Planning Policy Guidance Note (PPG) 7: The countryside and the rural economy*, HMSO, London.

Department of the Environment with Department of Transport (1994) *Planning Policy Guidance Note (PPG) 13: Transport*, HMSO, London.

Department of the Environment (1995) *Planning Policy Guidance Note (PPG) 2: Green Belts*, HMSO, London.

Department of the Environment (1996) *Planning Policy Guidance Note (PPG) 6: Town Centres and Retail Development*, The Stationery Office, London.

Department of the Environment (1997) *Planning Policy Guidance Note (PPG) 7: The Countryside: Environmental Quality and Economic and Social Development*, HMSO, London.

DETR (1999) *A Better Quality of Life, a strategy for sustainable development for the UK*, Cm 4345, The Stationery Office, London.

DETR (December 1999) *Planning Policy Guidance Note (PPG) 12: Development Plans*, The Stationery Office, London.

DETR (2000) Seminar on planning and agricultural diversification [www.dtlr.gov.uk/planning/seminar/01.htm] accessed 30 October 2000.

DETR (October 2000) *Planning Policy Guidance Note (PPG) 11: Regional Planning*, The Stationery Office, London.

DETR/MAFF (November 2000) Rural White Paper, *Our Countryside: The Future, A Fair Deal for Rural England*, Cm4909, The Stationery Office, London.

DETR (2001) Seminars on planning for farm diversification (GO-East Midlands and GOSW), personal communication with researchers at UWE, Bristol.

DETR (March 2001) *Planning Policy Guidance Note (PPG) 13: Transport*, The Stationery Office, London.

Elson M & MacDonald R, (1995) *Planning for Rural Diversification*, a report prepared for the Department of the Environment by Oxford Brookes School of Planning and PA Cambridge Economic Consultants, HMSO, London.

Elson M, Steenberg C and Wilkinson J (1995) *Planning for Rural Diversification: a good practice guide*, report prepared for the Department of the Environment by Oxford Brookes School of Planning,, HMSO, London.

Elson M, Steenberg C and Downing L (1998) *Rural Development and Land Use Planning Policies*, Rural Research Report No 38, a report prepared for the Rural Development Commission, Salisbury.

Ilbery B (1992) 'State-assisted farm diversification in the United Kingdom', Chapter 7 in Bowler I R, Bryant C R and Nellis M D *Contemporary Rural Systems in Transition Vol 1 Agriculture and Environment*, CAB, Wallingford, Oxon.

Ilbery B, Healey M & Higginbottom J (1997) 'On and off-farm business diversification by farm households in England' Chaper 9 in *Agricultural Restructuring and Sustainability: a Geographical Perspective*, CAB International, Wallington, Oxon.

Local Government Association (September 2000) *Local Government Charter for Agriculture*, LGA, London.

LUC (1995) *Planning Controls Over Agricultural and Forestry Development and Rural Building Conversions*, a report prepared for the Department of the Environment, HMSO, London.

LUC in association with Kernon Countryside Consultants (2001) *The Planning System and Sustainable Farm Diversification in the NALMI Area*, a report prepared for the Countryside Agency by Land Use Consultants, London.

MAFF (March 2000) *Strategy for Agriculture: An action plan for farming*, The Stationery Office, London.

MAFF, SERAD, DARD(NI), NAWADI (2000) *Agriculture in the UK 1999*, The Stationery Office, London.

MAFF (October 2000) England Rural Development Programme
www.maff.gov.uk/erdp/docs/national/agriculture.htm

MAFF (May 2001) *Task Force for the Hills*, A report prepared for the Minister of Agriculture by The Hills Task Force, MAFF, London.

Marsden T and Murdock J (1990) *Agriculture in Retreat: Implications for the Changing Control and Development of Rural Land*, Countryside Change Initiative Working Paper 9, University of Newcastle Upon Tyne, Newcastle.

Marsden T (1999) *Rural Sustainability*, Town & Country Planning Association, London.

McInerney J and Turner M (1991) *Patterns, Performance and Prospects in Farm Diversification*, Report No 236, Agricultural Economics Unit, University of Exeter, Exeter.

McLoughlin B (2000) 'Diversification of agricultural business: what farmers expect of the planning system and barriers to delivery', *Paper presented to the Planning and Agricultural Seminar at the Planning Officers' Society*, Oldham.

National Farmers' Union (July 1999) *Cutting Red Tape: An NFU Survey*, NFU Public Affairs Department , London.

National Farmers' Union North East Region (December 2000) *Farm diversification and planning delays – the Harrogate Experience*, NFU, York.

Neale J , Lowe P and Marsden T (1992) The Conversion of Agricultural Buildings: An Analysis of Variable Pressures and Regulations Towards the Post-Productivist Countryside, ESRC Countryside Change Initiative Working Paper 29, University of Newcastle Upon Tyne, Newcastle.

North Yorkshire County Council and Yorkshire Forward (November 2000) *A Planning Guide to Farm Diversification in North Yorkshire*, North Yorkshire County Council.

Objective One Partnership for Cornwall and Scilly (June 2000) *Task Force Strategy: Agriculture, Horticulture, Food and other land-based industries*, a report prepared for ONE by Duchy College and LANTRA, Cornwall.

RASE (1998) *Warwickshire Farm Business Guide: a guide to alternative farm businesses*, Rural Forum for Coventry and Warwickshire, RASE, Warwickshire.

Royal Town Planning Institute (March 2000) *Integrated Rural Strategies Good Practice Guide*, RTPI, London.

Scottish Executive (2001) *A Guide to Farm Diversification and Planning Permission in Scotland*, Scottish Executive Development Department, Edinburgh.

Shaw D and Hale A (1996) 'Realizing capital assets: an additional strand to the farm diversification debate' *Journal of Environmental Planning and Management*, 39(3), pp403-418.

Shorten J and Daniels I (September 2000) *Rural Diversification in Farm Buildings: An investigation into the relationship between the re-use of farm buildings and the planning system*, a report prepared for the Planning Officers' Society by the University of the West of England, Bristol.

Tarling R , Rhodes J, North J and Broom G (1993) *The economy and rural England*, Strategy Review Topic Paper 4, report prepared for the Rural Development Commission by PA Cambridge Economic Consultants, RDC, London.

Ward N & Lowe P (1999) *Agricultural Change and Rural Development in Northumberland*, a report prepared for Northumberland County Council by University of Newcastle upon Tyne, Centre for Rural Economy, Department of Agricultural Economics and Food Marketing, Newcastle.

APPENDIX 1

Methodology for choosing the sample of Local Planning Authorities (LPAs)

SAMPLING FRAME FOR THE SELECTION OF 21 LOCAL PLANNING AUTHORITIES (LPAS)

A1.1   As noted in Chapter 1, the 21 sample Local Planning Authorities (LPAs) have been chosen to reflect a range of different factors. In particular, they have been chosen to reflect the different development pressures that may be associated with different types of rural area relative to centres of population eg accessible and remote rural areas. They have also been chosen to reflect different geographical areas of England; different designations; different types of farming; and less favoured and disadvantaged areas.

Different types of rural area

A1.2   There are a number of standard classifications that have been used previously in major studies of rural economic and planning issues (Tarling et al, 1993; Bramley et al, 1995: Elson et al, 1995 &1998) to define different types of rural area:

- Tarling et al, (1993) is the model that was adopted by the former Rural Development Commission (RDC). It was used to determine the economic structures within different types of rural area as a means of identifying key threats and opportunities for the economy of rural England in the nineties. It was subsequently used in the recent report of the Policy and Innovation Unit (PIU) *Rural Economies* 1999 to define rural areas. The model identifies five types of LPA:

    - *metropolitan* (69 authorities);

    - *urban* (110 authorities);

    - *former coalfields* (10 authorities)

    - *accessible rural* (108 authorities) } taken by the PIU report to = rural areas

    - *remote rural* (63 authorities).

- Bramley (1995, RDC). This study examined rural incomes and housing affordability and drew on wards based on the 1981 OPCS categorisation developed by Craig (1987), as well as using a range of datasets. The model Bramley devised to predict patterns of income at the local level used two definitions – *deep rural* and *mixed rural* to contrast with *urban households* and *non-rural districts*, with a further sub division into zones by wards.

- Elson's (1995) study of rural diversification (DoE) incorporated an equal representation of *accessible and remote rural* authorities. In Elson's later research study on rural development and land use planning policies (RDC, 1998), LPAs examined were classified into three categories: deep rural for remote areas, mixed rural and urban fringe for more accessible areas.

A1.3 Since three of these studies were undertaken there has been local government reorganisation (1996) affecting local authority boundaries and structures.

A1.4 The approach adopted for this study draws on the above studies, using Tarling as the base. However, *urban* and *coalfield* are re-classified as *urban fringe* to take account of Green Belt designations and new peripheral forms of development occurring around the edge of many major cities and conurbations. *Accessible rural* and *remote rural* categories remain the same as defined by Tarling, allowing for local government re-organisation.

Other factors

A1.5 Other factors that influenced the choice of LPAs and the information used are as follows:

- **different geographical areas:** Incorporation of the eight English regions, with at least two LPAs in each region, but excluding London.

- **different environmental designations:** Coverage of a selection of 3 National Parks (8 National Parks nationally accounting for 7.6% of England's land area), a percentage of AONBs per region (37 AONBs nationally accounting for 15.6% of England's land area) – *source: The State of the Countryside 2000, The Countryside Agency.*

- **best and most versatile agricultural land:** Coverage of Best and Most Versatile agricultural land (Grades 1, 2 and 3a) as defined by MAFF Census data (*1997 Agricultural Land Classification*), Grade 1 accounts for 2.6% of England's land area, Grade 2 for 13.5% and Grade 3 for 43.6%.

- **different types of farming:** The datasets for this were too dispersed and local in nature but the sample was passed to MAFF for verification.

- **less favoured or disadvantaged areas:** Covering defined less favoured or disadvantaged areas (Rural Development Areas) and Objective 1, 2, and 5b funding areas.

- **farm diversification initiatives:** Finally, the sample sought to capture some areas where there are active farm diversification initiatives in place which may have encouraged greater support for farm diversification more generally – examples include the Bodmin and Forest of Bowland Upland Experiments, work in the Peak District National Park in support of Integrated Rural Development and the North Yorks. Moors National Park through a series of linked 5b initiatives, as well as the Countryside Agency's developing Land Management Initiatives.

A1.6 A sieve analysis provided a long list of 50 potential LPAs within the categories mentioned above, and this list was further refined to a short list of 36 LPAs. The final selection of 21 case study authorities was made following discussion with the DETR.

References

Bramley G & Smart G (1995) *Rural incomes and housing affordability*, Research Report No 20, Rural Development Commission, Salisbury.

Elson M & McDonald R (1995) *Planning for Rural Diversification*, a report prepared in conjunction with Oxford Brookes School of Planning and PS Cambridge Economic Consultants for the Department of the Environment, HMSO, London.

Elson M Steenberg C and Downing L (1998) *Rural development and land use policies*, Rural Research Report No 38, Rural Development Commission, Salisbury

Tarling R et al (1993) *The economy and rural England*, Strategy Review, Topic Paper 4, Rural Development Commission, London.

APPENDIX 2

Postal questionnaire to applicants

On Behalf of the Department of the Environment, Transport
and the Regions: Farm diversification and the planning system

This questionnaire is for important research into the relationship between the planning system and farm diversification The results of this questionnaire will be used for research purposes only. This information will be treated confidentially and the analysis of the data will ensure the anonymity of the individual cases.

Please complete this questionnaire.
It is very important that we find out about your experiences of the planning system.

This questionnaire is about your recent planning application (application number; mail merge).

Was it: approved ☐, refused ☐ or withdrawn ☐ *(tick)*?

The planning system – *to be completed for all applications*

Did you take any planning advice *(tick)*?

None ☐ Land agent ☐ Planning consultant ☐ NFU ☐

CLA ☐ Non professional (eg neighbour) ☐ Other ☐ _____

Did you have contact with the local authority before your planning application *(tick)*?

Phone conversation ☐ Letter exchange ☐ Meeting ☐ Site meeting ☐ None ☐

Who at the local authority did you contact for your planning application *(tick)*?

Development control ☐ Local planning ☐ Highways ☐ Farm liaison ☐ Other ☐

Did the farmer apply for planning permission? ☐

What was your experience of the treatment of your proposals by the planning authority?

_____

How do you think the way farm diversification proposals are dealt with by the planning system could be improved?

_____

Approvals – *only to be completed for approvals (refusals and withdrawals on next page)*

Has the development been implemented? Yes ☐ No ☐

If not, why not?

_____

What type of diversification activity? Please tick the box with brief description below.

Tourism ☐ Recreation ☐ Retail ☐ Horse Enterprise ☐ Workshop/ Manufacturing ☐

Food processing ☐ Storage / haulage ☐ Machinery/ vehicle repair ☐ Offices/ studios ☐ Agricultural Contracting ☐

Other/Description:

_____

If the development has not been implemented this is all you need to complete on the form

The Farm

Size of farm unit the diversification activity is on *(tick)*?

0–5ha ☐ 5–40ha ☐ 40–100ha ☐ 100ha+ ☐

Type of farm unit the diversification activity is on *(tick)*?

Working farm ☐ Farm no longer farmed ☐ Land/buildings sold away from working farm ☐

Relationship of diversification activity to the farm *(tick)*?

Related to agriculture on farm (eg farm shop) ☐

Additional income attached to farm (eg tourist accommodation, business units) ☐

Income through sale of land/buildings ☐

No relationship to farm ☐

If applicable what percentage of the farm income is provided through all diversification activities (approx)? _____

If applicable what percentage of the farm income is provided through this diversification (approx)? _____

Nature of this diversification business *(tick)*:

A new business ☐ Relocation of an existing business ☐ Expansion of an existing business ☐

Refusals – only to be completed for refusals

If planning permission was refused, either by the local authority or at appeal please give your views on this refusal and the reasons given for it

_____

Withdrawals – only to be completed for withdrawn applications

If you withdrew your application please explain why

_____

We will be following up a limited number of case studies in greater detail. Could you please provide a contact/s who if you are selected as a case study?

Name(s) and addresses

_____

_____

_____

Phone number(s)/e-mail(s)

_____

_____

_____

APPENDIX 3

Methodology for the farmer/ landowner telephone interviews

A3.1   In order to gather further information regarding planning and diversification issues a telephone survey of farmers and landowners was undertaken. This was carried out by Royal Agricultural College Enterprise (RACE).

A3.2   The aim of the farmer telephone survey was two fold. In the first instance it was to be used to collect the names of potential attendees for the subsequent workshops, and additionally, as contact was being made with farmers, to collect additional data of interest.

A3.3   Three of the LPA areas were selected, one urban fringe (Maidstone), one accessible rural (Stratford) and one remote rural (North Yorkshire Moors). From each of the areas telephone numbers for 125 farmers were accessed using a marketing database. The farmer selection was based on postcode regions relevant to the LPA. In the case of the North Yorkshire Moors an additional 125 telephone numbers were required in order to obtain sufficient responses.

A3.4   The telephone survey was carried out on the 7th to 10th November 2000. A copy of the questionnaire is attached. Calls to farmers were generally made between the hours of 9.00am and 5.00pm, although on one day calls were made in the evening to assess whether this would improve the success rate. Each contact number was attempted three separate times (usually non-consecutive days). If no response was received after the third attempt, then it was abandoned. The questionnaire is divided into nine sections following an initial screening question so that those farmers who had no experience of the planning system were not interviewed.

Section 1 examines farm structure

Section 2 assesses experience of planning and diversification

Section 3 discusses experience of successful planning applications

Section 4 was for those farmers who were in the process of an application

Section 5 discusses rejected applications

Section 6 examines cases where farmers had considered a diversification activity, and made contact with the LPA, but had not proceeded

Section 7 discusses diversification activities that are currently being considered but had not reached the planning stage

Section 8 asks whether farmers would be willing to attend a workshop

Section 9 asks for further comments about the planning process (whether or not related to farm diversification)

A3.5   The respondents were only asked to complete one of sections 3 – 7, and the interviewers prioritised these in the following order – 6, 5, 3, 4, 7. Section 6 was considered most important as the experiences of these farmers would not be available from other parts of the study, and they could provide vital information as to what barriers prevent farmers pursuing a diversification enterprise, and whether those barriers are related to planning and planning policy.

TELEPHONE QUESTIONNAIRE TO FARMERS/LANDOWNERS

Please may I speak to _____

Hello, my name is _____ from the Royal Agricultural College. We have been commissioned by the Department of Environment, Transport and Regions as part of the Government's Action Plan for Farming to carry out a survey related to the town and country planning system and farm diversification enterprises with the aim of trying to find ways of making the system more user-friendly. Please could you spare 10 minutes to complete a telephone survey.

Please may I assure you that all information you provide will be treated in strictest confidence, and your individual details will not be revealed in the study report or passed onto any third party.

(If asked assure the interviewee that the survey is certainly not aimed at uncovering any breach of planning law, and cannot be used as such)

Thank you

1. **Have you ever submitted a planning application related to a farm diversification exercise?** Yes ☐ No ☐

2. **Are you considering, or have you ever considered a diversification activity that might require planning permission, whether or not you may have proceeded with the scheme** Yes ☐ No ☐

If NO to both of the above then thank and terminate interview

I would like to ask some questions about your farm

SECTION 1: FARM STRUCTURE

3. **How big is the area of the farm:** *tick*

   0-20 ha ☐   0 – 50 ac ☐

   21 – 50 ha ☐   51 – 125 ac ☐

   51 – 100 ha ☐   126 – 250 ac ☐

   101 – 200 ha ☐   251 – 500 ac ☐

   201 – 400 ha ☐   501 – 1000 ac ☐

   > 400 ha ☐   > 1000 ac ☐

4. **Is the farm within any of the following designated areas?:** *[read list] tick all that apply*

   AONB (Area of Outstanding Natural Beauty) ☐

   National Park ☐

   Green Belt ☐

   Special Landscape Area ☐

   Other (Specify) [_____]

   Don't Know ☐

5. **Has a detailed agricultural land classification survey of your farm ever been carried out?**   Yes ☐ No ☐ Don't know ☐

   If no or Don't Know Go To Question 7

6. **What grades of agricultural land does your farm include according to the Agricultural Land Classification, and approximate proportions:**

   Grades 1/2/3a   ☐

   Grades 3b/4/5   ☐

   Don't Know   ☐

7. **What are the main enterprises on the farm?** *tick all that apply, and asterisk largest enterprise*

8. **Do you have any other enterprises, if so what are they?**

Arable – Cereal	☐	Field Scale Veg	☐
Arable – Root Crops	☐	Protected Cropping – veg	☐
Arable – other combinable crops	☐	Protected Cropping – salad	☐
Dairy cattle	☐	Protected cropping – other	☐
Beef	☐	Soft Fruit	☐
Sheep	☐	Tree Fruit	☐
Pigs	☐	Other 1 (Specify) [_____]	
Goats	☐	Other 2 (Specify) [_____]	
Poultry	☐	Other 3 (Specify) [_____]	

9. **How many full time employees does the farm have?** [_____]

10. **Are you:** *[Read List] tick*

    Owner   ☐

    Manager   ☐

    Tenant   ☐

    Other (specify) [_____]

11. **Which of the following age categories are you in?:** *[Read List] tick*

    20 – 30   ☐

    30 – 40   ☐

    40 – 50   ☐

    50 – 60   ☐

    60+   ☐

    SECTION END – GO TO SECTION 2

SECTION 2: DIVERSIFICATION QUESTIONS

12. **Do you have a farm diversification enterprise that required a planning application?**   Yes ☐   No ☐
    If yes Go To section 3

13. **Have you had a farm diversification enterprise that required planning permission, but is no longer in operation?**   Yes ☐   No ☐
    If yes Go To section 3

159

14. Have you received planning consent but not implemented the enterprise?　　Yes ☐ No ☐
If yes Go To Section 3

15. Are you in the process of Submitting a planning application for a farm diversification enterprise?　　Yes ☐ No ☐
If Yes Go To Section 4

16. Have you applied for planning permission for a farm diversification enterprise that has been refused?　　Yes ☐ No ☐
If yes Go To Section 5

17. Have you considered a farm diversification enterprise that would have required planning permission, but decided against submitting an application　　Yes ☐ No ☐
If yes Go To Section 6

18. Are you considering a farm diversification enterprise that will require planning permission, but have not decided whether or not to proceed　　Yes ☐ No ☐
If Yes Go To Section 7

If No to all of the above, thank and terminate interview

Interviewer: Only complete one of the Sections 3 through to 7. If the interviewee has said yes to more than one category, fill in the most important section according to the following ranking (1 most important)

Please circle the section you are going to complete

Section 6	1	Section 4	4
Section 5	2	Section 7	5
Section 3	3		

SECTION 3: SUCCESSFUL PLANNING APPLICATIONS

19. **What type of diversification activity was the subject of the planning application?** *[Read List if necessary]* Tick

Tourism	☐	Storage/Haulage	☐
Recreation	☐	Machinery/Vehicle Repair	☐
Retail (Farm shop and pick your own)	☐	Office/Studio	☐
Workshops	☐	Residential Lettings	☐
Agricultural Contracting	☐	Livery	☐
Manufacturing/Industry	☐	Energy (farm composting or wood fuel, NOT wind farms)	☐
Food Processing/Packing	☐	Other (specify) [_____]	

If more than one enterprise, say *"Please consider the most recent activity in the following questions"*

20. **What type of development was involved?** *[Read list if necessary]* tick

New buildings associated with a farm diversification activity ☐

Extension of an existing farm building ☐

Change of use of existing building ☐

Change of use of agricultural land ☐

Signs in support of a diversification activity ☐

Residential accommodation in support of farm diversification ☐

Other (specify) [_____]

21. **In what year was the application made?** [_____]

22. From whom did you take any outside advice prior to making the application and was this helpful:

Was advice taken from...tick   *Was this helpful*

Land Agent/Surveyor ☐   Yes ☐   No ☐

Planning Consultant ☐   Yes ☐   No ☐

NFU ☐   Yes ☐   No ☐

Non-professional (e.g. neighbour) ☐   Yes ☐   No ☐

Other (Specify) ☐   Yes ☐   No ☐

None ☐   ***Go to Question 24***

23. What was the nature of this advice? *tick*

On farm meeting ☐

Other meeting ☐

Letter ☐

Telephone conversation ☐

Other (specify) [＿＿＿＿＿]

24. Did you see, or try to obtain, any information about planning in the form of leaflets   Yes ☐   No ☐
or guidance booklets?   ***If No go to Question 27***

25. What was the title of these leaflets?

＿＿＿＿＿＿＿＿＿＿＿＿＿＿＿＿＿＿＿＿＿＿＿＿＿＿＿＿＿＿＿＿＿＿＿

＿＿＿＿＿＿＿＿＿＿＿＿＿＿＿＿＿＿＿＿＿＿＿＿＿＿＿＿＿＿＿＿＿＿＿

26. Did you find these leaflets useful?   Yes ☐   No ☐

27. Was contact made with the local planning authority before making the planning application and was this helpful:

Was advice taken from...tick   *Was this helpful*

Local authority planning officer/development control officer ☐   Yes ☐   No ☐

Local authority conservation officer ☐   Yes ☐   No ☐

Local authority farm liaison officer ☐   Yes ☐   No ☐

Local authority highways officer ☐   Yes ☐   No ☐

Unspecified (don't know who it was) ☐   Yes ☐   No ☐

Other (Specify) [＿＿＿＿＿＿＿＿＿＿]   Yes ☐   No ☐

None ☐   ***Go to Question 29***

28. What was the nature of this contact? *tick*

On Farm Meeting ☐

Meeting, other than farm ☐

Letter ☐

Telephone Conversation ☐

Other (specify) [＿＿＿＿＿]

29. Other than you, who was involved in preparing the planning application? *Tick all that apply*

Land Agent/Surveyor ☐

Planning Consultant ☐

Architect ☐

NFU ☐

Other (Specify) ☐

No-one ☐

30. Following the planning application did you have any further discussions with the local planning authority and were these helpful:

Was advice taken from...tick   *Was this helpful*

Local authority planning officer/development control officer ☐   Yes ☐ No ☐

Local authority conservation officer ☐   Yes ☐ No ☐

Local authority farm liaison officer ☐   Yes ☐ No ☐

Local authority highways officer ☐   Yes ☐ No ☐

Unspecified (don't know who it was) ☐   Yes ☐ No ☐

Other (Specify) ☐   Yes ☐ No ☐

None ☐

31. Was an appeal required?   Yes ☐ No ☐

32. Were any conditions placed on the permission?   Yes ☐ No ☐
(If NO Go to Q36)

33. What were the conditions related to?

_____

_____

34. Do you think these conditions were reasonable   Yes ☐ No ☐
If Yes, Go to Question 36

35. Why do you think the conditions were not reasonable?

_____

_____

36. Did you sign a Section 106 planning agreement?   Yes ☐ No ☐

37. If the diversification was not implemented or has ceased is this related   Yes ☐ No ☐
to planning conditions/issues?   *If No Go To Section 8*

38. Why did the planning conditions/issues cause you not to proceed with the diversification scheme?

_____

_____

SECTION END – GO TO SECTION 8

SECTION 4: IN THE PROCESS OF A PLANNING APPLICATION

39. **What type of diversification activity is the subject of the planning application?** *[Read List if necessary] Tick*

Tourism	☐	Storage/Haulage	☐
Recreation	☐	Machinery/Vehicle Repair	☐
Retail (Farm shop and pick your own)	☐	Office/Studio	☐
Workshops	☐	Residential Lettings	☐
Agricultural Contracting	☐	Livery	☐
Manufacturing/Industry	☐	Energy (farm composting or wood fuel, NOT wind farms)	☐
Food Processing/Packing	☐	Other (specify) [＿＿＿＿＿＿]	

40. **What type of development is involved?** *[Read list if necessary] tick*

New buildings associated with a farm diversification activity ☐

Extension of an existing farm building ☐

Change of use of existing building ☐

Change of use of agricultural land ☐

Signs in support of a diversification activity ☐

Residential accommodation in support of farm diversification ☐

Other (specify) [＿＿＿＿＿＿＿＿＿＿＿]

41. **Have you taken any outside advice prior to making the application and was this helpful:**

Was advice taken from…tick		*Was this helpful*	
Land Agent/Surveyor	☐	Yes ☐	No ☐
Planning Consultant	☐	Yes ☐	No ☐
NFU	☐	Yes ☐	No ☐
Non-professional (e.g. neighbour)	☐	Yes ☐	No ☐
Other (Specify)	☐	Yes ☐	No ☐
None	☐	*Go to Question 43*	

42. **What was the nature of this advice?** *tick*

On farm meeting ☐

Other meeting ☐

Letter ☐

Telephone Conversation ☐

Other (specify) [＿＿＿＿＿＿]

43. **Did you see, or try to obtain, any information about planning in the form of leaflets or guidance booklets?**   Yes ☐ No ☐
If No go to Question 46

44. **What was the title of these leaflets?**

_____

_____

45. Did you find these leaflets useful? Yes ☐ No ☐

46. Was contact made with the local planning authority before making the planning application and was this helpful:

Was advice taken from...tick *Was this helpful*

Local authority planning officer/development control officer ☐ Yes ☐ No ☐

Local authority conservation officer ☐ Yes ☐ No ☐

Local authority farm liaison officer ☐ Yes ☐ No ☐

Local authority highways officer ☐ Yes ☐ No ☐

Unspecified (don't know who it was) ☐ Yes ☐ No ☐

Other (Specify) [_____] Yes ☐ No ☐

None ☐ *Go to Question 48*

47. What was the nature of this contact? *tick*

On Farm Meeting ☐

Meeting, other than farm ☐

Letter ☐

Telephone Conversation ☐

Other (specify) [_____]

48. Other than you, who was involved in preparing the planning application? *Tick all that apply*

Land Agent/Surveyor ☐

Planning Consultant ☐

Architect ☐

NFU ☐

Other (Specify) [_____]

No-one ☐

49. Following the planning application did you have any further discussions with the local planning authority and were these helpful:

Was advice taken from...tick *Was this helpful*

Local authority planning officer/development control officer ☐ Yes ☐ No ☐

Local authority conservation officer ☐ Yes ☐ No ☐

Local authority farm liaison officer ☐ Yes ☐ No ☐

Local authority highways officer ☐ Yes ☐ No ☐

Unspecified (don't know who it was) ☐ Yes ☐ No ☐

Other (Specify) [_____] Yes ☐ No ☐

None ☐

SECTION END – GO TO SECTION 8

SECTION 5: UNSUCCESSFUL PLANNING APPLICATION

50. What type of diversification activity was the subject of the planning application? *[Read List if necessary] Tick*

Tourism	☐	Storage/Haulage	☐
Recreation	☐	Machinery/Vehicle Repair	☐
Retail (Farm shop and pick your own)	☐	Office/Studio	☐
Workshops	☐	Residential Lettings	☐
Agricultural Contracting	☐	Livery	☐
Manufacturing/Industry	☐	Energy (farm composting or wood fuel, NOT wind farms)	☐
Food Processing/Packing	☐	Other (specify) [_____]	

If more than one enterprise, say *"Please consider the most recent activity in the following questions"*

51. What type of development was involved? *[Read list if necessary] tick*

New buildings associated with a farm diversification activity ☐

Extension of an existing farm building ☐

Change of use of existing building ☐

Change of use of agricultural land ☐

Signs in support of a diversification activity ☐

Residential accommodation in support of farm diversification ☐

Other (specify) [_____]

52. In what year was the application made? [_____]

53. From whom did you take any outside advice prior to making the application and was this helpful:

Was advice taken from...tick   *Was this helpful*

Land Agent/Surveyor	☐	Yes ☐	No ☐		
Planning Consultant	☐	Yes ☐	No ☐		
NFU	☐	Yes ☐	No ☐		
Non-professional (e.g. neighbour)	☐	Yes ☐	No ☐		
Other (Specify) [_____]		Yes ☐	No ☐		
None	☐	*Go to Question 55*			

54. What was the nature of this advice? *tick*

On farm meeting ☐

Other meeting ☐

Letter ☐

Telephone Conversation ☐

Other (specify) [_____]

55. Did you see, or try to obtain, any information about planning in the form of leaflets or guidance booklets?   Yes ☐ No ☐

If No go to Question 58

56. What was the title of these leaflets?

_____

_____

57. Did you find these leaflets useful?   Yes ☐ No ☐

58. Was contact made with the local planning authority before making the planning application and was this helpful:

Was advice taken from...tick   *Was this helpful*

Local authority planning officer/development control officer ☐   Yes ☐ No ☐

Local authority conservation officer ☐   Yes ☐ No ☐

Local authority farm liaison officer ☐   Yes ☐ No ☐

Local authority highways officer ☐   Yes ☐ No ☐

Unspecified (don't know who it was) ☐   Yes ☐ No ☐

Other (Specify) [_____] ☐   Yes ☐ No ☐

None ☐   *Go to Question 60*

59. What was the nature of this contact? *tick*

On farm meeting ☐

Off farm meeting ☐

Letter ☐

Telephone conversation ☐

Other (specify) [_____]

60. Other than you, who was involved in preparing the planning application? *Tick all that apply*

Land Agent/Surveyor ☐

Planning Consultant ☐

Architect ☐

NFU ☐

Other (Specify) [_____]

No-one ☐

61. Following the planning application did you have any further discussions with the local planning authority and were these helpful:

Was advice taken from...tick   *Was this helpful*

Local authority planning officer/development control officer ☐   Yes ☐   No ☐

Local authority conservation officer ☐   Yes ☐   No ☐

Local authority farm liaison officer ☐   Yes ☐   No ☐

Local authority highways officer ☐   Yes ☐   No ☐

Unspecified (don't know who it was) ☐   Yes ☐   No ☐

Other (Specify) [_____]   Yes ☐   No ☐

None ☐

62. Was there an appeal against the refusal?

No Appeal ☐   *GO TO Q64*

Public Inquiry ☐

Informal Hearing ☐

Written Representation ☐

63. Was advice taken for the appeal?

No advice ☐

Land Agent/Surveyor ☐

Planning Officer ☐

Planning Consultant ☐

NFU ☐

Other (Specify) ☐

64. Following the refusal, have you had any further discussions with the planning authority about the diversification proposal?   Yes ☐   No ☐
If No Go To Question 66

65. Have these discussions been helpful?   Yes ☐   No ☐

66. Do you think you are likely to submit a further planning application, either for a similar or different diversification scheme, in the foreseeable future?   Yes ☐   No ☐

SECTION END – GO TO SECTION 8

SECTION 6: NOT PROCEEDED

67. What type of diversification activity was considered? *[Read List if necessary] Tick*

Tourism	☐	Storage/Haulage	☐
Recreation	☐	Machinery/Vehicle Repair	☐
Retail (Farm shop and pick your own)	☐	Office/Studio	☐
Workshops	☐	Residential Lettings	☐
Agricultural Contracting	☐	Livery	☐
Manufacturing/Industry	☐	Energy (farm composting or wood fuel, NOT wind farms)	☐
Food Processing/Packing	☐	Other (specify) [_____]	

If more than one enterprise, say *"Please consider the most recent activity in the following questions"*

68. What type of development was involved? *[Read list if necessary] tick*

New buildings associated with a farm diversification activity ☐

Extension of an existing farm building ☐

Change of use of existing building ☐

Change of use of agricultural land ☐

Signs in support of a diversification activity ☐

Residential accommodation in support of farm diversification ☐

Other (specify) [_____]

69. What year did you consider this enterprise? [_____]

70. Did you take any outside advice and was this helpful:

Was advice taken from...tick		*Was this helpful*	
Land Agent/Surveyor	☐	Yes ☐ No ☐	
Planning Consultant	☐	Yes ☐ No ☐	
NFU	☐	Yes ☐ No ☐	
Non-professional (e.g. neighbour)	☐	Yes ☐ No ☐	
Other (Specify)	☐	Yes ☐ No ☐	
None	☐	*Go to Question 72*	

71. What was the nature of this advice? *tick*

On farm meeting ☐

Off farm meeting ☐

Letter ☐

Telephone conversation ☐

Other (specify) [_____]

72. Was contact made with the local planning authority and was this helpful:

Was advice taken from...tick   *Was this helpful*

Local authority planning officer/development control officer ☐   Yes ☐   No ☐

Local authority conservation officer ☐   Yes ☐   No ☐

Local authority farm liaison officer ☐   Yes ☐   No ☐

Local authority highways officer ☐   Yes ☐   No ☐

Unspecified (don't know who it was) ☐   Yes ☐   No ☐

Other (Specify) [＿＿＿＿＿＿＿＿＿＿＿]   Yes ☐   No ☐

None ☐   ***Go to Question 77***

73. What was the nature of this contact? *tick*

On farm meeting ☐

Off farm meeting ☐

Letter ☐

Telephone conversation ☐

Other (specify) [＿＿＿＿＿＿]

74. Did you see, or try to obtain, any information about planning in the form of leaflets   Yes ☐   No ☐
or guidance booklets?   ***If No go to Question 77***

75. What was the title of these leaflets?

_____

_____

76. Did you find these leaflets useful?   Yes ☐   No ☐

77. What was the reason for deciding not to proceed?

Discussions with local planning authority – conflict of policy   ☐

Attitude of local planning authority – helpful/sensible advice   ☐

Attitude of local planning authority – unhelpful/dismissive advice   ☐

Costs of Proceeding with Planning Application   ☐

Other Professional advice   ☐

Enterprise not feasible (detail)   ☐

Opposition from locals   ☐

Other (specify) [＿＿＿＿＿＿＿＿＿＿＿]

78. If the decision not to proceed was planning related was it in relation to? *[READ LIST]*

Highways and access (road safety) ☐

Traffic generation ☐

Noise/Pollution ☐

Local objection ☐

Contrary to environmental designated policy ☐

Site suitability ☐

Design & Suitability of Buildings/Land ☐

Other (specify) [_____]

79. At what stage did you decide not to proceed?

_____

SECTION END – GO TO SECTION 8

SECTION 7: CURRENTLY CONSIDERING

80. What type of diversification activity is being considered? *[Read List if necessary]* Tick

Tourism ☐   Storage/Haulage ☐

Recreation ☐   Machinery/Vehicle Repair ☐

Retail (Farm shop and pick your own) ☐   Office/Studio ☐

Workshops ☐   Residential Lettings ☐

Agricultural Contracting ☐   Livery ☐

Manufacturing/Industry ☐   Energy (farm composting or wood fuel, NOT wind farms) ☐

Food Processing/Packing ☐   Other (specify) [_____]

81. What type of development would be involved? *[Read list if necessary]* tick

New buildings associated with a farm diversification activity ☐

Extension of an existing farm building ☐

Change of use of existing building ☐

Change of use of agricultural land ☐

Signs in support of a diversification activity ☐

Residential accommodation in support of farm diversification ☐

Other (specify) [_____]

82. Have you take any outside advice and has this been helpful:

Was advice taken from...tick   *Was this helpful*

Land Agent/Surveyor ☐   Yes ☐   No ☐

Planning Consultant ☐   Yes ☐   No ☐

NFU ☐   Yes ☐   No ☐

Non-professional (e.g. neighbour) ☐   Yes ☐   No ☐

Other (Specify) ☐   Yes ☐   No ☐

None ☐   *Go to Question 84*

83. What was the nature of this advice?

On farm meeting ☐

Off farm meeting ☐

Letter ☐

Telephone conversation ☐

Other (specify) ☐

84. Has contact been made with the local planning authority and has this been helpful:

Was advice taken from...tick   *Was this helpful*

Local authority planning officer/development control officer ☐   Yes ☐   No ☐

Local authority conservation officer ☐   Yes ☐   No ☐

Local authority farm liaison officer ☐   Yes ☐   No ☐

Local authority highways officer ☐   Yes ☐   No ☐

Unspecified (don't know who it was) ☐   Yes ☐   No ☐

Other (Specify) ☐   Yes ☐   No ☐

None ☐   *Go to Question 86*

85. What was the nature of this contact?

On farm meeting ☐

Off farm meeting ☐

Letter ☐

Telephone conversation ☐

Other (specify) ☐

86. Have you seen, or tried to obtain, any information about planning in the form of leaflets or guidance booklets?   Yes ☐   No ☐

If No go to Section 8

87. What was the title of these leaflets?

_____

_____

88. Did you find these leaflets useful?   Yes ☐   No ☐

SECTION END – GO TO SECTION 8

SECTION 8: RESEARCH WORKSHOP

89. As part of this study we are carrying out a research workshop involving farmers in your area.
    Would you be willing for somebody to contact you about attending such a workshop?   Yes ☐   No ☐

If Yes – "Please could you give us your details so that we can contact you"

Name: _____

Address: _____

_____

_____

_____

Tel: _____

Fax: _____

email: _____

SECTION 9: RESEARCH WORKSHOP

90. Do you have any other brief comments about recent experience, positive or negative, of dealing with your local planning authority, whether on diversification proposals or other development?

_____

_____

_____

[IF RESPONDENT ASKS FOR CONTACT DETAILS GIVE TELEPHONE NUMBER 01285-889929 AND INDICATE THEY SHOULD ASK FOR GRAHAM SMITH OR, IN HIS ABSENCE, BILL HOWARD]

"That is the end of the survey. Thank you very much for your time and co-operation"

APPENDIX 4

Results of the farmer/landowner telephone interviews

Respondent Profile

A4.1   Of the 554 farmers contacted only 67 were available, fitted the criteria (i.e. had experience of a diversification enterprise) or were willing to complete the survey (Table 1).

Table 1: Farmers contacted and response rate for questionnaire

	Stratford	Maidstone	North Yorks	Total
Attempted	126	128	300	554
No Response	36	28	119	183
Refusals	29	25	38	92
No Planning Experience	41	45	126	212
Completed Questionnaire	20	30	17	67

A4.2   Of those that completed the questionnaire 58.2% of respondents had successfully submitted an application (although a number of those enterprises had not been implemented). A further 34.3% were either in the process of an application, or are currently considering submitting an application (Table 2).

Table 2: Profile of Respondents Involvement in Diversification Enterprise

	Stratford	Maidstone	North Yorks	Total
Successful Planning Application	14	15	10	39
In the Process of an Application	2	6	4	12
Unsuccessful Planning Application	1	1	0	2
Considered an Enterprise but not Proceeded	0	2	1	3
Currently Considering	3	6	2	11

A4.3   It can be seen from Table 2 that only three respondents had considered a diversification enterprise but had decided against proceeding with an application. The low number of respondents in this category suggests that very few farmers are being put-off applying for planning permission, or that those that have been put-off did not wish to complete the questionnaire. The number of respondents who have had permission refused is also very low. Other research by Royal Agricultural College Enterprise has shown that respondents who have an opinion or a grievance about such an issue tend to complete surveys of this type. The existence of barriers that prevent farmers pursuing a potential diversification scheme will be examined further in the research workshops.

A4.4   Figure 1 shows the farm size profile for those that completed the questionnaire. This varies from the June 1999 MAFF census figures for the UK (Table 3), with a lower percentage of small farmers. This could be due to a number of reasons:

● Farmers in the smaller size classes are less likely to answer telephone surveys (because, for example, they are part-time or let the land to a larger holding)

● Farmers in the smaller size classes are not involved in diversification

● The lists used to collate the sample do not cover smaller holdings

Figure 1: Farm Size Profile of Respondents

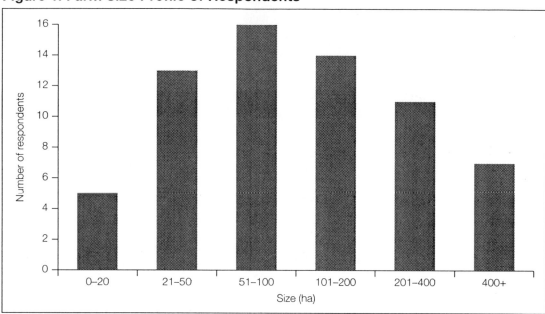

Table 3: Percent of holdings and land within size classes, England 1999 (From MAFF June 1999 census)

Size (ha)	Per Cent of Holdings	Per Cent of Land
0-20	45.3%	5.3%
21-50	21.1%	11.2%
51-100	16.1%	18.5%
101-200	11.0%	24.6%
201-500	5.4%	25.8%
500+	1.1%	14.6%

A4.5   Figure 2 shows the agricultural enterprises managed by the respondents. The majority of those that completed the questionnaire had an arable enterprise, the second most common enterprises being beef and lamb. Dairy is under-represented, and a higher than expected number of fruit growers are included. This is perhaps as a result of the importance of farm diversification in these sectors.

A4.6   Figure 3 shows that nearly all of the respondents were owners of the land, and only a small number were tenants. Again this could be a function of the sample, but this has not been evident in other work that has used the same data source. It may be more likely that tenant farmers are less prepared to enter into a diversification enterprise.

Figure 2: Respondent enterprises

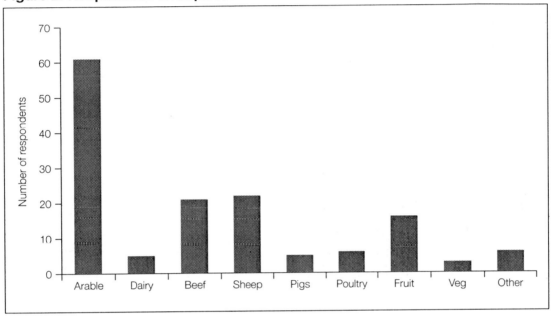

Figure 3: Management of holding

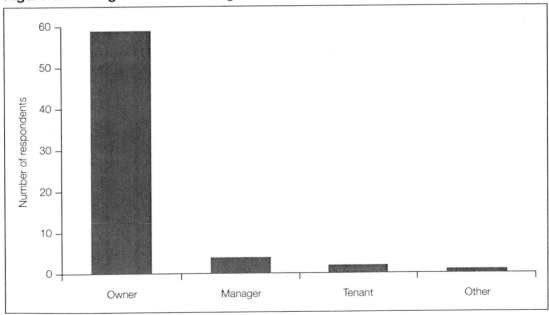

Profile of diversification schemes

Table 4: Types of diversification and development

	Stratford	Maidstone	North Yorks	Total
Type of Diversification				
Tourism	2	6	11	19
Recreation	2	1	0	3
Retail	2	0	5	7
Workshops	2	7	2	11
Agricultural Contracting	1	0	0	1
Manufacturing/Industry	2	2	1	5
Food Processing/Packing	1	2	1	4
Storage/Haulage	3	4	1	8
Machinery/vehicle repair	3	0	1	4
Office/studio	0	9	3	12
Residential lettings	2	9	3	14
Livery	1	4	2	7
Energy	0	0	0	0
Other	2	0	2	4
TOTAL	**23**	**44**	**32**	**99**
Type of Development				
New Buildings	0	5	4	9
Extension of Buildings	1	3	1	5
Change of use of buildings	15	21	19	55
Change of use of land	3	4	2	9
Signs	4	3	2	9
Residential accommodation	0	0	0	0
Other	0	1	0	1
TOTAL	**23**	**37**	**28**	**88**

A4.7 Table 4 shows the types of diversification activity and types of development covered by Section 3 – 7 of the questionnaire amalgamated. It should be noted that most respondents gave more than one response to this question. The most common type of diversification activity was tourism (19.2%) followed by residential lettings (14.1%) and office/studio (12.1%). There are, however, significant differences between the areas. For example, in the North Yorks area over 34% of the diversification activities include a tourism element, whereas in Maidstone the most common type of diversification would appear to be residential letting and office/studios. In the Stratford area there appears to be a greater range of enterprises considered. The great majority of developments considered were for the change of use of buildings (62.5%) compared to 10.2% for the erection of new buildings. It is noteworthy that of the nine developments involving new buildings, none were located in the Stratford area. It should also be noted that none of the respondents discussed residential accommodation as a type of development, suggesting that all those enterprises that involved residential lettings required a change of use of building rather than new building.

A4.8 The following analysis concentrates only on that group of farmers who currently have successfully completed a planning application and received permission (39 in total), although each respondent often consulted more than one expert. The analysis of the other groups is not considered appropriate due to the small numbers, and the fact that the respondents were at various stages of consideration or application, leading to potential confusion in the interpretation of the data. The very small size of the contacted group that decided not to proceed with an application means that the data cannot be further analysed.

Advice prior to and subsequent to planning application

A4.9   Table 5 shows the number of respondents who took advice prior to making the application, from whom they took that advice, and the proportion who stated that the advice was helpful.

Table 5: Advice taken prior to submitting an application (not LPA)

Source of Advice	Stratford		Maidstone		North Yorks		Total	
	No.	found helpful	No.	found helpful	No.	found helpful	No.	found helpful
Land Agent/Surveyor	1	100%	7	86%	1	100%	9	89%
Planning Consultant	7	100%	6	67%	3	67%	16	81%
NFU	2	100%	3	100%	2	100%	7	100%
Architect	1	0%	1	100%	4	100%	6	83%
Non-professional	2	100%	3	67%	3	67%	8	75%
Other	2	0%	7	71%	4	25%	13	50%
None	2	n/a	0	n/a	1	n/a	3	n/a

A4.10   This shows that the majority of those considering an enterprise took advice prior to making the application. Only three said they took no advice. The most popular source of advice is a planning consultant, except in Maidstone where the Land Agent/Surveyor was considered most important. In general the applicant felt the advice given at this stage was helpful. Table 6 shows that in most cases this advice involved an on-farm meeting, with telephone contact, letters and other meetings being less common.

Table 6: Nature of advice taken prior to application (not LPA)

Nature of Advice	Stratford	Maidstone	North Yorks	Total
On Farm Meeting	79%	80%	100%	85%
Other Meeting	7%	33%	30%	23%
Letter	21%	33%	30%	28%
Telephone Conversation	29%	80%	70%	59%

A4.11   Table 7 shows that a high proportion of applicants also took advice from the LPA prior to submitting an application, with the majority speaking to the planning officer. The second most consulted person was the highways officer, although this was mostly in the Stratford area. In most cases the advice from the LPA was considered to be useful. Care needs to be taken in interpreting some of the percentages quoted due to the low number of responses. Of the 35 farmers who had contact with the LPA prior to submitting their application, 29 took the advice in the form of a meeting at the farm, and 4 arranged meetings at a site other than the farm. This suggests that the advice given was substantial.

Table 7: No. of applicants taking pre- application advice from the LPA

Source of Advice	Stratford		Maidstone		North Yorks		Total	
	No.	found helpful	No.	found helpful	No.	found helpful	No.	found helpful
Planning Officer	11	73%	11	82%	9	78%	31	74%
Conservation Officer	2	100%	2	100%	0	-	4	100%
Farm Liaison Officer	0	-	1	100%	0	-	1	100%
Highways Officer	5	100%	1	0%	1	100%	7	86%
Unspecified	0	-	3	33%	1	100%	4	50%
Other	0	-	2	50%	2	50%	4	50%
None	2	n/a	2	n/a	0	n/a	4	n/a

Making a planning application

A4.12 The majority (35 of the 39) of those applying for planning permission involved outside advice in completing their application. The most commonly used source of assistance was an architect, but land agents and planning consultants were also typically used (Table 8). It is not uncommon for the applicant to consult more than one source of advice.

Table 8: Who is involved in making the planning application

Source of Advice	Stratford	Maidstone	North Yorks	Total
Land Agent/Surveyor	3	5	3	11
Planning Consultant	4	5	1	10
NFU	1	2	0	3
Architect	6	2	8	16
Non-professional	0	1	3	4
Other	3	5	1	9
None	3	0	0	3

Contact with the LPA after making a planning application

A4.13 Table 9 shows the frequency of contact by applicants with different LPA officers following the submission of the planning application. This shows that a large number of applicants retained contact with the authorities, mostly with the planning officer, but also with the highways officer (especially in the Stratford region), only 15% saying they had no subsequent dealings with the LPA. However, the percentage of those who felt the advice or information given was helpful was lower than when contact was made prior to the application. This can possibly be related to some of the responses given in the final comments section, when many respondents suggested that the planning authorities were 'contradictory' or were 'flexing their muscles'.

Table 9: Contact with the LPA following the application

Source of Advice	Stratford		Maidstone		North Yorks		Total	
	No.	found helpful	No.	found helpful	No.	found helpful	No.	found helpful
Planning Officer	11	46%	8	63%	3	33%	22	50%
Conservation Officer	2	50%	1	0%	0	-	3	33%
Farm Liaison Officer	0	-	3	0%	0	-	3	0%
Highways Officer	4	75%	3	0%	1	100%	8	50%
Unspecified	1	100%	2	100%	1	0%	4	75%
Other	0	-	1	100%	1	100%	2	100%
None	1	n/a	1	n/a	4	n/a	6	n/a

Conditions placed on planning permission

A4.14 All but four of the permissions granted had conditions, other than the standard time conditions, placed on them. Many of these related to highways and parking, seasonality of letting, and appearance of the building or landscaping. Of those respondents, 66% felt that these conditions were acceptable. A common reason for feeling the conditions were unreasonable came from believing that the planning department may not understand the situation fully. For example: 'when the buildings were in agricultural use we were doing more of activities [more traffic] than will be, but now restricted'. Additionally, in some cases the respondents felt that restrictions on future ownership were unhelpful in terms of inheritance "unable to split the farm to pass onto children, as the title of the cottage could not be separate".

General comments on the planning system

A4.15 The final section of the questionnaire asked for general comments on the planning authorities and the farmer's dealings with them. Of the 58 respondents who made a comment 18 said they found the LPAs helpful, or that they had a positive experience. The comment was often made that the situation was made better if the authorities were involved in the early stages, or if a third party was used for the dealings. A range of negative comments were given related to dealings with the LPAs, most of these are unsurprising – 10 respondents said that the LPA was inflexible, six said that the process took too much time, and four felt they were receiving contradictory messages, three said the process was too expensive and a further nine also had negative experiences. The respondents often mentioned that they felt that the LPAs were less interested in the small applications, and only wanted to deal with the big developers. If this is true then it is certainly something that should be of concern relating to farm diversification. A full list of (verbatim) comments is attached. (Table 10). The highlighted cells are the comments of those farmers that considered an application, but did not pursue it. Due to the nature of the sampling technique there may be some comments that do not relate directly to the correct LPA.

Table 10: Individual comments made by farmers regarding the planning system

Area	Comment
Stratford	Positive. Planners are sticking to the book/don't help through the process. Natural reaction is NO until you ask, then they start to think – not flexible enough
	Applied 4 times before getting permission. It is a lottery and if your face fits
	Negative, plans vary from barn conversion to barn conversion
	Positive – everyone involved was helpful in getting project going. Negative – when applying to a building adjacent to all other buildings, unhelpful
	Have not put enough money into project. Applied for a grant but did not succeed. Therefore, have not started work
	Positive, but planning officer on holiday for two weeks and no-one else to deal with. Public meeting held during this period which was difficult – inflexible
	Length of time to deal with application
	Very slow
	Govt encouraging diversification BUT planners difficult to deal with and cause difficulties
	Presumption that diversification will go ahead but LPA not always co-operative
	To go to appeal is a massive undertaking (experience on another project) relevant professionals in consulting and planning bought in + MP & NFU (project to raise height of roof of buildings)
	Govt need to change planning directive 1995/1997. Temp permissions. Planning officers need more flexible tier system
	Negative
	With Perseverance and keeping a civil tongue usually get what you want
North Yorks	Hope they will be more helpful rather than restrictive or negative.
	Had trouble with LPA as they seemed to behave in a contradictory manner and were very strict – inflexible
	No problem with planning as very close to village and the authorities wanted houses on the land anyway.
	Very obstructive and exceedingly slow and have hanged minds on restrictions on extension to original shop which will stick
	Friends of theirs were being bullied – ridiculous behaviour Plus more "flexing of muscles" & flat refusals rather than negotiating/considering and offering helpful advice
	Positive Experience
	(National Park Planning) Do the opposite to what you want
	Positive Experience
	Hard going different planning views depending on who you are. (National Parks)
	Matter of Speed trying to swim through treacle, go around and around.
	Spoke to National Park Planning Authority about having electricity – no grant available
	National Parks helpful except listed buildings. Head in sand when it comes to keeping listed building in use/repair
	Not easy to deal with and Planners are very inflexible (e.g. a tied cottage – won't reassess worker only status to allow him to let it out). Use hard rules rather than considering options and using discretion.
	Found him to act as though "flexing muscles", "I am God". Not willing to enter into discussions/negotiations.

Area	Comment
	They have chicken houses on land which the village is growing around and are having difficulty with planning and developing this block.
	10 years ago found them OK as she went to them early in process
	Had no problems – were not very slow
	Didn't get as far as putting in application, but LPA said they did not have a problem with what was planned for site
	National Park Authorities – very difficult to deal with. People have to find things out for themselves rather than providing the information. Holiday cottages are everywhere and market is flooded but that is all the authorities will allow planning for
Maidstone	They do seem to want to keep same regime going – no new buildings in countryside. Seem to be prepared to work alongside big developers, but not smaller individual enterprises. Also tend to pull out book and refer to 'old decision' rather than reviewing current situation
	At time when farming is bad and P.M is saying "have to diversify" – should be more amenable. Process is very long & have to work hard at it. Took 2yrs to get permission.
	Problems with SEEDA grants, builders do not want to take on tight schedule
	LPA etc could not think of anything to do with now redundant buildings. Not in suitable area for B&B not enough traffic for passing trade
	Had difficulty/refusal for building house for son on farm – came up with very unreasonable proposals and had to go for more expensive option of buying a cottage elsewhere. (This was many years ago) were more reasonable with use of existing buildings
	People want BIG SPACE. Guidelines are too stringent and should be eased so that, for example, old buildings can be used economically
	Quite happy with process, has been on parish council for 30 years
	They have been very positive although very slow – overall happy with progress
	Don't be scared of them – within reason they are quite helpful
	Very Helpful
	Have difficulty making up their mind about what they are trying to achieve – mixed from central government
	In light of new guidelines – they will be hopefully looking with new eyes. Thinks on the whole (senior planning officers at least) take a fairly sensible view.
	---- Borough Council – rated worst in paper had dealings for 30 yrs. Never had recommendation for approval. Appealed 3-4times. Delaying tactics, but never lost a case – what does that say about councillors. Never bother to read evidence properly
	Have been involved several times, has always consulted planning officers at earliest possible stage. Like to be asked advice, will stop you going down blind alley and will offer alternative ideas/solutions
	Like most councils, not very helpful
	Surprisingly simple – had a good person allocated to case
	LPA pain in neck – not at all helpful. Have only ever offered farmers markets & in all dealings with them has had to spend lots of money
	Not helpful – unbelievably slow – telling regulators and negative aspects rather than being supportive or putting forward useful advice
	If goes to appeal – costs more money which is good for council. "They are really up against it"
	Very hard to deal with – not helpful advice, drag the process out to get more money he can ill afford to spend. (Process is expensive and time consuming)
	Not for the individual – need good professional support

Area	Comment
	Have yet to implement, but if building regs too onerous may need to revise application for different use. May have to look at heating issue. Feel that planning dept have too much control, should lie more with local and parish councillors
	Obstructive in the process, message isn't filtering down (to aid diversification) from upper level government
	Quite helpful if you involve them at an early stage. By same token, don't know how they will react to this plan.
	Not as yet – is considering holiday lets perhaps in the future. (For Farm buildings)

Conclusions of the telephone survey

A4.16 The survey reveals that only a very small number of farmers feel that the planning system is a major barrier to beginning a farm diversification enterprise. If farmers did feel there was a significant issue, especially if it had affected them individually, then it is likely that they would have wanted to express an opinion. However, this would not appear to be the case.

A4.17 The survey, however, cannot be considered to entirely disprove the hypothesis that farmers find the planning system to be a barrier to farm diversification, as this was not its purpose. There are a number of reasons that the survey is not adequate for this purpose, despite using sound methodologies:

- The sample size is small (although the number of holdings in the LPA areas are not readily available, the MAFF June Census (1999) shows 2,489 holdings in Warwickshire, 4,103 in Kent and 8,521 in North Yorkshire, thus the coverage of the survey was only 3.6% (5.0% in Warwickshire, 3.0% in Kent and 3.5% in N Yorks) in these counties). If we consider those that actually fully completed the questionnaire then the proportion is reduced to 0.4%. In order to reduce the level of error in the results to below 5% a sample size of 500 (completing the questionnaire) is required. If the response rate from this survey is extrapolated, a total of 6,000 farmers would be need to be contacted. Robustness of the survey could also be increased by surveying more LPAs.

- The survey was structured in such a way that farmers who did not have experience of planning and diversification were not interrogated. This means that it is not possible to carry out a complete analysis of the sample to ensure that it was appropriate (i.e. we cannot compare the farm structure of those with and without diversification experience to see whether the sample used is representative of the farming community)

A4.18 It should be emphasised, however, that out of the 280 farmers spoken to only 3 (1.1%) had not pursued an enterprise that they had considered. Of those three only one stated that the reason they had not pursued the application was planning related. In addition, further evidence collected via the workshops (described elsewhere), supported the findings of the telephone survey.

A4.19 The comments from respondents do show that there is evidence of problems in the planning system. These were further analysed in the stakeholder and farmer workshops.

A4.20 It may be true that the planning system is a perceived problem, and that farmers may not seriously consider an enterprise with this being one of the reasons. However, such farmers may not have had any contact with the LPAs to discuss this. It is unlikely that this group would want to complete the questionnaire. For example, a number of respondents who said they had not considered an enterprise (and therefore did not complete the questionnaire) qualified the response saying they 'had not seriously considered' an enterprise, and as such did not want to complete the questionnaire. A more detailed analysis of this group may be of interest, but at the same time accessing them would prove difficult.

Agent and farmer workshops

A4.21   In order to discuss the issues in more depth two research workshops were held in each region. The first was for 'stakeholders', who had experience of a wide range of planning applications and dealings with the LPAs. Those attending these workshops were generally land agents, NFU and CLA representatives and planning consultants. The second workshop was for farmers themselves who had experience of farmer diversification enterprises that required planning permission. The invited attendees of these workshops were taken from the responses of the telephone survey. For the stakeholder survey between six and ten people were invited, and for the farmer workshops between nine and twelve farmers were invited (and agreed to attend). Unfortunately, for a number of reasons the attendance at some of the workshops was poor (Table 11). In the case of the farmer workshop in N Yorks, this is probably due to the large size of the area, the very bad weather at the time and farmers not wishing to travel long distances – despite having agreed to. In order to get a better understanding of the issues involved from the stakeholders, a series of telephone interviews were carried out subsequent to the workshops. The results of these workshops and telephone calls are reported in the main report.

Table 11: Dates and number of attendees at research workshops

Region	Date	Number of Stakeholders	Additional stakeholder telephone interviews	Number of Farmers
Maidstone	27 November 2000	4	1	9
Stratford	29 November 2000	3	2	9
North Yorks	4 December 2000	3	3	2

APPENDIX 5
Plans reviewed

Regional Planning Guidance

Region	Extant RPG	Review document examined
North East	RPG7 1993	Draft Regional Planning Guidance for the North East, Association of North East Councils, May 1999
North West	RPG13 1996	People, Places & Prosperity, Draft Regional Planning Guidance for the North West, North West Regional Assembly July 2000
Yorkshire & Humberside	RPG12 1996	Advancing Together, Towards a Spatial Strategy, Regional Assembly for Yorkshire & Humberside, Draft 1999
West Midlands	RPG11 1998	none
East Midlands	RPG8 1994	Draft Regional Planning Guidance for the Spatial Development of the East Midlands, East Midlands Regional Local Government Association, Public Examination Draft 1999
East of England	RPG6 2000	none
South West	RPG10 1994	Draft Regional Planning Guidance for the South West, South West Regional Planning Conference, Consultation Draft 2000
South East	RPG9 1994	Draft Regional Planning Guidance for the South East, GOSE, GOEE, GO for London, March 2000

Structure Plans

Plan	Status	Date
Cheshire 2011 Replacement Structure Plan	Adopted	1999
Replacement Cornwall Structure Plan	Adopted	1997
Derby and Derbyshire Joint Structure Plan	Written Statement and Proposed Modifications	2000
County Durham Structure Plan 1991-2006	Adopted	1999
East Sussex and Brighton and Hove Structure Plan 1991-2011	Adopted	1999
Hampshire County Structure Plan Review	Adopted	2000
Kent Structure Plan	Adopted	1996
Lancashire Structure Plan	Adopted	1997
Leicestershire Structure Plan	Deposit Draft and Explanatory Memorandum	2000
Lincolnshire Structure Plan Deposit Draft	Proposed Modifications and Proposed Further Modifications	2000
Norfolk Structure Plan	Adopted	1999
Northumberland Structure Plan	Adopted	1996
North Yorkshire County Structure Plan	Adopted	1995
Somerset and Exmoor National Park Joint Structure Plan Review	Adopted	2000
Warwickshire Structure Plan	Deposit Draft and First Modifications	2000
Worcestershire Structure Plan	Deposit Draft	2000

Local Plans

Plan	Status	Date
Bath & North East Somerset Council Local Plan	Written Statement Adopted	1997
Wansdyke District Council Local Plan	Written Statement Deposit Version	1995
Basingstoke & Deane Borough Council Local Plan 1991 – 2001	Adopted	1998
Blaby District Council Local Plan	Written Statement Adopted	1999
Berwick upon Tweed District Council Local Plan	Proposed Modifications Adopted	1999
Caradon District Council Local Plan	Proposed Modifications Adopted	1999
	Deposit Version Adopted	1994
Eastleigh Borough Council Local Plan 1991 – 2001	Adopted	1997
East Lindsey District Council Local Plan	Alteration adopted	1999
Ellesmere Port & Neston Borough Council	Deposit Draft	1998
	Proposed Modifications	2000
Exmoor National Park Authority Local Plan	Written Statement Adopted	1997
Harrogate Borough Council District Local Plan	Deposit Draft incorporating Proposed Modifications	2000
Maidstone Borough Council – Borough Wide Local Plan	Deposit Draft	1997
North Norfolk District Council Local Plan	Adopted	1998
North York Moors National Park Authority Local Plan	Deposit Draft	1999
Peak District National Park Authority Local Plan	Provisionally adopted	1999
Ribble Valley Borough Council – District Wide Local Plan	Adopted	1998
Sedgemoor District Council – District Local Plan 1991 – 2011 Sedgemoor District Council Cheddar Area Local Plan Sedgemoor District Council Bridgwater Area Local Plan	Revised Deposit Draft Adopted Adopted	2000 1994 1995
Stratford-on-Avon District Local Plan	Adopted	2000
Warwick District Council – Warwick District Local Plan	Adopted	1995
Wealden District Council Local Plan	Adopted	1998
West Lancashire District Council Local Plan	Adopted	2000
Wychavon District Council Local Plan	Adopted	1998

APPENDIX 6

Applications database structure

DATABASE OF PLANNING APPLICATIONS

Planning register details (all applications)

1. Reference number of application

2. Name and address of applicant and, if applicable, agent

3. Site address, if different

4. Description of development

5. Diversification activity:

   - tourism
   - recreation
   - retail (farm shop)
   - workshop
   - manufacturing/industry
   - food processing
   - storage/haulage
   - machinery/vehicle repair
   - office/studio
   - energy
   - equestrian/livery
   - other

6. Type of development

   - new building
   - extension of an existing building
   - building re-use
   - change of use of land
   - residential accommodation in support of farm diversification
   - signage
   - other

7. Planning decision

   - Withdrawn
   - Approved with conditions
   - Approved subject to S106
   - Refused

8. Date of decision/withdrawal

9.   Appeal decision (where applicable)

Additional details (all applications) – unlikely to be on the planning register

10. Date of submission

11. Who determined:

- Committee
- Delegated decision

12. Officer recommendation to Committee

- Approve with conditions
- Refuse
- Approve with conditions and S106

13.a Conditions imposed

- number of employees
- noise/sound proofing
- parking
- limits on type of tools/no power tools
- access/traffic
- occupational restrictions eg only to be let to tourists
- design/materials
- improve appearance of existing building (PPG7)
- (residential) completion of enterprise prior to residential occupation
- restrictions on future extensions/growth (PPG 7)
- removal of Part 2 Permitted Development Rights
- landscaping/screening
- removal of Part 6 Permitted Development Rights (PPG 7)
- restrictions on activities/use
- personal permission/occupancy
- limits on operating hours
- tying the building to the land of the holding (PPG 7)
- limits on use of internal space
- limits on use of external space
- other

13.b Reasons for refusal

- not appropriate within designated area
- non structural suitability of building for re-use
- inappropriate development in the countryside
- relationship to neighbours
- landscape/visual impact
- noise
- other environmental impacts (wildlife habitats/trees etc)
- highway safety eg dangerous entrance
- traffic generation
- size of building
- sustainable transport issues
- over intensification/cumulative impact
- other
- retail issues

13.c Use of S106 Agreements

- tying building or land use to the remainder of the unit
- use/occupancy of building
- traffic/highways issue
- financial contribution (memo box for type of contribution)
- other

14. Planning application fee

15. Date of appeal submission (if applicable)

16. Appeal decision

- appeal conditions imposed (repeat 13 a)
- reasons for refusal (repeat 13 b)
- Section 106 agreements required (repeat 13 c)

Additional details for sample applications (from case files)

17. Pre-application advice discussions

- Yes/No
- Comments box (who was the consultation between/issues involved?)

18. Summary of proposal

- Comments box (i.e. what the application is for, including area covered by the application; floorspace created; likely number of employees; car parking spaces to be provided.)
- In the case of building re-use, involving:
    - a traditional farm building
    - a modern farm building

19. History of site/building

- Comments box

20. Location/Accessibility

- Within or on the edge of a settlement
- Within 5 miles of a town
- Within 5 miles of A road
- Part of farmstead in open country
- Isolated building in open country
- Land in open country
- Other

21. Relationship to farm unit

- Within or on the edge of active farmstead on active farm unit (same ownership)
- Within or on the edge of redundant or largely redundant farmstead on active farm unit (same ownership)
- Other building on active farm unit (same ownership)
- Land forming part of active farm unit
- In building(s) sold away from the farm i.e. no longer forming part of an active farm
- On land sold away from the farm i.e. no longer forming part of an active farm unit

22. Applicant

- Farmer/landowner
- Farm manager
- Tenant farmer
- Land agent
- Developer
- Private business enterprise
- Other

23. Specialist advice sought by the LPA

- Comment box

24. Designations

- within World Heritage Site
- within Green Belt
- within National Park
- within AONB
- within local Landscape Designation eg AGLV
- within Conservation Area
- within a listed building
- on Best and Most Versatile Land
- within/adjacent to RAMSAR site, SAC, SPA
- within/adjacent to National Nature Reserve/SSSI/Local Nature Reserve
- within/adjacent to an ancient woodland
- affecting a scheduled ancient monument or site of archaeological interest
- other

25. Summary of key planning issues

- landscape/visual impact
- design/appearance
- other environmental issues
- traffic generation
- sustainable transport issues
- noise

- intensification/cumulative impact
- size/scale
- neighbours
- other
- Comment box

26. Summary of representations received

- number of representations
- landscape/visual impact
- design/appearance
- other environmental issues

- intensification/cumulative impact
- size/scale
- neighbours
- other

APPENDIX 7

Application details by local authority

Table 1: Farm diversification applications and outcome recorded for each local planning authority

	Total Applications (incl. Withdrawn etc)	Withdrawn	Applications Determined (=100%)			
			Approved		Refused	
Basingstoke and Deane	62	9	42	67.7%	9	14.5%
Bath and N E Somerset	15	2	6	40.0%	5	33.3%
Berwick upon Tweed	22	0	19	86.4%	1	4.5%
Blaby	25	0	17	68.0%	3	12.0%
Caradon	23	1	19	82.6%	2	8.7%
East Lindsey	41	2	30	73.2%	9	22.0%
Eastleigh	27	1	16	59.3%	9	33.3%
Ellesmere Port and Neston	21	0	11	52.4%	8	38.1%
Exmoor National Park	53	0	49	92.5%	4	7.5%
Harrogate	60	6	45	75.0%	8	13.3%
Maidstone	70	0	42	60.0%	27	38.6%
North Norfolk	128	4	101	78.9%	10	7.8%
North York Moors National Park	139	6	111	79.9%	22	15.8%
Peak National Park	125	9	99	79.2%	15	12.0%
Ribble Valley	38	4	29	76.3%	3	7.9%
Sedgemoor	44	4	32	72.7%	8	18.2%
Stratford on Avon	162	21	119	73.5%	19	11.7%
Warwick	71	5	51	71.8%	15	21.1%
Wealden	89	11	69	77.5%	9	10.1%
West Lancashire	80	9	62	77.5%	8	10.0%
Wychavon	102	6	70	68.6%	26	25.5%
Total	**1397**	**100**	**1039**		**220**	

Table 2: Farm diversification applications by population and geographical area of each local planning authority

	Total Applications	District population (1991 Census)	Applications per 10000 population	District area (hectares)	Applications per 1000 hectares
Basingstoke and Deane	62	144,790	4.28	63,411	0.98
Bath and N E Somerset	15	158,692	0.95	35,112	0.43
Berwick on Tweed	22	26,731	8.23	97,606	0.23
Blaby	25	82,700	3.02	13,043	1.92
Caradon	23	76,516	3.01	66,407	0.35
East Lindsey	41	116,957	3.51	176,201	0.23
Eastleigh	27	105,999	2.55	7,967	3.39
Ellesmere Port and Neston	21	80,873	2.60	8,800	2.39
Exmoor National Park	53	10,494	50.51	69,147	0.77
Harrogate	60	143,526	4.18	132,089	0.45
Maidstone	70	136,209	5.14	39,368	1.78
North Norfolk	128	90,461	14.15	96,614	1.32
North York Moors National Park	139	25,500	54.51	143,474	0.97
Peak National Park	125	38,000	32.89	143,734	0.87
Ribble Valley	38	51,767	7.34	58,444	0.65
Sedgemoor	44	97,763	4.50	56,775	0.77
Stratford on Avon	162	105,586	15.34	97,740	1.66
Warwick	71	116,299	6.10	28,253	2.51
Wealden	89	130,214	6.83	83,659	1.06
West Lancashire	80	107,978	7.41	33,165	2.41
Wychavon	102	101,716	10.03	66,612	1.53

APPENDIX 8
Case studies

INDEX

Approved by Local Planning Authority
Equestrian:

1. Erection of 292m² stable block with staff living accommodation in a field next to an ex indoor riding school.

2. Use of existing land and buildings for livery, including extension to existing barn to accommodate stables and provision of sand paddock.

Typical Examples of Future (Non-Traditional) Types of Diversification:

3. Conversion of barn and outbuildings to B1(a) use.

4. Change of use of existing out-building to farm shop to sell own produce and related produce from neighbouring site.

5. Conversion of existing redundant traditional farm buildings to provide a business complex.

Large Scale/Expansion:

6. Change of use of existing farm buildings to craft workshops, plus the use of one unit for plant sales.

Other:

7. Change of use from agriculture to grow and buy in plants, trees and accessories to sell from the farm, specialising in wild plants and flowers.

8. Change of use of existing agricultural barn to use as an agricultural engineer's workshop and wrought iron workshop.

Recommended for Refusal but Approved

9. Change of use of redundant agricultural building to three offices/stores.

Refused and then Approved on Appeal

10. Change of use of agricultural building (modern calf-rearing unit) to a general storage facility.

Refused by Local Planning Authority – Appeal Dismissed

11. Change of use of three redundant modern steel and asbestos agricultural buildings to class B1 uses including 35 car parking spaces.

12. Proposed change of use of existing modern barn to industrial units class B1 and B8.

Approved by local planning authority

Equestrian

CASE STUDY 1:

Approved by local planning authority

Farm size and status: County Council Smallholding Tenanted farm of 25 hectares plus 28 hectares private farm, near Leicester. Within 5 miles of an A road, and 5 miles of a settlement.

Main enterprise: Council Smallholding: wheat and grass for hay. Land owned: not cultivated/developed into caravan storage park, golf course, stables and indoor arena, which is now used as industrial units.

Length of occupation: Tenant since 1969 on Agricultural Holdings Act Tenancy. Bought private land in 1977.

Tenure: Owner–occupier and tenant.

Type of diversification: Erection of 292m² stable block with staff living accommodation in a field next to an ex indoor riding school.

Date: Application: 11/08/1998
Approval: 28/09/1998

Site history and reasons for diversification: The site lies on the edge of Leicester. The applicant first erected a stable block in 1980 on land in their ownership. In 1990-91 planning permission was granted for the construction of an indoor arena for animal shows and competitions. This was implemented. Based on an agricultural exemption, the rates for this were £200 a month, but increased to £600 a month when it was clarified that the agricultural exemption did not apply. The requirement for back payments left the applicant with a debt of £12,000. This, plus the new business rate, forced the applicant to start up a summer riding school with an instructor living on site in a mobile home. The applicant went on to apply for planning permission to put up more permanent accommodation for the instructor. This was refused, and an enforcement notice served to remove the mobile home. With this, the riding school was no longer viable and so the applicant converted the indoor arena into industrial units, following planning approval in 1998. Prior to this, in 1995 planning permission had been granted to erect a stable block on the same footprint as the case study proposal, but without residential accommodation.

The planning process: The applicant used an agent to make the application on his behalf and found this invaluable in terms of complying with building regulations etc. There were pre-application site visits from both the Highways Authority and LPA, which were helpful. The Highways Authority recommended that the access should be via the new road serving the industrial units, while the LPA advised that a new stable block with ancillary accommodation was acceptable, taking into account the outstanding planning consent for a stable block given in 1995. Planning permission was granted subject to conditions restricting the occupation of the accommodation to employees of the equestrian use and removing permitted development rights for extensions.

Other factors: Although the applicant was satisfied with the planning process for the most recent planning application, he felt that more generally the planning system had backfired. If ancillary accommodation for the indoor arena had been allowed in the first place, then the arena would not have been converted into industrial units, and there would have been no need for the most recent planning application. Thus the building which is being erected now could have been avoided, helping to retain the open aspect of the Green Wedge which was the LPAs primary concern. In general, the applicant thought that planning Committees should be de-politicised.

Effects of diversification: The stable block has just started to be erected. Upon completion it will house the applicant's son, who will work with the stables and also on the farm. Therefore no extra employment will be created as a result. It will also account for a very small percentage of the applicant's overall income, taking account of the considerable diversification that has already taken place on the applicant's land.

Conclusion: This application demonstrates effective use of an agent and pre-application discussions with the Local Planning Authority, leading to a positive decision in less than seven weeks. The only area of concern is the apparent lack of clear communication between the Local Planning Authority and applicant about coordination of wider activities on the site.

CASE STUDY 2

Approved by local planning authority

Farm size and status: 13 hectares in North West England, redundant farm. On the edge of a settlement and just over 5 miles from an A road.

Main enterprise: Some land is let for sheep grazing, but the farm is now entirely used as a livery.

Length of occupation: One and a half years.

Tenure: Owner–occupier

Type of diversification: Use of existing land and buildings for livery, including extension to existing barn to accommodate stables and provision of sand paddock.

Date: Application: 28/10/1999
          Approval: 02/03/2000

Site history and reasons for diversification: The applicant bought the property with a view to converting it to a livery, there was never an intention to retain it as a working farm.

The planning process: The applicants employed a planning consultant to deal with their application. They felt the consultant was helpful and resulted in the application being dealt with much more quickly than would have been the case if they had made the application themselves. The applicants had been in contact with the LPA about three times prior to the application, seeking advice on the suitability of various properties the applicants were considering buying for conversion to a livery. A planning officer was also contacted about this specific application. The applicants felt the planning officers were generally not very helpful, were discouraging of diversification proposals and asked more questions than offered advice, although they felt the planning officer was more positive about this application after a site visit had been made. The concerns of the planning officers appear to have related wholly to the farm's location in the Green Belt and the potential impacts of the proposed activity on the Green Belt. This is reflected in the committee report, which makes no mention of agricultural or diversification policy. The applicants felt that the mismatch between the very negative and discouraging pre-application advice from planning officers, and the relative ease of obtaining planning permission was a common problem. Modifications to the application were requested by the LPA regarding the retention of a tree. One objection was received that the applicant was able to view at the Council offices. No response was made by the applicants.

The applicants felt the outcome of their application was reasonable apart from the condition to retain the tree, which they did not really understand the need for and note is half dead. Their main reservation with the planning process is that it took too long, 18 weeks in this instance, and they felt that the speed with which applications are dealt with needed to be improved. The long processing time appears to have been largely the result of their originally scheduled Committee planning meeting being deferred to allow a site visit, and a request for modification to the application. The applicants were somewhat frustrated

by the site visit as they felt that the 15 people (the Planning Committee) that attended only asked questions to which the applicants felt they had already provided the answers in the planning application.

Other factors: The most difficult aspect of setting up the business has been in trying to attract the customers after the livery was set up. The conversion is privately funded.

Effects of the diversification: The livery is a new business and provides almost 100% of the unit's income, with the exception of a small amount of income received from letting some pasture for sheep grazing. The application has been implemented with the exception of the provision of a new building, which has not been built yet. The livery has 2 part-time local employees, in addition to the wife who works full time, and husband who works part-time. The length of the planning process has resulted in some financial difficulties for the applicants, as the delays resulted in the loss of some trade and income that could have been accumulated over the winter months – the busiest period for liveries. Although the applicants eventually received planning permission in March, they were unable to attract any significant trade until the following September.

Conclusion: The apparent change in attitude of the LPA after a site visit highlights the difficulties for officers in giving pre-application advice without such a visit. Again the positive benefits of employing a professional agent are illustrated. The potential delays due to committee cycles and member site visits are reflected by the lengthy determination time for this scheme.

Typical examples of future (non-traditional) types of diversification

CASE STUDY 3:

Approved by local planning authority

Farm size and status: Working farm of 24 hectares, in Hampshire. Within 5 miles of an A road, and 5 miles of a settlement.

Main enterprise: Arable (farmed by son in conjunction with other land)

Length of occupation: 30 years

Tenure: Owner–occupier

Type of diversification: Conversion of barn and outbuildings to B1(a) use.

Date: **Application:** 8/12/1998
  Approval: 24/3/1999

Site history and reasons for diversification: The site is situated within 5 miles of the A340. The farm was bought 30 years ago, and the farmhouse sold off. The farmyard includes a combination of buildings, including those forming this application which were the subject of a planning approval for B1 use 10 years ago – this was not implemented and has lapsed. A re-application has been made to provide an alternative source of income. Another building within the complex was converted into a packing complex 15 years ago and subsequently into offices.

The planning process: The agent acting on behalf of the applicant, with whom the site is in trust, described the planning process as "*straight forward, very reasonable and professional*". The agent, who runs a property development consultancy business, took an active role in preparing and making the planning applications, and no pre-application advice was sought from the LPA or Highways Authority. Post application site visits by the LPA and Highways Authority went smoothly, with no areas of concern identified. However, a condition was applied to the approval limiting working hours and limiting the change of use to B1(a). This condition was not considered reasonable as another development opposite had not had this condition imposed, nevertheless it was properly explained.

Other factors: Four letters of objection by local villagers were received by the LPA concerning the conversion of the buildings. The agent thought that the condition, limiting hours of use and type of development of the site, was implemented to placate these objections and control the nature of traffic generation.

Effects of diversification: Since the planning permission was granted, the barn has been converted, generating £10,000 per year and employing 7 people. The outbuildings have yet to be converted. Upon conversion they have been estimated to generate £15,000 per year, and employ up to 15 people.

Conclusion: The agent appears satisfied with the processing of this application, despite it taking 15 weeks. His advice to the applicant appears to have been clear and accurate, given the lack of subsequent problems with the application. The Local Planning Authority appears to have reached a balanced view, taking account of objections, and made appropriate and justified use of conditions.

CASE STUDY 4

Approved by local planning authority

Farm size and status: 3 hectare working farm in North West England in a Green Belt. On the edge of a settlement and within 5 miles of an A road.

Main enterprise: Poultry farm.

Length of occupation: 32 years.

Tenure: Owner–occupier

Type of diversification: Change of use of existing out-building to farm shop to sell own produce and related produce from neighbouring site.

Date: Application: 01/2000
      Approval: 03/2000

Site history and reasons for diversification: Diversification prompted by the desire for more income. The applicant felt it made sense to sell a proportion of their products directly to the public, and also a proportion of the product supplied from a neighbouring site. There are several other farm shops in the locality and the applicant felt there would be a market for their products as well.

The planning process: The application was submitted by the applicants. Initially they sought the advice of local planning officers, who sent them policy extracts from the local plan. The applicant understood from the local plan that they might establish a farm shop, a second call to the planning officers clarified that it would require planning permission. After submitting an application to sell their own produce and that of the neighbouring site, the applicants were advised by planning officers that they could not sell their neighbour's product as some of it had been processed in another part of the county. The applicants approached an ex-local councillor who was supportive of their application. Planning officers eventually decided that the enterprise was of a sufficiently small-scale, that selling their neighbour's produce would not present a problem, and permission was granted for sale of both the applicants and the neighbours produce. A condition was attached that the permission be personal to the applicant.

The applicants felt the outcome was reasonable, but that they should not have had to appeal to a third party for help, particularly in light of the local planning policy that states support for farm shops, and the number of other farm shops in the locality. The location of the farm in the Green Belt was noted as a particular problem. The applicant also noted that the planning process was too long, as by the time permission is granted for such developments, the market for the product has often moved on. The application took just over 10 weeks to decide – two weeks more than the Government's eight week target.

Other factors: The applicant felt that the planners make it as difficult as possible for farmers in the area to get added value for their products as any form of added value is often counted as an industrial process, and therefore not allowed on site.

Effects of the diversification: The farm shop has not proven as successful as the applicants had anticipated and contributes only 1–2% of the farm's income. The applicant feels this is because although there is periodically a large volume of foot traffic past their property due to near-by car-boot sales, those people have not turned out to be an appropriate market for their produce. No additional people are employed as a result of the farm shop.

Conclusion: The location of this farm in the Green Belt and the proposal to sell goods processed in another part of the county presented a barrier to the establishment of this small diversification scheme. The pre-application advice, whilst of some use, does not appear to have fully explained to the applicant the relatively complex planning issues associated with retail uses. Although there was a positive outcome, the applicant appears not to fully appreciate the reasons for imposing the conditions. The case study does however demonstrate the positive role that members can play in liasing between applicants and officers.

CASE STUDY 5

Approved by local planning authority

Farm size and status: 146 hectare working farm in South West England. Within 5 miles of a town and within 5 miles of an A road.

Main enterprise: A mix of sheep, dairy, beef and arable.

Length of occupation: Has been a family farm since the grandparents owned it.

Tenure: Owner–occupier

Type of diversification: Conversion of existing redundant traditional farm buildings to provide a business complex.

Date: **Application:** 11/01/2000
   Approval: 15/02/2000

Site history and reasons for diversification: The yard in which the business complex is proposed was becoming redundant as it was not very useful for modern farming methods. The applicants were aware that grants were available for converting to offices, so they decided to explore the option.

The planning process: The applicants employed an architect to present their initial planning application and have subsequently engaged a new firm to advise them on detailed architectural drawings and applications for grants. The applicants feel they could never have negotiated the grants system without the professional help. Although the application was for full planning permission, it was largely exploratory on the applicant's part. There were no third party representations and the application was approved by delegated powers and without modification. Contact was made with the LPA prior to application. They spoke with both planning officers and the Council's business resource manager. The applicants received advice on access and parking issues, establishing offices, the letting of offices and general information relevant to their proposal. The applicants found the advice very helpful, had no problems and were generally surprised with the ease and speed of negotiating the planning process. Conditions were imposed relating to parking, access and restriction of uses of the buildings, which the applicants considered were reasonable.

Other factors: The applicants have found obtaining grants the most difficult part of establishing their diversification proposal, largely due to the sheer number of grants available and the conditions of many of the grants that proposals be purely speculative. 45% of the funding for this proposal has come from grants.

Effects of the diversification: The commercial units are to be leased out and will be completely separate businesses to the farm enterprise. The application has only very recently begun to be implemented and the applicant is not sure what percentage of the farm income will eventually be derived from the proposal. The applicant notes that the farm is only just breaking even at present and so any profit as a result of the diversification will be significant. As the proposal is speculative, the applicant does not know how many people might be employed on the site.

Conclusion: This case is notable for the helpful attitude of the LPA, good communication between the applicants and the LPA prior to and during the application process, and for the smooth and very swift processing of the planning application. The involvement of the LA's economic development (business resources) officer was also seen as being of value. The applicant's difficulties in securing grant aid illustrate both the variety of bodies that can be involved in the diversification process, and the benefits that could be realised through a more comprehensive and coordinated approach.

Large scale/expansion

CASE STUDY 6

Approved by local planning authority

Farm size and status: 283 hectare working farm in the middle of England. On the edge of a settlement and adjacent to an A road.

Main enterprise: Until 3 months ago the farm was a dairy unit. Now the unit supports a mix of beef cattle, arable and diversification activities.

Length of occupation: 50 years.

Tenure: Owner–occupier

Type of diversification: Change of use of existing farm buildings to craft workshops, plus the use of one unit for plant sales.

Date: **Application:** 22/02/2000
       Approval: 23/05/2000

Site history and reasons for diversification: The farm initially began diversifying 10 years ago when the applicant's daughter wanted to establish a farm shop. The applicants seem to have fallen into diversification, restoring derelict farm buildings as they went along.

The planning process: The applicant appointed an architect to help with the planning application and found the architect to be very good. The applicant was generally happy with the planning process and overall demonstrated a good understanding of the process and a willingness to listen and negotiate with the LPA. The LPA officer made two to three visits to the farm through the course of the application. The applicant noted that in addition to showing as much of the proposal as possible to the officer, it was also important to *"listen to what he says"*. The officer offered some verbal advice in addition to written communications to the architect, including a request for further information on the intended use of the site and potential traffic generation. The applicant found the planning officer's advice very helpful and felt that the application would have been refused if he had not heeded the advice. Modifications were requested by the LPA and negotiations were undertaken right up to the planning committee itself on issues of retail space and highway safety and possible related conditions that might be imposed. The applicant felt the outcome of the application, and the conditions that were attached, were reasonable, largely because everything had been negotiated previously and he therefore expected the conditions that were imposed.

Other factors: There were two third party representations objecting to the proposal and an objection from the County Highway Authority on the basis of traffic safety issues. The planning officer recommended refusal of the application on grounds of the need to control retail development and highway safety. The planning committee decided against this advice following a site visit, considering that the access was well-used without any problems already and that the proposal was unlikely to result in any new problems. An important factor in the applicant's understanding of the planning process was his experience from previous planning applications for similar diversification activities on the farm. The applicant noted that the planning process had been improved recently by the LPA to the extent that applicants and third parties have the option of addressing the planning committee in person for 3 minutes. The planning committee was in turn able to ask questions. The applicant felt this was very useful as it enabled him to address any objections in person.

Effects of the diversification: Approximately 40% of the farm's turnover comes from diversification activities, though the applicant was unable to estimate what percentage of the farm's income this specific application would contribute. He notes that while the set-up costs of converting the agricultural buildings are expensive, they are subsequently cheap to maintain and profit is therefore good. The applicant's farm is in a good location for craft businesses, with a lot of tourist traffic in the area, a relatively affluent local population and a large amount of foot traffic from the nearby canal in summer. 22 people are employed by businesses leasing units on the farm, plus the applicant's daughter who runs a farm shop, and a son who has a garden furniture business. Most of the businesses on site are start-up businesses. Not all the employees are local. Whilst the applicant gives preference to local people, the need to have profitable units is important and the skills necessary for running good businesses cannot always be sourced locally. The most difficult aspect of diversifying has been the loss of privacy as the craft units are located around his house.

Conclusion: The openness of the LPA in negotiations and committee meeting has been rewarded with a positive view from the applicant, despite an officer recommendation for refusal. This case study illustrates the problems occurring due to highways objections, but also the greater willingness of members than officers to be flexible about highway standards.

Other

CASE STUDY 7:

Temporary permission from local planning authority for four years

Farm size and status: 81 hectare working farm in North York Moors National Park. Within 5 miles of an A road and within 5 miles of a settlement.

Main enterprise: Hay for sale.

Length of occupation: Been in the family for five generations. The applicant took over the farm 20 years ago.

Tenure: Owner–occupier.

Type of diversification: Change of use from agriculture to grow and buy in plants, trees and accessories to sell from the farm, specialising in wild plants and flowers.

Date: Application: 12/1/1999
         Approval: 11/3/1999

Site history and reasons for diversification: This site forms part of an isolated farmstead in open countryside. The applicant has always supported conservation and was one of the first farmers to join the Countryside Stewardship Scheme in the area. Having given up sheep farming with the downturn in income, the applicant wanted to diversify, developing his love of nature into a viable, all-day visitor attraction, growing and selling wildflower seeds and opening up the wildflower meadows on the farm to the general public. The main development has been conversion of a redundant sheep barn into a potting shed and selling area. All other activity is outside. The applicant is committed to retaining a working farm.

The planning process: Before making the planning application, the applicant employed ADAS horticultural division to undertake a full feasibility study (£650) for which he received a 50% grant under Objective 5b. Business Link also prepared a whole farm business plan. The planning application was made by the applicant without the use of an agent as this was seen as too expensive (this is an area where the applicant felt that financial assistance would be useful, even if only as an interest free loan).

On receipt of the application the LPA was concerned about the lack of clarity as to the size, scale and nature of the proposed operation, and minded to refuse, but through on-going liaison with the applicant a compromise was sought. The Committee report accepts that the proposal is well located in relation to other activities and involves no new building. However, it highlights concern with the retail element of the proposal and notes that it should not 'operate in a manner tantamount to a retail garden centre'. In consequence, a temporary four year permission was recommended and subsequently granted.

The applicant felt that the planning process had been fair throughout and that the LPA was helpful in its negotiations. Nevertheless a temporary permission offers no security when the site needs an investment of £20,000.

Other factors: Two letters of objection were received from neighbours about traffic generation, but these were sufficiently far away for the LPA to override this consideration. Over the last ten years the applicant has also developed a small hotel/ bed and breakfast on the site, which caters for up to 15 people. Since being granted planning permission, the applicant has found it difficult to gain horticultural training, as all courses are full time. The applicant now hopes to enrol on an internet-based learning course.

Effects of diversification: The applicant has now been operating his business for two out of the four years. Pre-application advice from ADAS predicted that long term the business would generate £40,000 per year. However, the applicant has started small scale, with earnings of £6,000 to date and with the aim of increasing this to £20,000 in the next two years to meet establishment costs – the time demands of farming activities, mean that the business plan is behind schedule.

Conclusion: Addressing a planning concern by use of a temporary consent has clearly created financial uncertainty. However, the case shows a positive attitude from the Local Planning Authority in addressing a legitimate planning concern, where the proposal may otherwise have been refused. The applicant appears to be fully aware of the reasons for the retail concerns but is less sure about planning issues, for example appearing unaware that he could apply for permanent consent now.

CASE STUDY 8:
Approved by local planning authority [but not implemented]

Farm size and status: 21 hectares working farm in Lincolnshire, but land rented out to applicant's brothers. Farmstead in open countryside.

Main enterprise: Arable and grass (8ha sheep)

Length of occupation: 10 years

Tenure: Owner–occupier

Type of diversification: Change of use of existing agricultural barn to use as an agricultural engineer's workshop and wrought iron workshop.

Date: **Application:** 21/8/1997
          Approval: 28/10/1997

Site history and reasons for diversification: This site lies in open countryside near the village of Minting. It used to be part of a larger farm, but was divided into three between the applicant and his two brothers when the applicant's father died. The applicant's farm was not big enough to make a living, so the applicant trained to become an agricultural engineer, renting the land out to his brothers, who continued to farm. The applicant applied for planning permission to convert one of his agricultural barns to a workshop for him and one employee. This would have been the first step, with future plans including rebuilding part of the barn and extending the workshop to include one other barn. Until then he was subcontracting from another premises. The conversion was planned to produce a turnover of £40,000 per year.

The planning process: The application was submitted by the applicant with an accompanying plan drawn by an architect but only as part of another proposal for a bungalow on an adjoining site. There were no pre-application discussions with the LPA or Highways Authority as the applicant was unaware that this advice was available. The applicant was also unaware that an agent could submit an application on his behalf, although he would not have followed this route because of the expense involved.

The application was approved with conditions that there should be a landscaping scheme; that before the change of use was implemented the existing vehicular access should be improved in accordance with details submitted to the LPA; and only as long as the associated dwelling was occupied by a person employed in the business permitted. The applicant was disappointed with the highway condition and unaware that it would be applied – this was not made clear during the post-application site visits by the LPA and Highways Authority. However, they did express concern at the time that lorries would be using the site, despite the applicant's view that the expected increase in traffic would be no more than four cars and that heavy duty agricultural equipment was already using the access.

Other factors: At the same time as making the planning application, an application was made for a 3-phase power upgrade to the electricity supply. This was expected to cost around £800 based on previous experience and that of neighbours, but the quote was for £10,000 as the power line required upgrading. There were also some newly built industrial units close to the site, which the applicant felt that the LPA was keen for him to use instead of his own buildings. He suspected that it was for this reason that the planning process and subsequent conditions were *"very hard work"*. However, the applicant did not want to use these units as he was disillusioned with the Council, the rents were too high, and it would require travelling by car which would not suit the person he was proposing to employ from the local village.

Effects of diversification: The applicant has not implement the planning permission because of: the expense of upgrading the entrance to full public road specifications (£2–3000); the expense of 3-phase power; his declining economic situation; and the decreased demand for wrought iron.

Conclusion: The applicant is clearly unhappy with the Local Planning Authority, despite receiving an approval in less than ten weeks. Seeking professional advice would undoubtedly have increased the applicant's awareness of the planning system and given greater understanding of the likely outcome. The financial costs of complying with the conditions do not appear onerous when seen against the other financial problems with the scheme.

Recommended for refusal but approved

CASE STUDY 9:

Recommended for refusal by officers, but granted consent at planning committee [but not implemented]

Farm size and status: 243 hectares working farm in Norfolk. On the edge of a settlement, and within 5 miles of an A road.

Main enterprises: Arable and sugar beet. Organic eggs: separate enterprise from farm.

Length of occupation: Over 100 years in family, but this occupant since 1970.

Tenure: 17 ha Farm Business Tenancy, 226 ha successional tenancy held under the Agricultural Holdings Act (1st generation).

Type of diversification: Change of use of redundant agricultural building to three offices/stores.

Date: **Application:** 23/11/1999
        Approval: 6/3/2000

Site history and reasons for diversification: This site lies in on the edge of a settlement, down a private track which can be accessed from the middle of the village of Great Ryburgh. The applicant has already successfully diversified into Bed and Breakfast in the farmhouse itself. The aim of further diversification was to increase the farm income by an estimated £3,500 per annum per unit, which would have boosted their falling income from agriculture. The son also runs a successful enterprise of organic egg production, but this is treated as a separate enterprise from the farm. The three offices/stores would have all been converted out of the one traditional single storey building, with each unit employing up to four people once rented out. This site lies within an Objective 5b area and upon making this application the applicant had secured an Objective 5b grant of £20,000. The total cost of the change of use was estimated at £70,000.

The planning process: The applicant sought informal pre-application advice from a farm diversification expert and Objective 5b advisor (un-paid). The LPA and Highways Authority also made a pre-application visit. The applicant was alerted that highways would be a problem, but as the amount of traffic to be generated was likely to be small, decided to proceed with the application. As the son had trained in countryside planning, no agent was used to make the application.

The Highway Authority formally objected to the application once received and recommended refusal on highway safety grounds because of the restricted nature of the surrounding road network. The case officer's report makes it clear that apart from this the proposal complied with planning policy. The case officer contacted the Highways Engineer to discuss ways in which highways objections could be overcome. Committee members felt that additional traffic would be minimal and that the proposal would create local employment. Thus they approved the application subject to a condition requiring improvement to the existing passing places on the private lane leading up to the proposed development site prior to implementation of the development. According to the applicant, the LPA was very reasonable.

Tenancy considerations: Prior to making the application the landlord was contacted and following liaison and a site visit, the landlord provided a letter of consent, although he refused to contribute to the capital investment. Under the Agricultural Holdings Act, any investment made by the tenant is written off over a period of ten years. Thus, in return for allowing the change of use and economic activity of the building, after a period of ten years all investment made in the building would transfer to the landlord.

Effects of diversification: The applicant has decided not to implement the planning permission for the following reasons:

- The cost of converting one unit was estimated to be £25,000 by the builder when planning was applied for, however this subsequently increased to £45,000.

- The building works were delayed by 2–3 months by which time they had decided not to go ahead with the project.

- The returns on investment would not have justified an expenditure of £70,000, especially as ownership would have reverted to the landlord in 10 years' time.

- The proposed occupant for Unit 1 was not very 'secure' and, after the planning application was approved, withdrew.

None of these decisions were therefore related to the planning process.

Conclusion: The applicant sought a range of pre-application advice, which successfully highlighted the key highways area of concern. Both the case officer and committee members appeared keen to address and overcome the concerns. Failure of implementation was not due to planning issues, but due to the nature of the applicant's tenancy agreement, an inaccurate quotation by a building contractor and their proposed occupant withdrawing.

Refused and then approved on appeal

CASE STUDY 10:

Refused by local planning authority. Allowed on appeal.

Farm size and status: 8 hectare redundant farm in the West Midlands. Within 5 miles of a settlement and within 5 miles from an A road.

Main enterprise: The only farming activity that occurs now is selling grass for silage.

Length of occupation: 11 years.

Tenure: Owner–occupier

Type of diversification: Change of use of agricultural building (modern calf-rearing unit) to a general storage facility.

Date: Application: 19/05/1998
Refusal: 02/07/1998
Allowed on appeal: 06/04/1999

Site history and reasons for diversification: Calf-rearing became uneconomic after the BSE crisis, the owner felt forced to look for income from other areas. The main activities on the farm are now a mix of storage, workshops and some machinery hire.

The planning process: This application is a re-submission of a retrospective application that had previously been refused. Refusal of this application took 2 months. The application was refused by the LPA because the adjacent dwelling has an agricultural occupancy condition and it was felt the change of use of the former calf-rearing unit would deprive the dwelling of its main justification for agricultural need. The LPA was also concerned about setting a precedent for similar proposals in the area. On appeal, the Planning Inspector felt that the application met the requirements of PPG7, but restricted the type of storage materials and removed Schedule 2, Part 6 permitted development rights as conditions of approval.

The applicant employed a planning consultant to deal with his planning application, but dealt with the appeal himself. The applicant feels that the LPA was unhelpful and unreasonable, particularly in light of the financial problems the farm is experiencing. He felt the LPA had not properly explained its opposition to his application. The applicant is also under the impression that unless applicants are represented by professionals, the LPA does not want to deal with them. The applicant did not have any direct contact with the LPA prior to submitting this planning application, primarily because of "bad experiences" dealing with the LPA over previous planning matters (the property had been the subject of a series of agricultural-related planning applications previously, some of which were unsuccessful). The applicant did receive support from a local councillor when he approached her for support while the second application was being considered.

In fairness to the LPA, the applicant appears to have a limited understanding of the planning process and the existence of the agricultural occupancy condition on the applicant's dwelling is particularly problematic. The LPA is currently taking enforcement action against the applicant on the basis of the contravention of the agricultural occupancy condition (a separate process to the planning application examined in this case study). The relationship between the applicant and the LPA appears to have deteriorated to the point of distrust and some degree of animosity.

Other factors: This application was brought about by the threat of enforcement action against the use of the calf-rearing unit for storage purposes without planning permission. Two other current applications relating to similar diversification activities have been bought about as a result of enforcement action by the LPA. No modifications to this planning application were suggested by the LPA officers, and no advice was received from enforcement officers visiting the property. No third party representations were made, other than by CPRE. The applicant feels that clearer information from the LPA on what people can or cannot do is required, in particular to avoid the expense of employing planning consultants.

Effects of diversification: Approximately 90% of the applicant's income derives from renting out former agricultural buildings. The applicant estimates the subject of this planning application provides 20% of his income. No persons are directly employed by the applicant, apart from some casual labour if help is needed with maintenance of the buildings. The applicant estimates approximately 20 people move on and off the site in association with the various diversification activities, though only 3-4 people are actually based on-site.

Conclusion: The farm reported in this case study has been subject to a long and difficult planning history resulting in a poor relationship between the LPA and the applicant, a problem which appears to hinder the planning process. The presence of a dwelling with an agricultural occupancy condition presents a particular barrier to the diversification scheme proposed by the applicant, which would effectively render the farm redundant.

Refused by local planning authority – appeal dismissed

CASE STUDY 11:

Refused by local planning authority. Appeal dismissed

Farm size and status: 36 ha, rented out to adjoining farm. 6 ha in hand. Farm in an AONB in East Sussex. Within 5 miles of an A road and 5 miles of a settlement.

Main enterprise: Arable and grazing.

Length of occupation: 6 ha 44 years, remainder 30 years.

Tenure: Owner–occupier

Type of diversification: Change of use of three redundant modern steel and asbestos agricultural buildings to class B1 uses including 35 car parking spaces.

Date: Application: 20/12/1999
       Refusal: 15/2/2000
       Dismissal of appeal: 15/6/2000

Site history and reasons for diversification: This site is in open countryside within the High Weald Area of Outstanding Natural Beauty. Until ten years ago the buildings were rented out, employing 8-10 people under a personal planning permission to the buildings' tenant, which ceased when the business went bankrupt. The applicant wanted to put the buildings to use to stop them deteriorating further, and to gain an income to supplement his pension.

The planning process: The applicant used an agent to make the planning application, costing £6000. No pre-application discussions were held with the LPA or others. Once the application was submitted site visits were made by the LPA and Highways Authority. Both the applicant and the agent were extremely surprised when the planning permission was refused, and the subsequent appeal dismissed. They thought that the application was virtually guaranteed success as the farmer at the other end of the lane had been granted planning permission to convert farm buildings to offices. The applicant therefore did not think that the planning process had been reasonable although the reasons for refusal were well explained by the LPA.

The LPA gave five reasons for refusal, covering: AONB issues, appearance of the buildings, impact upon the locality's character and amenities, and highways concerns. On appeal the Inspector considered that the proposal would generate significant traffic movements which would have a harmful effect on the AONB and rural environment, the noise and fumes generated would have a harmful impact on neighbours; and highway safety would be compromised by an increased number of vehicles on narrow roads.

Other factors: Six letters of objection were received by the LPA from adjoining occupiers. A range of traffic, noise, disturbance and amenity issues were raised, including objections that existing commercial activities on the site caused noise and breached existing planning conditions. The applicant claimed that it was these representations that caused the appeal to be dismissed, rather than the planning restrictions themselves.

Effects of diversification: Due to the expense involved, after the appeal was dismissed the applicant did not pursue the matter further. He did not discuss possibilities of scaling down the application with the LPA. The amount of employment which would have been created as a result of this diversification, and the amount of income that would have been generated, were never finalised.

Conclusion: Given the range of concerns identified by the Local Planning Authority, Inspector and objectors, the refusal does not seem too surprising. The application and subsequent appeal were both dealt with relatively quickly. The failure of the agent to undertake pre-application discussions seems to have been a significant factor. The outcome, or at least cost to the applicant, may have been different had more reliable advice been received.

CASE STUDY 12:

Refused by local planning authority. Appeal dismissed

Farm size and status: 4.5 hectare redundant farm in the South West in a Green Belt. On the edge of a settlement and within 5 miles of an A road.

Main enterprise: The applicants now rely entirely on the income they receive from letting light industrial units.

Length of occupation: 15 years.

Tenure: Owner–occupiers.

Type of diversification: Proposed change of use of existing modern barn to industrial units class B1 and B8.

Date:

Application:	04/1997
Refusal:	06/1997
Dismissal of appeal:	11/1997

Site history and reasons for diversification: The applicants state they were forced to diversify years ago as the farm unit was not economic.

The planning process: Application refused on the grounds of inappropriate activity in the Green Belt, encroachment on the countryside, potential impacts on residential amenity and inadequacy of parking provision. All former agricultural buildings on the property are now let as light industrial units (from a previous single planning application) apart from the building subject to the planning application. The property is located in the Green Belt, immediately adjacent to a residential area. The applicants were generally unhappy with the planning process as they felt the LPA was unreasonable and not particularly consistent in its decision-making. The applicants did not fully understand some of the reasons why the LPA refused planning permission, though they recognised that their case was difficult due to their proximity to neighbouring residents and the Green Belt designation. They particularly disagreed with the Council and Inspector's assessment of traffic impacts. The applicants had employed a planning consultant to deal with their application. No direct contact was made between the applicants themselves and the LPA. The consultant's advice was apparently unhelpful as he advised that they would not have a problem getting planning permission. The application received considerable opposition from neighbouring residents. Generally the applicants felt that the planning process was too slow, that applications needed to be dealt with more quickly. This application was dealt with in 10 weeks.

Other factors: The proposed development is privately funded. The applicants appear to have a reasonable understanding of the planning process, though not necessarily the planning issues at hand. They feel they have been put in a very difficult position with regard to the remaining redundant agricultural building as a result of poor advice from planning consultants and from historical decisions by the LPA not to allocate the land for housing.

Effects of the diversification: The building proposed for conversion is one of the larger buildings on the property and the applicants estimate that if it were converted, it would contribute approximately 15% of the farm income. It is proposed the building be let to a light engineering company that is already located on the site and wishes to expand. Approximately 70–80 employees currently work from the site, most of whom are local residents, none of whom are directly employed by the applicants.

Conclusion: There is already substantial commercial use of the site and again the main concern in this case appears to be inadequate professional advice prior to and during the planning application process.

APPENDIX 9

Appeals

METHODOLOGY

The sample of planning appeals was found with the help of the Planning Inspectorate. The Planning Inspectorate undertook a search of their database for all planning appeals with 'change of use' in the title for the three-year period February 1997-February 2000 (a more specific search for 'farm diversification' was not possible). From this process over 9000 appeals were found, of which summaries were sent to the consultants.

Of these appeals, a manual trawl identified 300 that were potentially associated with farm diversification. Thirty sample appeals were selected from this list by looking at different forms of development (in terms of development types and development activity), and geographical spread, and then taking a representative sample. The Inspector's Report, and where appropriate, the Secretary of State's decision letter, for each of these was requested. From these thirty, the final twelve were chosen as case studies.

1. Cherwell District Council
Farm, Weston-on-the-Green, Bicester.

Planning permission refused for change of use of part of an agricultural barn into a depot for a horticultural/landscape contractor, including some demolition works and a "portacabin" as an office. Within Green Belt.

Date of appeal decision: April 2000.

Appeal decision: **Allowed with conditions.**

Background
The appeal relates to a Dutch barn within a redundant farmstead on a holding of 180 hectares, situated in open countryside to the west of Bicester. There has also been another appeal within the same farmstead for change of use of a former dairy building into consulting rooms for a physiotherapist. The farmstead already accommodates a nursery school and a residential conversion. The appeal was retrospective – the change of use had already taken place and the 'portacabin' building erected in association with the contracting business using it. However, further works were envisaged. The remaining section of the barn would still be used for agricultural purposes.

LPA's view
The farm is located on the south-eastern side of an unclassified road close to the M40/A34 junction. The appeal site also lies within the designated Oxford Green Belt. The application was therefore considered to go against policies G1, G2, G4 and E4 of the

Oxfordshire County Structure Plan and policies GB1, GB5, EMP4 and TR10 of the Cherwell District Local Plan regarding appropriate development in the countryside. The LPA considered that the needs of the business operating in the Dutch barn would require construction of side walls at some stage in the future. This could result in major reconstruction to the detriment of the character and appearance of the area, and of a scale which was inappropriate in the Green Belt. The LPA was also concerned regarding the risk and consequences of outside storage, as the farmyard area adjacent to the appeal building is exposed and open to view from the public highway.

Appellant's view
The appellant's view was not quoted.

Inspector's report- main issues
The inspector considered that the main issues in this case were

- *Whether the proposal represents appropriate development in the Green Belt.* The inspector was satisfied that the building was redundant and that the re-use was not inappropriate development subject to certain criteria being met. He stated that in fact the conversion could avoid the building being left vacant and falling into disrepair. The use would not have a greater impact than when it was in agricultural use.

- *Whether the proposal warranted an exception to the normal policies of restraint applicable to development within the Green Belt.* The proposed use would not involve significant changes affecting the character of the building, and could even serve to enhance the surroundings if open storage was controlled. No major reconstruction would be necessary.

- *The free flow of traffic in the area and highway safety:* The appeal proposal would not be detrimental to the safety and convenience of road users, with refusal of planning permission not justified on highway safety grounds alone. However, the inspector recognised that in order to keep the building's use from changing, planning permission should limit the use to the named tenant and to a time limit in keeping with that of the existing contract.

The Inspector allowed the appeal with the following conditions:

- *Use permitted carried out only by Continental Landscapes Ltd and for 7 years only.*

- *Use restricted to only the eastern section of the building.*

- *Parking area shall be confined to 9 car parking spaces to the east of the building.*

- *No goods, materials, plant or machinery shall be stored, repaired or operated in the open without prior consent of the LPA.*

- *Within 9 months the junction of the site access with the public highway shall be improved which shall be agreed with the LPA. The scheme shall relate to the provision of improved visibility splays and access.*

2. Teignbridge District Council

Farm, Longdown, Exeter.

Planning permission refused for the use of part of an existing building for a self-catering holiday unit.

Date of appeal decision: October 1999.

Appeal decision: **Allowed with conditions.**

Background

The application was for the use of part of an existing building for self-catering accommodation, with no material change to the external appearance of the building or to existing facilities. The building is a substantial modern structure, fitted with windows and rooflights that was erected as a result of planning permission granted in 1992 for agricultural and ancillary domestic use. The part proposed for conversion already currently provides office and utility space on the ground floor.

LPA's view

The Council's view is not explicitly stated, although through the quoted planning policies of both the Teignbridge Local Plan and the Devon Structure Plan First Review, the concerns appear to relate to adverse impact on traffic, road safety, and local landscape impact. The LPA suggests that should the partial conversion be allowed, occupancy should be limited to no more than 3 months of the year. The Highway Authority was concerned that this development could be seen to set an undesirable precedent for other proposals in the locality, especially as the site is in an Area of Great Landscape Value (local designation).

Appellant's view

The appellant's view is not quoted. One reason that was put forward in favour of the appellant was that there is an under-supply of rural self-catering accommodation in the district.

Inspector's report- main issues

The inspector considered that the main issue in this case was whether the proposed change of use of part of the building would be justified, bearing in mind:

- *the strict controls on development in the countryside:* The inspector stated that he did not consider that the proposals would erode the character or appearance of the countryside beyond that which had already been permitted there.

- *the free flow and safety of traffic in the area:* The appeal could not be refused on the basis of the additional traffic that would be generated by one holiday unit.

The Inspector allowed the appeal with the following condition:

- *The development shall only be used as holiday accommodation.*

3. North York Moors National Park Authority
Agricultural Buildings at Staintondale

Planning permission refused for the adaptation and re-use of redundant agricultural buildings to form one unit of Class B1 workspace with ancillary residential accommodation.

Date of appeal decision: October 2000.

Appeal decision: **Dismissed.**

Background
The proposal relates to three buildings, including two disused barns, which stand in an isolated location well outside the village of Staintondale. The buildings would be partially converted into residential use, and partially converted into one unit for light industrial use. This would entail only very minor changes to the exterior of the buildings.

LPA's view
The LPA stressed that the appellants had not offered to enter into a legal obligation which would enable the Authority to control the development of a residential curtilage. With regard to the use of the buildings for light industrial use, the proposal was in clear conflict with Policy G2 of the North York Moors Local Plan which seeks to safeguard the natural and built environments of the Park. The amount of new building and repair work required and the new wall needed to screen car parking spaces would give the site a very harsh and inappropriate appearance in the landscape. The proposal was also not in accordance with Policy EM4, which allows for the conversion of redundant buildings outside villages for industrial or business purposes if the buildings are worthy of retention in themselves or make a significant contribution to the landscape. In this regard the buildings were not particularly well built and did not have any obvious outstanding architectural features.

Appellant's view
The appellants argued that the buildings were of a style that is quite distinctive in the North York Moors and that they had historic merit. Their contribution to the landscape was also significant and thus the proposal was in accord with Local Plan Policy EM4.

Inspector's report- main issues
The inspector considered that the main issues in this case were:

- *Whether the buildings could be converted without substantial rebuilding:* This was concluded not to be the case. All the buildings were in poor condition, and at least 30% of the fabric of the buildings would need to be rebuilt or replaced.

- *Whether the buildings were of sufficient merit and importance to the local landscape to merit retention:* Again this was dismissed, as the buildings in question were not exceptional in the area, and in light of the scale of development could only partially be 'retained'.

- *Whether the appearance of development and its associated activity would detract from the natural beauty of the National Park and the North Yorkshire and Cleveland Heritage Coast:* The amount of repair work would detract from the landscape as well as traffic generated. There were also vacant buildings more suitable not too distant from the site.

4. North Wiltshire District Council
Farm, Yatton Keynell, Chippenham

Planning permission refused for the development of a recycling unit for processing stone and timber.

Date of appeal decision: July 2000.

Appeal decision: **Dismissed.**

Background
The proposal concerns the conversion of two modern buildings to a recycling unit for processing stone and timber within a farmyard complex which includes another barn and farmhouse. Car parking spaces would be some distance from the other buildings. The eastern boundary of the site is not defined. Storage and crushing of raw materials would take place in the open yard at the rear of one building.

LPA's view
There is no direct statement of the LPA's views but reference to Policy F16.3 and emerging Policy RE20.1 and .8 of the North Wiltsthire Local Plan suggest that the key concern is maintenance of the character of the countryside. The highway authority states that visibility at the site access and at the junction affected by the proposal is substandard compared to national recommendations.

Appellant's view
The site access is the subject of a dispute as it is not a through road but serves several properties. The appellants say HGV movements would not increase.

Inspector's report- main issues
The inspector considered that the main issues in this case were

- *Implications for highway safety on surrounding roads:* On the evidence of the submitted plan it would not be possible to achieve adequate visibility and increased HGV use was inevitable despite the appellant's claim. This would give rise to unacceptable hazards on approach roads to the site.

- *The effect on the rural character of the area:* Highway improvements necessary would alter the characteristic pattern of roadside hedges and narrow lanes, and stone and timber processing are likely to be noisy and dust-creating activities. Taken together these would detract unacceptably from the rural character of the countryside in the vicinity of the site.

5. Restormel Borough Council

Farm Buildings, Pentewan – within an AONB

Appeal against imposition of condition No.1 on planning permission given for the change of use from agricultural storage of cattle and fodder to caravan and boat storage.

Date of appeal decision: September 2000.

Appeal decision: **Allowed and planning permission varied.**

Background

This appeal regards the change of use of an agricultural building in support of camping and caravanning, connected with the business of Pentewan Sands Ltd. The condition in dispute was that: 'The use hereby permitted shall be carried on only by Pentewan Sands Ltd and shall be for a limited period being the period of two years from the date of this permission following which all boats and caravans shall be removed from the land.' The reason given for the condition was: 'To allow the Local Planning Authority to further monitor the use of the land to assess the visual impact in the Area of Outstanding Natural Beauty'. Both main parties agree that the use of the appeal building for storage of boats and caravans is an acceptable use. The Council wished, however, to limit the permission to a trial period to assess the effect of the development on the area. Pentewan Sands Ltd already has a caravan park and camping site opposite the appeal site, which extends towards the sea.

LPA's view

The LPA was concerned that the appeal site would conflict with Structure Plan Policy ENV1 of the Cornwall Structure plan, which seek to protect the landscape character of the coast and countryside. Its criterion 1 gives priority to the conservation and enhancement of AONBs, while also having regard to the social and economic well being of the area. There is also concern over the emerging Local Plan Policy 13, which reflects the Structure Plan in giving priority to the preservation and enhancement of natural beauty in AONBs, and PPG7, regarding development in the countryside and AONBs. Trial planning permission was granted due to there being insufficient evidence to enable the authority to be sure of the effect of the use.

Appellant's view

The appellant questioned the relevance of the condition, its enforceability and, in relation to the short time period and the need for capital expenditure, its reasonableness.

Inspector's report- main issues

The inspector considered that the main issue in this case was:

- *The effect on the character and appearance of the surrounding area, of varying condition No. 1 to allow the permitted use to be for an unlimited period.* Restricting the permitted use to a limited period of two years is unnecessary as condition 3 already passed prevents any storage other than inside the appeal building, and this would limit the associated levels of activity, not significantly increasing it from previous agricultural activity. Thus the permitted use would not affect the character and appearance of the surrounding area.

The Inspector allowed the appeal with the following conditions substituted for condition No. 1:

- *The use hereby permitted shall be carried out only by Pentewan Sands Ltd.*

6. Suffolk Coastal District Council
Farm, Dunwich, Suffolk – within AONB and Heritage Coast.

Planning permission refused for the change of use to mixed use comprising two residential dwellings, two holiday letting units, and functions room for occasional courses/workshops for community use.

Date of appeal decision: April 2000.

Appeal decision: **Dismissed.**

Background
The appeal buildings are situated in the open countryside about 150 metres to the north-west of the defined limits of the coastal village of Dunwich. The proposal concerned an extensive range of buildings, totalling 8,000 square feet of floor space. The decision notice describes the proposal as including the change of use of a cart shed, barn and stable block, together with the use of a modern barn which would be weather boarded and roofed in pantiles to match the existing buildings. In addition the site plan indicates that existing car parking to the barn would be used as a stable/tack room/pony trap.

LPA's view
The application is contrary to Policies LP1, LP11A and LP65 of the Local Plan and other policies and guidelines which seek to ensure that proposals for conversion respect the character and appearance of existing buildings and incorporate minimal external change.

Appellant's view
The appellant draws attention to the fact that he intends to live and work on the site, including operating their mail order business. The appellant has also suggested conditions regarding completion of the letting units and function rooms, and would be prepared to agree detailed changes by way of imposed conditions.

Inspector's report- main issues
The inspector considers the main issues to be:

- *The restriction of development in the countryside:* The part of the appeal linked to residential development is not farm diversification and so will not be covered here. In regard to the provision of two holiday letting units and function rooms, the inspector recognises that they are a form of farm diversification. However, in terms of additional employment the benefits from both uses are small.

- *Whether there are any material considerations in this case sufficient to justify the proposals and outweigh policy:* Although the use is suitable in light of the suitability of the buildings for conversion, the lack of significant overall employment benefits and material considerations still do not justify allowing this appeal contrary to local and national policy.

- *The effect of the proposal on the character or appearance of the Dunwich Conservation Area, the Heritage Coast and AONB:* The barns occupy a prominent position and make a positive contribution to the Dunwich Conservation Area and to the character of the surrounding countryside. The degree of change necessary in their conversion would be evident over a considerable distance. The proposal would therefore fail to preserve or enhance the character of the area.

7. Calderdale Metropolitan Borough Council

Farm, Clifton, Brighouse – within Green Belt.

Failure to give notice within the prescribed period of a decision on an application for planning permission. Development proposed is the change of use from agricultural to B2 and B8 use.

Date of appeal decision: September 2000.

Appeal decision: **Dismissed.**

Background

The appeal site consists of four former agricultural buildings, their surrounding yard and roadway, and access drive to Highmoor Lane. The buildings are former cattle sheds, and Units 1-3 are ranked side by side, encircled by a concrete roadway. There is also access to Unit 4 plus some hardstanding and a silage pit. The complex of massive buildings occupies an elevated position on rising ground above the village of Clifton, and the combined lengths of Units 3 and 4 are starkly visible on approach from the south-west along the A643. The site contains no landscape planting, and insufficient space to accommodate an effective landscape screen. The appeal is made by a manufacturing company which intends to use the site. Farm traffic is recorded as still using the site. The evidence is that commercial vehicle movements would be in the order of two or so per day.

LPA's view

The appeal site is within the Green Belt. Policies N105, N13 and E3 are quoted which concern appropriate development, re-use of buildings, the re-use of buildings in the Green Belt, and appropriate new industrial or commercial development for employment with local job opportunities and accessibility to the Primary Employment Areas. It is also stated that on 4 July 2000 the Council's Planning Committee accepted the recommendation that the appeal should not be opposed but that the Inspector be requested to attach the conditions if minded to allow the appeal.

Appellant's view

This is not stated. The appellant offers a minibus service to the site to avoid transport generation, but has not submitted a 'Section 106' undertaking to provide such a service.

Inspector's report- main issues

The inspector states that the main issues are

- *The appropriateness of development in the Green Belt:* Although when in agricultural use the appeal units could be considered appropriate, they are not themselves in keeping with their rural surroundings. Any improvements to the external appearance of the building would not be adequate to overcome the harmful impact of their mass in the landscape. Although vehicle generation is stated as being unusually low, the site also has the capacity and the potential to generate large numbers of commercial lorry movements, and could constitute encroachment upon the countryside. Lorries parked would also be visible, conflicting with the openness of the Green Belt.

- *Special circumstances sufficient to outweigh the consequent harm with any other harm which may be identified:* The proposal would bring with it 100 jobs. However, it is not clear whether some or all of these would be relocated from existing premises. There is also no evidence that access to employment is especially difficult in this part of the District. Also the appellant is currently the subject of a planning application for four large poultry houses, and there is no evidence that the appeal buildings are unsuitable for poultry purposes. If both the appeal and application were allowed, this would result in a further decline in the openness of the Green Belt in this prominent location.

8. Mid-Bedfordshire District Council
Farm, Clophill

Planning permission refused for the change of use of farm building to B1 use.

Date of appeal decision: September 2000.

Appeal decision: **Allowed with conditions.**

Background
The farm was used for mushroom growing from 1988 until 1996 when it ceased due to a depressed market and ill health. The appeal building was used for packing, sales and staff facilities. Since then there has been a low level of activity on the farm, although from a site visit there was no indication of any agricultural use being made of the building.

LPA's view
The LPA is concerned that the building may be required for future agricultural enterprise, and if developed the loss of this building to agriculture would result in a need for additional buildings.

Appellant's view
The appellant's view is not stated.

Inspector's report- main issues
The inspector reports that there is one main issue in this case:

- *Whether the use of this building for non-agricultural purposes conflicts with Council policy/ Government advice in respect of the re-use of rural buildings:* PPG7 advises that there should be no reason for preventing the conversion of rural buildings for business re-use, subject to a number of provisos. The LPA's policies reflect this advice. The LPA's main reason for refusal is the potential need of the building for further agricultural use. However, the inspector states that under PPG7 it should not normally be necessary to consider whether the building is no longer needed for its present purposes. The building is suitable for adaptation to business use, and the area is not subject to any specific landscape designation and the site is not prominent. Any further development would be subject to separate planning permission, and so the proposed change of use is acceptable in planning terms.

Therefore the appeal proposal would accord with the development plan and Government advice, and should be allowed with the following condition:

- *Notwithstanding the provisions of the Town and Country Planning (General Permitted Development) Order 1995 (or any order revoking and re-enacting that Order with or without modification), no extension shall be added to the building without the prior written consent of the Local Planning Authority.*

9. Winchester City Council

Farm Barns, Boarhunt, near Wickham.

Planning permission refused for change of use from redundant agricultural barns to livery yard and headland exercise routes.

Date of appeal decision: September 1999.

Appeal decision: **Allowed with conditions.**

Background

The two appeal buildings are part of the existing group of buildings around the farm, which is situated off a long private track about 1 km south of the village of North Boarhunt. The headland exercise routes are around the perimeter of the approximately 20 hectare holding, which is in agricultural and/or grazing use. By the time of the hearing one of the two barns had been partially converted to stables. Commercial livery use had not yet commenced. However, the inspector determined the appeal as if the application was made under Section 73A for the continued use of the barns for the stabling of horses, the retention of paddocks and the continued use of headland rides in association with the proposed use of the barns as a livery yard.

LPA's view

Proposal RT8 of the Local Plan states that the development of various types of equestrian enterprises in the countryside will be permitted subject to the satisfaction of various criteria. These include: the re-use, where possible, of existing buildings, the relationship to existing and proposed bridleways and the avoidance of conflicts between equestrians, vehicles or pedestrians; the avoidance of harm to nearby properties or land uses. The development of dwellings in connection with equestrian development will be considered only where an essential need can be demonstrated. In considering applications for such development regard will be had to the need for on-site accommodation and the adequacy of existing residential development. The refusal is made with reference to this proposal.

Appellant's view

Again this is not stated.

Inspector's report- main issues

The main issues which the inspector considers are whether the development would accord with adopted development plan policy having regard to:

- *Its relationship to existing or proposed bridleways:* The LPA and local objectors state that the buildings are too far from the existing bridleway network and to other areas where horses might be exercised. However, a full network of bridleways is a rarity. In regard to vehicular access, the Highway Authority has no objection to the use of the access track, and the proposed conversion to provide 12 stables would limit the number of horses. The presence of headland rides and tracks, and use as a serviced livery yard would limit the chances of conflicts between horses, pedestrians and vehicles.

- *Its impact on the living conditions of nearby residential properties:* There may be some additional noise. Additional traffic would be no more than for agricultural usage. The area is too small for use as an indoor school and subject to satisfactory floor treatment the inspector considers that the proposed use need not give rise to serious disturbance to adjoining residents. The LPA was concerned about the need for external lighting, but the inspector recommends that this is controlled by condition.

- *Whether there may be a need for on-site living accommodation in association with the proposed use that should be considered at this stage as part of the principle of development.* The inspector considers that the LPA has an adequate policy framework to control the development of dwellings which might be needed in connection with rural activities. It is clear that the appellant is aware of the constraints this may place on the development of the use. This is therefore not a reason to withhold planning permission.

The Inspector allowed the appeal with the following conditions:

- *Limit the number of horses to be stabled to 12 and the type of equestrian use to that stated.*

- *Control external lighting and implement an agreed scheme of landscaping.*

- *Ensure the proper provision of car parking.*

- *Implement approved details of the means of disposal of horse manure.*

- *Approve details of the construction of the remaining stables and the treatment of the indoor exercise area.*

- *Control the use of the paddocks for jumping of horses.*

10. East Hertfordshire District Council
Farm, Epping Green – within Metropolitan Green Belt.

Planning permission refused for the change of use of a piggery to a studio/office.

Date of appeal decision: July 1999.

Appeal decision: **Allowed with conditions.**

Background
The building is at least 30 years old and is of a simple functional agricultural appearance. The building is not visible from any public viewpoint and is well screened from the road by

an area of protected woodland. There is an adjoining paddock to the northeast. A car park is also proposed to accommodate six vehicles, and would be largely situated on an existing hardstanding to the side of the building, where it appears that servicing was undertaken when the building was in use as a piggery.

LPA's view

The LPA assessed the application with reference to criteria in PPG2 and the draft East Hertfordshire Local Plan. The LPA considered that the increase in traffic and general activity would have a materially greater impact than the present use on the openness of the Green Belt, and introduce an urban use into a rural area. Concern was also expressed over the use of surrounding land, which could be in conflict with the openness of the Green Belt. The LPA states that the building is not of any intrinsic merit and does not reflect local styles. There was no objection based on the effect on the landscape. However, the LPA expressed concern that this proposal would set a precedent for other schemes, which would be detrimental to the character and openness of the Green Belt. The LPA recommended that any permission be made personal to the appellant.

Appellant's view

The appellant stated that the studio/office would be likely to be only occupied by up to eight people, although not all of these would be present at any one time, and that deliveries of stationery and similar goods might amount to one van each week.

Inspector's report- main issues

The inspector states that there is one main issue:

- *Appropriateness of development in the Green Belt and any special circumstances if not:* The inspector states that the proposal would be unlikely to generate significantly greater traffic or general activity than the previous use, or represent the harmful introduction of a use more suited to urban areas. External alterations necessary would not make the building appear out of keeping with its surroundings. The inspector also stated that the appeal should not fail on a generalised fear of precedent. Personal planning permission would not be reasonable as it is intended that the building be occupied by persons in addition to the appellant, and there are no personal circumstances which would justify such a condition.

The Inspector allowed the appeal with the following conditions:

- The submission and approval of further details prior to occupation regarding design and materials for the external appearance of the building, and on the car parking area and the hard surfaced area between the studio/office and the existing concrete yard with development carried out in accordance with these details.

- The protection and preservation of trees.

- No external storage of goods, articles or materials other than within the enclosed compounds, the details of which shall previously have been submitted to and approved in writing by the LPA.

11. Boston Borough Council
Farm, Kirton Holme, Boston

Planning permission refused for change of use from agricultural land to a site for touring caravans.

Date of appeal decision: June 2000.

Appeal decision: **Allowed** with conditions.

Background
The site is already largely screened from the north by the farm house, an outbuilding to the rear, and existing trees and hedges. From the south, views are obscured by another dwelling. To the rear, oblique views into the site would be obtainable from various points, but most land is in agricultural use. However, the site is most exposed to view at close quarters from the front, from Holmes Road. Hedgerow plants and trees are still immature and do not provide any practical screening.

LPA's view
The adopted Boston Local Plan shows the site within countryside where, under Policy C01, development will not be permitted unless supported by other Local Plan policies. Policy R12 states that the development of a touring caravan site will be permitted, with criteria, including that it should not harm local amenities due to its appearance, that there should be no significant detriment to visual amenity, and that it should include a satisfactory landscaping scheme incorporating means of future management. The application was refused due to the front exposure of the site leading to the caravan site constituting an intrusive element in the rural landscape.

Appellant's view
The appellant's view is not stated.

Inspector's report- main issues
The main issues in this case are:

- *The effect of the proposal on the character and appearance of the area:* The site would only have a significant effect from one side. That side is capable of being screened; and a substantial amount of planting has already taken place in advance of the development.

- *If harm is found in relation to the first issue, whether it would be appropriate to grant permission in the absence of mature screen planting at the site:* It would be unreasonable to withhold permission for development which otherwise is acceptable solely because necessary landscaping is immature. However, the visual impact of the proposal could and should be reduced in the short term. Present landscaping could be reinforced by additional planting, and possibly by the incorporation of more mature specimens. Additional screening, by means of earth mounding, or fencing could also be temporarily added.

The Inspector allowed the appeal with the following conditions:

- *No caravan shall be placed on the site until the first 10m of the access road has been hard surfaced.*

- *No development shall take place until full details of both hard and soft landscaping have been submitted to and approved in writing by the LPA, and development carried out in accordance with these details.*

- *No development shall take place until a schedule of landscape maintenance for a minimum period of 5 years has been submitted to and approved in writing by the LPA, and development carried out in accordance with these details.*

- *Tree protection and preservation.*

- *Restriction of occupation both in terms of length of stay and time of year.*

12. London Borough of Bromley Council
Piggery, Cudham – within Metropolitan Green Belt.

Planning permission refused for change of use from agricultural (piggery) to light industrial use (motor vehicle repairs with ancillary office and stores).

Date of appeal decision: December 1999.

Appeal decision: **Dismissed.**

Background
The site is within both the Green Belt and an Area of Special Landscape Character (local designation). It lies behind the frontage of residential development on the fringe of Cudham. Despite sporadic, loose-knit development of dwellings and farm groups, the predominant character of the area is open and rural. The site is elevated on the east side of a small valley. It is occupied by a small complex of former agricultural buildings, a concrete yard to the south of these and grassland around the west and south sides of the site. The site is served by a shared concrete drive, which runs between two residential properties. The most modern of the buildings is used as a workshop, with attached store. This generates a need for parking and vehicle activity at and around the site. There is an extensive area of hardstanding, but the extent of this activity creates an urbanising effect. The remaining buildings provide mess facilities and limited storage, such as of old oil.

LPA's view
The urbanising effect of the site erodes the character and attractive, rural quality of the Area of Special Landscape Character, contrary to policy G12 of the development plan. Local residents also complain of noise from the use of compressed air equipment and from banging at the site.

Appellant's view
The appellant's view is not stated.

Inspector's report – main issues
According to the inspector the main issues are:

- *The impact on the character and amenity of the surrounding area:* The inspector agrees with the LPA's view.

- *The impact on residential amenities:* The impact on residential amenities due to noise and disturbance from work within the building would not be unacceptably harmful due to noise attenuation measures in place and the site's distance from other dwellings. However, traffic associated with the development unacceptably harms the amenity of local residents, contrary to development plan policy G17.

- *Whether the development is appropriate in the Green Belt, and if not whether there are any very special circumstances:* The associated activity around the building has an urbanising effect and introduces commercial activity, contrary to a purpose of including land in the Green Belt to protect the countryside from encroachment. No good circumstances to justify this inappropriate development have been advanced.